PHILOSOPHY OF THE STATE AS EDUCATOR

Matri Dei Amabili

PHILOSOPHY
of the STATE
as EDUCATOR

THOMAS DUBAY, S.M.

THE BRUCE PUBLISHING COMPANY
MILWAUKEE

NIHIL OBSTAT:

EARL F. NIEHAUS, S.M.
Censor deputatus

IMPRIMI POTEST:

DANIEL C. O'MEARA, S.M.
Provincial

NIHIL OBSTAT:

JOHN F. MURPHY, S.T.D.
Censor librorum

IMPRIMATUR:

✠ WILLIAM E. COUSINS
Archbishop of Milwaukee
May 20, 1959

Library of Congress Catalog Card Number: 59–13483

© 1959 REV. THOMAS E. DUBAY, S.M.
MADE IN THE UNITED STATES OF AMERICA

PREFACE

THE competing factions that strive in the world's marketplaces for the minds and hearts of men without exception bid ardently for the attention and allegiance of youth. This phenomenon coupled with the rapidly growing fact of compulsory instruction makes of modern education a matter of no trifling consequence. In bygone centuries relatively few went to school and the same few ran public business. Yesterday, the school left small trace on the population masses. Today in civilized nations the school leaves an indelible mark on the minds and hearts of the vast majority.

The significance of contemporary education can scarcely be exaggerated. Nor can the significance of its sponsors. The modern world has witnessed and is still witnessing a sharp switch from family and church sponsorship of education to a state sponsorship. Not that the former is dying; rather it is a question of the latter sprouting, and sprouting on a world-wide and grand scale.

In view of this vast expansion of public educational enterprise in the past century and the present one as well, one marvels that so little philosophical thought has been injected into the process. My investigations into the matter have not turned up a single thorough and professedly philosophical analysis of the state's function in education.

The growth of state-sponsored education, whether for weal or for woe, has been singularly short on principled foundations. To a large extent the public school movement in the United States has been one of expediency. It is doubtful that even the stanchest advocate of public education would pretend that the American movement is the natural flower of a philosophical plant. It is rather a flower of the pressures arising from a pluralistic society.

Since no man enjoys having the label of expediency tacked on to the work of his hands, it would seem that we moderns should be industriously seeking for public education a solidly based foundation in political science. If public education has a solid basis — and we are convinced that it has — we ought to find it and lay it bare to the eyes of men. Yet remarkable is not too strong a word to describe the thoroughness with which current secular educational literature avoids

v

any excursion into the political philosophy of the agencies of education.

The present study has singled out one of these three agencies, the state, and seeks to explore the functions of that agency in the field of education. Our examination is philosophical in that the whole structure of it grows out of an analysis of the nature and functions of the state as a state. This approach, we believe, affords a logical and well-knit foundation for our consequent investigation of the state's educational role. Once the foundation is laid, the implications and ramifications of the state's relationships to education are deduced philosophically from the state's nature and function as a state.

The study is partially legal in the sense that the various functions of the state in education, first philosophically analyzed, are then illustrated from the actual practices of the nations of the world. These practices are largely drawn from the constitutions, legislation, and judicial decisions of these nations. In our choice of legal illustrations we have tried to be unbiased. We have used illustrations just as our research has turned them up, whether or not the practices indicated accorded with our position.

Among the unconsciously attained byproducts emerging from this investigation perhaps the most significant is the appearance of legal positivism as shorn of its angel-of-light role. By all standards of human dignity and freedom, countries which have pushed legal positivism to its logical conclusion present a tragic educational picture indeed. But the greatest tragedy is that the positivist cannot logically call these tragedies tragic. For if there be no law but state law, if the state is the sole norm of right and wrong, a governmentally originated educational tragedy is of course strictly impossible. Legal positivism stands starkly exposed as inadequate.

The only salvation of the individual in his relationships with the mighty hand of the state is the natural law. If there be no inviolable right planted in the very nature of man, the state can crush his mind and body with impunity. But given an inviolable right, given a natural law, the whole of mankind can rise in moral indignation and condemn the ruthless to international disgrace.

The state's educational function presents a contemporary urgency not shared by its other functions. In its instructional role the state does not merely administer programs and allot monies. It touches directly the intellects and wills of men, for it teaches, and teaches most effectively. This single truth that the state as educator is the state as soul-former renders imperative a thoughtful examination of bases and ends and means.

The fields of knowledge taught by modern governments in their public schools are not exhausted by the liberal arts and the vocational sciences. Philosophy and religion, often the philosophy and religion of secularism, do not lie beyond the sweep of the state's teaching influence. They cannot. Even the denier of metaphysics constructs a metaphysics in building his denial. The pragmatist uses absolutes to destroy absolutes. The question is not whether one shall be a metaphysician, an absolutist or not — supposing he is going to think at all. The question is rather what kind of metaphysics and what kind of absolutes he is going to embrace. States which exclude philosophy and religion from their curricula to do so on the basis of a philosophy and a religion all their own. Philosophical and religious neutrality is the purest myth. It can be found in no school system the world over, public or private.

Among the more crucial problems included in any state's philosophy is the view it takes of itself and of its educational function. The state cannot fail to take a stand on its own basis, its aims, and the means it shall use to implement those aims. It must face up to the problem of its educational function: what is the foundation of that function, what are its purposes and rights and duties and limitations. Answers to these problems have profound consequences, consequences that reach into eternity. It is therefore imperative that those answers be correct.

In its original form this study was presented to the Graduate School of Arts and Sciences of The Catholic University of America in partial fulfillment of requirements for the doctor's degree, and an abstract of it was printed by the Press of the same institution. Since that time I have revised it in a considerable number of minor points and have in a few instances supplemented both philosophical and legal aspects of the work. In none of these cases, however, has there been need to modify any of the philosophical principles or conclusions posited in the original study.

I wish to take occasion here to thank sincerely Doctors Bernard T. Rattigan, F. J. Houlahan, Charles McCoy, and George Donovan, all of Catholic University, for their critical reading of the text and for their helpful suggestions. Appreciation is likewise due to my confrere, Father Earl F. Niehaus, S.M., of Notre Dame Seminary, who wedged into an already heavy round of duties an adept criticism of the manuscript. I wish finally to acknowledge gratefully the aid and encouragement always forthcoming from another confrere, Father John L. White, S.M., of Marist College, Washington, D. C.

Notre Dame Seminary
New Orleans, Louisiana

CONTENTS

PART I

PHILOSOPHY OF THE STATE

CHAPTER I

THE NATURAL LAW, MAN, AND SOCIETY

CONCEPT OF NATURAL LAW

IN OUR efforts to analyze the state's role in education we must, to be complete and thorough, explore the bases of society and of the state as found in the very nature of man. For this reason our attention must be directed first of all to a concept of the natural law. Even though common sense recognizes in its own rudimentary way the natural law character of morality, and despite the fact that the atrocious crimes of modern nations have shaken any positivistic explanation of morality, the precise meaning of natural law ethics is not always understood. We do not, however, intend to detail our explanation or to prove it to the reader. That has been done elsewhere.[1] Our aim is merely to cast a foundation for the chief purpose of this study.

The natural law teaching on right and duty is unmistakably teleological.[2] The principle of finality runs through typical explanations of natural law philosophers. Zalba, writing from Spain, speaks of the natural law as "the necessary and divine ordering of the rational creature to its natural ultimate end, which ordering is necessary, expressed in the nature itself, and perceived by the natural light of

---

[1] J. Messner has done a fine piece of work in his *Social Ethics* (St. Louis: B. Herder Book Co., 1952). Heinrich Rommen has produced two books pertinent to this question: *The Natural Law* (St. Louis: B. Herder, 1948) and *The State in Catholic Thought* (St. Louis: B. Herder, 1950).

[2] I suspect that many shy away from a teleological philosophy because they really do not understand it. It seems to them static and rigid. This, however, is far from the case, for natural law ethics makes ample provision for change, development, and progress. We shall note this fact below.

3

reason."³ A French writer compresses the same ideas into fewer words. For him the natural law is defined as the "divine ordering of the rational creature to its last end, engraven in human nature and perceived by the light of reason."⁴ From the United States we have Renard who speaks of the natural law simply as finality: "Natural law is the finality of nature inclining man not only to his last end but also to due acts. . . ."⁵

What does this finality in human nature mean? Every agent or doer acts for an end or purpose or he would not act at all. If a man did not have an end or purpose in digging a hole, he would not dig it. The first Cause of all reality, God, is also the cause of human nature. Like any other doer, therefore, God has an end in view in his creation of a human person. He impresses that end in the very nature he creates. Just as a watchmaker's end can be extracted from the watch by an examination of its nature, so also can God's end in making man be extracted by a careful analysis of the nature of man.

In order to discover the intent of the Creator in bringing the rational creature into being, the tendencies or drives of that latter must especially be studied. It is through these tendencies that God naturally reveals what He wants this being to do. There is, for example, in man the drive to self-preservation; and through it God clearly indicates that He expects man to nourish his body by food and drink and to protect himself and others from undue danger. Negatively, this same tendency bespeaks the moral evil of mutilation, suicide, and gluttony. The drive to self-propagation likewise suggests, and even more, makes imperative, a whole group of precepts dealing with sexual and family life. Man's social inclinations point to the necessity of the state and to the manifold relationships of right and duty toward his fellows.

It would be a mistake, however, to assume that any of man's *isolated* tendencies creates an obligation to follow it out. As a moral norm, each of man's drives must be viewed in the context of his whole nature. The human person is neither mere body nor mere soul. Attention to the one with a neglect of the other can lead to nothing

³ E. F. Regatillo and M. Zalba, *Theologiae Moralis Summa* (Matriti: Biblioteca De Autores Cristianos, 1952), I, No. 330.
⁴ A. Molien, "Lois," *Dictionnaire de Theologie Catholique,* ed. A. Vacant, E. Mangenot, E. Amann, IX (1926), 878.
⁵ Henri Renard, *Philosophy of Morality* (Milwaukee: The Bruce Publishing Co., 1953), p. 207.

better than self-defeat. Anything snatched out of context may be distorted. So also human action. Modern paganism too clearly brings out this lesson in its refusal to see as the whole purpose of the sex drive not only the happiness of husband and wife, but also, and primarily, the procreation and full formation of children, which formation involves physical, moral, intellectual, and spiritual elements.[6]

Since our purpose here is not a complete treatise on natural law, but rather a concise summary, we will indicate only briefly a number of observations that flow from this concept of it.

The natural law binds all men without exception, since all have the same rational nature from which it flows. It is not, therefore, a "Catholic" law, but one as universal as is human nature. This law is termed natural, not only because it is based on nature, but also because it is a law promulgated by human reason. Man by his own intelligence can recognize and reason out at least the basic stipulations of it.

It follows then that the fundamental principles of natural law are immutable in the sense that they could be changed only by changing human nature itself. Given the nature of man, the natural law cannot be altered even by God Himself. This is not to say, however, that the application of these principles does not change with changing times and situations. To argue, as do some positivists, that the natural law is a closed system and therefore not amenable to adaptation to new circumstances is to fell a straw man. The openness of the natural law is indicated by the fact that its basic principles do not automatically dictate in concrete applications what is good or evil or what one is to call murder or theft or adultery.[7] Nor do these principles do away with the necessity of a constantly changing positive law, which itself flows out of the natural law.

The law of nature is, however, the measure of human positive laws. A positive law of man which contradicts the natural law and thus is an unjust law, is really no law at all. It consequently induces no obligation.

---

[6] This illustration may serve to remind us of the often overlooked fact that Catholicism has a comprehensive, balanced, and beautiful philosophy of sex. Although this matter is related to our investigation, an amplification of it would lead us too far astray. See Joseph Buckley, *Christian Design for Sex* (Chicago: Fides Publishers, 1952) or Arthur Vermeersch, *De Castitate* (Rome: Gregorian University, 1921).

[7] William J. Kenealy, "Whose Natural Law?" *The Catholic Lawyer,* I (October, 1955), 262.

Natural law is real because it is founded on the stark nature of things. That is why what is good economics or good politics must be morally good and what is morally bad cannot be genuinely good economics or politics. This fact will have considerable bearing on our present study in its normative and critical aspects.

It follows from the preceding observation that the natural law is not a burden capriciously imposed by God on man for some set of reasons unknown by the latter. Messner, an Austrian political scientist, points out that this erroneous concept is strengthened by philosophers who give the natural law a theological foundation by suggesting that God arbitrarily imposes it on men through an act of His free will. Since God moves and governs all the rest of creation by having things operate according to their natures, there is no reason to suppose that He has not done the same in the case of man.[8] Because this is so, we may conclude that the observance of the natural law is a means for the attainment of man's terrestrial happiness as well as his celestial destiny, for he cannot be happy except by living up to his own true nature, which is merely to say by being what he is supposed to be.

Yet not all of the principles of natural law are equally evident. The utterly basic imperatives are known to every intelligent man: good must be done, evil avoided; do to others as you would have them do to you, and so on. Derivative principles (e.g., the obligation to restore lost goods to the rightful owner when this is possible) are not so clear and may go unrealized even by an intelligent man. One of the services of positive law is to call these latter to the attention of the community.

We ought not to view natural law as a legal strait jacket determining all details of morality. Much discretion is left to human lawmakers to decide what here and now, all things considered, is the preferable course of action. Much also is left to the individual's prudence in judging the applicability of a principle to the concrete situation. We may note with a recent writer that "there can be no universal file of proximate norms for behavior. The proper precepts of individual actions are to be found in the particular precepts of prudence — not in the law, which, natural or human, retains a certain degree of generality."[9]

---

[8] *Op. cit.,* p. 37.

[9] Charles de Koninck, "General Standards and Particular Situations in Relation to

A just law made by men (a positive law) is either a restatement or a determination of the natural law. It is a restatement if it merely repeats what is already contained in natural law (e.g., the proscription of murder). It is a determination when it specifies an obligation that is contained in the natural law in a general way only. Thus the right to private property is of natural law, but this latter does not determine how that property is to be acquired. Positive law does the determining. Even if all men were of perfectly good will, the natural law would need this determination of positive law. This is so because our intellects are deficient and we often do not know what ought to be done in a particular set of circumstances.[10]

Natural law, furthermore, possesses a dynamism of its own in that it binds men to seek to improve their social and political institutions, since these need constant readjustment to changing conditions.[11] Thus while principles remain constant, applications need repeated revision. The pertinence of this truth to the problems of the state's role in education is readily discernible.

Just as physical laws carry with them a sanction, so also does the natural law. The penalty for the latter's violation may not be paid immediately, but it is paid in the long run. One writer has remarked in this connection that

a nation despising the first principles of natural law will perish; justice remains the foundation of the state. Wherever a nation, in contempt of natural law, lets the crusaders of birth control or the cynics of libertinism corrupt the sexual and family life, this may produce in the short run easy solutions of economic or social dilemmas. But once loose practices become national habits, such a nation will become senile, will become extinct by losing its identity through subjugation or immigration by more vigorous nations. Natural law has stood at the deathbed of many a nation which had contempt for that law in the heyday of materialistic hedonism.[12]

We might add that besides the sanction attached to natural law, positive law often adds one of its own to a restatement or a determination of that natural law.

---

the Natural Law," *Proceedings of the American Catholic Philosophical Association,* XXIV (1950), 29.

[10] See Karl Kreilkamp, *The Metaphysical Foundations of Thomistic Jurisprudence* (Washington: The Catholic University Press, 1939), pp. 97–98.

[11] Messner, *op. cit.,* pp. 81–83 and 206–207.

[12] Rommen, *The State in Catholic Thought,* pp. 206–207.

Our study of the state's educational role will be based almost exclusively on natural law principles, for God has not seen fit to promulgate divine positive laws dealing with this problem.

EXISTENCE OF THE NATURAL LAW

For the man in the street a proof of the natural law is superfluous; he takes it for granted; its existence is obvious. Unlike the mere animal, he can know things and he can know what fits them and what does not. In his eminently common sense view of reality the ordinary man knows full well that some things are good and some bad regardless of what the state may say or may not say about them. Rommen shrewdly remarks that "the juridically non-educated is fully aware that there is a difference between what is just and what is formally legal, between what is unjust and what is illegal. This appeal to the idea of justice, to 'the law' as distinguished from the mere factual will of the lawgiver, is an irrefutable witness to the conviction of the existence of natural law."[13]

The teleology in human nature cannot be missed — it is planted everywhere in the human person: in his body, his senses, his mind, his whole composed and unified being. Man's intellect can see that the disregarding of this finality involves the violation of an order, the frustrating of human nature, the slighting of the will of the Designer. It sees the natural law.

For the legal positivist there is no basis for distinguishing a just from an unjust law, good government from tyranny, since for him human law alone is the norm of good and evil. However, "it often happens that, when grave issues of justice are at stake, we see the most determined positivist changed into a believer in natural law appealing to the idea of justice as superior to all statute books."[14] The positivist, if he is caught unaware, will condemn a state action as cruel or unjust using as his basis for judgment the plain wrongness of the act. That plain wrongness is nothing but light shed from his awareness of the natural law. Common sense can never be completely shaken off oneself.

The positivistic denial of a natural basis for morality is defective on another count. If the masses accepted the theory of legal positivism

---

[13] *Ibid.*, p. 169.   [14] *Ibid.*

as their practical norm of morality, they would disrupt society. The chief reason most men obey laws is moral, not legal. It has been pointed out that "in the courts this denial of the natural moral law has made law penal — a trap for the unwary and unwise. It has made legal process a game with artificial rules where dexterity of action is more prized than consistency of principle."[15] If the ordinary man lost his common sense grasp of the natural law, society at large would be in sad straits. In this way the truth of the natural law can be verified experimentally. Living according to it produces individual contentment and social peace, whereas living at variance with it produces individual ennui and social tragedy. History and personal experience are twin witnesses to this oft-repeated phenomenon.

In conclusion we may note that the natural law gives final and satisfying answers to the problems of morality, whereas positivistic systems offer only partial and intellectually unsatisfying solutions. Legal positivism declares that murder is wrong because civil law says so. Dewey would say it is wrong because the consequences are bad. But one immediately wonders what would happen if the state should decide that some murders are good. Or he may ask who is to decide which consequences are good and which bad. Embarrassing questions! Neither can be answered without recourse to natural law, whether that recourse be admitted or not.

SOCIAL NATURE OF MAN

Among the tendencies or drives designed in human nature by its Author is the social drive. Men of every age have been unmistakably inclined to group together in societies of widely varying types: families, clans, tribes, guilds, labor unions, literary associations, churches, cities, states. Unlike mere animals which congregate under the motive force of a necessary impulse, men associate under the free direction of intellect and will. This is evident from the fact that their societies are uniform only in broad outline and consequently show numerous differences in ends and means.

In its generic sense we may define a society as an organized association of persons pursuing voluntarily a common end through the fulfillment of various duties and under the direction of authorized

---

[15] Laurence J. McGinley, "Natural Law," *Thought*, XXVII (Winter, 1952), p. 568.

leadership. It will be noted that society is made up of persons, not mere irrational units. A group of mere animals, being units and not persons, cannot make up a society in the proper sense of the term. They cannot work for a known and willed common end nor do they benefit from the group as individuals of inviolable worth and dignity but merely as parts. They further have no duties nor proceed under a directing leadership. In addition, it will be seen that a mere juxtaposition of persons does not suffice to form a society. A theater full of people does not embrace a special society, for as theater goers they have neither a common end nor a common leadership. However, an adjacent hall housing a labor union meeting does embrace a genuine society fulfilling all of the notes we have given in the definition.

Even though its unity is only accidental, a unity of order,[16] society is more than the mere combination of individuals who make it up, and yet it has no being independently of those individuals. A house is more than the bricks and wood that make it up, and yet it has no being independently of those materials.[17] So also is an organized team of athletes something more than a mere assemblage of athletes.[18] Hence, even though society enjoys only an accidental, nonsubstantial unity, it is for all that more than the mere sum of the persons who make it up. This fact becomes even clearer when we consider that society does and produces much more than the sum of the individuals could do and produce working as individuals in an unordered and unintegrated way. Mass production, schools, museums, social protection are only a few instances of the greater effectiveness of concerted and united effort.

As has been already suggested, man's sociability is rooted in his very nature and that in a twofold manner. Man is intended to live with his fellows, first of all, because he is rational. As a thinking and willing being he wishes to communicate knowledge, goodness, and love to those of his kind. The animal bestows none of these on the members of its group, but is for the most part a rugged individualist. Man's faculty of speech betrays his communicative and thus social nature as rooted in the very depths of his being.

Man is social, secondly, because he needs completion or complemen-

---

[16] "The whole which is civil society or the domestic family has only a unity of order and thus is not unqualifiedly one." St. Thomas, In Ethic., I, 1.

[17] Messner, op. cit., p. 109.

[18] John F. Cox, A Thomistic Analysis of the Social Order (Washington: Catholic University Press, 1943), pp. 46–47.

tation both for survival and for full development. Unlike the brute, the human offspring is for many years almost wholly dependent on the family for physical welfare. Moral, intellectual, and spiritual growth require an even longer and more intense supplementation. The supernatural order likewise evinces man's sociability, for the attainment of his final end can in God's providence be achieved only through the social agency of the Mystical Body of Christ, His Church.[19] So deeply rooted in man's nature is his sociability that Aristotle was able to say in his oft-quoted dictum: "He who is unable to live in society, or has no need because he is sufficient for himself, must be either a beast or a god."[20]

From the twofold source of man's social nature and the many diverse ends which he can propose for himself arise the many different associations, clubs, organizations, and societies that fill the earth. These in turn should be united and subordinated and co-operative in procuring the common good of society at large.

From all that has been said we may conclude that society exists for the individual and not the individual for society as Marxian theory and practice would have it. It follows, secondly, that since society and its order are drawn from the very nature of man, he cannot plan that order according to his own whim and without reference to its natural basis.[21]

END OF SOCIETY: THE COMMON GOOD

Intimately bound up with the nature of society is, of course, the end of society or the common good. Being the *raison d'être* of society, we must do our best to obtain a clear concept of it. The common good may be defined as the aggregate of those conditions and helps provided by the group's co-operation which aid individuals in the attainment of their proximate and remote ends. Thus industrial peace

---

[19] One recent writer seems unduly to play down wants as a basis of man's sociability, although he admits they have some role. He argues that all material beings have "wants" (e.g., moisture, food), but it is clear that subhuman beings do not have wants to nearly the extent that man has them. Moreover, the plant and the animal are much more independent in satisfying their wants than is man. Cf. William F. Drummond, "Roots of Sociability," *Social Order,* II (March, 1952), 107.

[20] *Politics,* I, Ch. 2. Richard McKeon, ed., *The Basic Works of Aristotle* (New York: Random House, 1941), p. 1130.

[21] Messner, *op. cit.,* p. 112.

as guaranteed by the community is a modern day condition without which the worker cannot secure his temporal welfare. Schools are helps made possible only by group co-operation and are aimed at aiding the individual members of the group in achieving moral, intellectual, and spiritual integration otherwise unobtainable.

Each society has a common good of its own: the family, the state, the church, a commercial business, a hospital. The individual members by their mutual co-operation create the very helps which revert back to them but which they could not obtain by individual effort. In relation to the common good of the whole of society the common good of a lesser society must be viewed as a particular good and consequently subordinated (when in the same genus of goods) to the good of the greater.

The genuine notion of the common good — and this has important implications for education — must be preserved from both the statist and the individualist corruptions of it. For the former the state is an end in itself entitled to deprive the individual of basic rights in order to serve its interests. Thus the ancient Spartan state deprived parents and children of basic human rights by taking the male children from the home at the age of seven and assigning them to barracks where they received an official state upbringing. Statism further exhibits an exaggerated concept of its position by usurping activities that can be and are well handled by private individuals. The modern concept of the paternal state points in this direction as does the totalitarian notion of state monopoly in education.

On the other hand, individualism understands the common good as the mere protection of free interplay among citizens.[22] It minimizes the place of the state and makes the common good the mere total of individual goods. Individualism "overlooks the fact that social organizations can contribute to the welfare of individuals."[23]

While placing the common good of society at large on a higher level than the particular good of the citizen, natural law social thought does not endanger the fundamental rights of the individual person. While discussing the respective values of virginity and matrimony, St. Thomas makes the interesting observation that "the common good is to be preferred to the private if it is in the same genus; but

---

[22] *Ibid.*, p. 134.
[23] John F. Cronin, *Catholic Social Principles* (Milwaukee: The Bruce Publishing Co., 1950), p. 120.

it can happen that the private good is better according to its (superior) genus. In this way virginity dedicated to God is preferred to carnal fecundity."[24] For this reason a man may not be forced to act against his conscience, since his spiritual and eternal welfare must be preferred to any merely temporal good.[25] Rommen brings out this truth when he remarks that

> the state, as distinguished from the whole of the individual citizens and their families, is a servant. Its end, the common good, can be realized only by enabling the citizens to fulfill their ultimate and transcendent end, the salvation of their souls, in pursuing their secular task in peace and security and in mutual help. Therefore, it is not true that under all circumstances the end of the state must prevail in case of conflict.[26]

However, when the common good and the particular good lie in the same genus, the latter must cede to the former. When, for example,

---

[24] *Summa Theologica*, II, II, 152, a. 4, *ad* 3. Other philosophers explain this same truth by saying that the private good in question is ordained to a higher *common* good and hence that virginity is preferable to marriage *if* it is consecrated to God.

[25] Thus we see in advance one reason why the state may not force parents to send their children to schools which neglect the work of spiritual formation.

[26] *Op. cit.*, p. 307. Pope Pius XII has lucidly spotlighted this dignity and immunity of the individual as against undue invasion by the state. "It must be noted that, in his personal being, man is not finally ordered to usefulness to society. On the contrary, the community exists for man. . . . Considered as a whole the community is not a physical unity subsisting in itself, and its individual members are not integral parts of it. Considered as a whole, the physical organism of living beings, of plants, animals or man, has a unity subsisting in itself. Each of the members, for example, the hand, the foot, the heart, the eye, is an integral part destined by all its being to be inserted in the whole organism. Outside the organism it has not, by its very nature, any sense, any finality. It is wholly absorbed by the totality of the organism to which it is attached.

"In the moral community and in every organism of a purely moral character, it is an entirely different story. Here the whole has no unity subsisting in itself, but a simple unity of finality and action. In the community individuals are merely collaborators and instruments for the realization of the common end.

"What results, as far as the physical organism is concerned? The master and user of this organism, which possesses a subsisting unity, can dispose directly and immediately of integral parts, members and organs within the scope of their natural finality. He can also intervene, as often as and to the extent that the good of the whole demands, to paralyze, destroy, mutilate and separate the members. But, on the contrary, when the whole has only a unity of finality and action, its head — in the present case, the public authority — doubtlessly holds direct authority and the right to make demands upon the activities of the parts, but in no case can it dispose of its physical being." Discourse to the First International Congress on the Histopathology of the Nervous System, September 13, 1952, N.C.W.C. News Service, *National Catholic Almanac* (Paterson, N. J.: St. Anthony's Guild, 1953), p. 68. *A.A.S.*, 1952, pp. 786–787. The Holy Father dealt with the same problem in his 1956 address on corneal transplantation, *The Pope Speaks*, Autumn, 1956, pp. 200–201. *A.A.S.*, 1956, pp. 459–467.

the material welfare of the community clashes with that of the individual, the former must prevail. If a city judges it opportune for the general welfare to condemn property for the building of an adequate road, the citizen must acquiesce to the action. Manifestly, of course, he has a right to a just recompense for his property. A man may be required also to sacrifice his very life for the common good, but even in this case his ultimate destiny remains untouched and so his rights are not violated.[27]

The concept of the citizen's sharing in the fruits of the common good gives us a solid basis for our later discussion of distributive justice as a duty of the state. Then, too, we may note that there must be a proportionate equality in the various shares of the social benefits produced by society.[28] Mathematical equality is out of the question, but justice requires that one segment of society be not unreasonably favored at the expense of another or one penalized with the other's consequent benefit. We have here one of the fundamental reasons why a government which taxes all citizens for education fails in distributive justice, if it refuses aid to parents who with good reason choose a private school for their children. To this question we shall return later.

---

[27] The materialist by denying the spiritual in man is hard put to explain how in this case there is no violation of man's right to life.

[28] Messner, *op. cit.*, p. 129.

CHAPTER II

THE STATE AND SUBSIDIARITY

NATURE OF THE STATE

IT MIGHT appear to the casual observer that the delineation of society, nation, and state as distinct and really different realities is nothing but the merest quibbling. And yet a faulty concept of state may easily arise from an unrealized identification of these terms. In our first chapter we have explained what we mean by society. It remains for us now to differentiate the remaining two concepts,[29] and then to investigate more closely the nature of the state.

A nation is a group of persons that finds its basis for mutual adhesion as a nation not in political authority but in a number of less tangible commonly held realities: territory, language, attitudes, customs, religion, and history. Often a nation will be bound together also by the bonds of the political organization known as the state, but it likewise happens that several nations are combined into one state. Soviet Russia is an instance of the latter in that it embraces a plurality of nations in one sovereign state.

A state, on the other hand, is an organized group aimed at the carrying out of the ends of society. Manifestly, the whole community cannot direct and supervise the achievement of the common good, which, as we have explained, is the end of society. The state is the community to which this direction and supervision is committed. The state is, therefore, that group of persons which carries out the two functions of protection and promotion. The state through its organ-

---

[29] We might point out that not all sociologists make this distinction. Later on in this present study we will use the terms, state and nation, interchangeably in order to avoid a deadening repetition of the same word. It is nonetheless well to realize that in their strict meanings the words are not identical. Maritain explains these concepts at some length in *Man and the State* (London: Hollis and Carter, 1954), pp. 1–17.

ization and its coercive power assures internal and external peace, thus laying the absolutely basic condition for the attainment of human ends. It exercises its promotive function by supplying the help and direction the individual needs for the achievement of his purposes.[30]

Root of the State

Thomas Hobbes saw the root of the state in the need of the individual to protect himself from other individuals, and in this Hobbes was consistent with himself since he viewed each man as being at war with every other man. Jean Jacques Rousseau placed the origin of the state in some ancient, perhaps unexpressed social contract whereby men surrendered voluntarily some of their freedom in order to supply government with the authority it needs and enjoys. Natural law philosophy, on the other hand, does not seek the root of the state in an artificial man-made arrangement but in the very nature of man himself. We have already seen how society springs from the make-up of man as a communal being needing and capable of bestowing supplementary help. To show that the state itself likewise springs from this same make-up we need advance only one step further. Society at large cannot bestow this supplementation without organization, direction, and authority. Hence, if man's ends are to be achieved, the whole social body must be organized and directed authoritatively by some special group. This group is the state and thus it takes its rise from the very requirements of human nature — which is merely to say from human nature itself.

At this point we think it well to indicate explicitly what we have implicitly supposed throughout our whole development of the natural law foundation of morality, society, and the state. Since the natural law is merely a participation of a rational being in the eternal law of God, morality, society, and the state ultimately take their rise from

---

[30] Natural law philosophy does not favor one kind of state to the exclusion of others. Throughout the course of history many variations have been developed from the three fundamental forms of monarchy, aristocracy, and democracy. As long as a government is based on justice and a capacity to serve the common good, it may not be ruled out as necessarily unacceptable. See, for example, the scholastic philosopher, Boyer, who explicitly sets up and proves the thesis that these three forms of government (whether in simple or mixed forms) are legitimate. Charles Boyer, *Cursus Philosophiae* (Paris: Declee de Brouwer et Soc., 1937), II, 562–564.

the will of God. By the eternal law God directs all creation to its end: the glory of the Creator. Like any agent, God must have an end when He acts and there is no end worthy of Himself but Himself. This finality God impresses on each creature by making it to be what it is: a finite reflection of the divine goodness. The rational creature, in our case man, reflects that goodness by being fully a man, that is to say by acting according to his nature and the ends designed in it. Because God founded that nature and its finality, anything demanded by that nature arises originally and ultimately from Him. God is thus the prime source of the state and the authority it enjoys.[31]

FUNDAMENTAL RESIDENCE OF THE STATE'S AUTHORITY

Even though God is the ultimate source of any power the state possesses, we may ask the further question as to just what *in the state* is the fundamental residence of that power. Does the state's authority take its rise in a summation of each individual's private authority or in the collective will of the majority to accept the dominion of the state? If so, the stability of a government must necessarily lie at the mercy of the majority's whim and caprice. Or does God directly intervene each time a ruler or a government is seated and immediately bestow political authority? For this latter view there is no proof. Furthermore, it cannot face successfully the objection that God usually operates through secondary causes in His dealings with men and not immediately.

The truth, as is so often the case, will be found between the two extremes. In the state the fundamental residence of authority is to be found in the political community. Society is of natural law and hence as soon as men consent to live in society, the authority that is necessary for achieving the common end of that society arises and rests in it. "As soon as men by their free will and consent, though in consequence of the urge of their social nature and by force of the necessity of perfecting the good life, unite into a body politic, authority is simultaneously born and rests in the body politic."[32]

---

[31] In saying that the natural law depends on the divine will we are not suggesting, of course, that the natural law could be anything but what it is. God could not change basic natural law without first changing the human nature from which it flows.

[32] Rommen, *The State in Catholic Thought*, p. 448. St. Robert Bellarmine held that

This residence of political authority in the people is interestingly and diversely reflected in many of the constitutions of modern states. The constitution of Brazil states that "all power emanates from the people and shall be exercised in its name."[33] Finland puts the matter in much the same way: "Sovereign power in Finland belongs to the people represented by their delegates assembled in Diet."[34] Communistic, antinatural law political philosophy shines through the Czechoslovak formulation of sovereignty: "The People are the sole source of all power in the State."[35] On the other hand natural law principles are clearly reflected in the statements of Pakistan and Ireland: "Whereas sovereignty over the entire universe belongs to God Almighty alone and the authority which He has delegated to the State of Pakistan through its people for being exercised within the limits prescribed by Him is a sacred trust. . . ."[36] "In the Name of the Most Holy Trinity, from Whom is all authority and to Whom, as our final end, all actions both of men and States must be referred. . . .[37] All powers of government, legislative, executive, and judicial, derive, under God, from the people. . . ."[38]

As Suarez observed,[39] the community is at first a democracy of all the people, since in them is to be found the authority needed to organize and rule. Later the community through its free consent transfers this authority to a select few, and civil government as we know it comes into being. It will be seen, therefore, that political authority does not take its being from the will of the people. It exists in them independently of their will. Because the people do not enjoy absolute sovereignty, they cannot change their government at will. For this reason political writers commonly assign severe limits to the

---

political authority is originally in the whole people only by "universal essence" and needs to be specified as to some particular form of government. Suarez' position is that political authority is originally in the whole people in such a way as to constitute them a form of government (direct democracy) as soon as they unite into a body politic.

[33] *Constitution of the United States of Brazil*, Sept. 24, 1946, article 1, found in Amos J. Peaslee, *Constitutions of Nations* (Concord, N. H.: Rumford Press, 1950), I, p. 181.

[34] *Form of Government of Finland*, July 17, 1919, article 2. Peaslee, I, p. 777.

[35] *Constitution of the Czechoslovak Republic*, article 1, No. 2, Peaslee, I, p. 603.

[36] *Objectives of the Pakistan Constitution*, Mar. 7, 1949, Peaslee, III, p. 691.

[37] *Constitution of Ireland*, Dec. 29, 1937, Preamble. Peaslee, II, p. 239.

[38] *Ibid.*, article 6.

[39] *Def. Fidei*, III, c. 2, n. 9.

circumstances in which a community may use active resistance (revolution) to remove a legitimate government.[40]

LIMITATIONS ON STATE AUTHORITY

The reader will readily note that the section we now approach bears pointedly on our later analysis of the state's role in education. If the state can be criticized at all, it is because it is not omnicompetent and omnipotent; it is not a law to itself. While the political community is in a real sense sovereign (it is the highest temporal authority for internal affairs within its borders), it is not absolutely so. Limitations lie upon what it may and may not do.[41] These limitations we will now indicate in a general way, reserving particularizations for our later discussion of educational problems.

The first is the natural law. That the state is bound by the principles of natural law is clearly evident. Even the political positivist who sees in civil law the source of every obligation is driven to admit in practice that the state can be wrong, unjust, tyrannical. This he could not do if there were no norm of morality outside and independent of the political community, a norm by which the community itself can be judged. This norm can be nothing but the natural law. Most by far of our judgments on the state's role in education will be founded on natural law principles.

A second limitation on the state is the positive divine law.[42] Catholic political thought has traditionally held that the state is subject to the will of God as expressed in revelation.[43] The reason is not difficult to discover: men organized into a nation and state are just as much

---

[40] See, for example, the moral theologian, Noldin, *Summa Theologiae Moralis* (Oeniponte diag. Lipsiae: Felicianus Rauch, 1941), II, No. 312.

[41] The Japanese constitution adopted in 1946 explicitly recognizes this truth: "We believe that no nation is responsible to itself alone, but that laws of political morality are universal and that obedience to such laws is incumbent upon all nations which would sustain their own sovereignty and justify their sovereign relationship with other nations." Preamble. Peaslee, II, p. 307.

[42] By positive divine law we mean an ordination promulgated by God through revelation and one often further determining natural law. Thus man is bound from the very nature of the divine-human relationship to worship God (natural law), but that he formally execute this worship on a particular day of the week (positive law) is a determination of the natural obligation and was known to the Jews through revelation.

[43] See among others the French philosopher-theologian, Garrigou-Lagrange, *De Revelatione* (Rome: F. Ferrari, 1931), II, p. 440 ff. and Rommen, *The State in Catholic Thought*, p. 257.

subject to God as they are taken singly and individually.[44] It follows necessarily, therefore, that since individuals are bound by the positive law of God, the state is likewise so bound. This position has been the ordinary doctrine of Catholic philosophers and theologians throughout the ages. Recent attempts[45] to deny the direct obliging force of positive divine law on the state assert that Leo XIII (who was quite clear on the question) was speaking for one age and that his principles need not be applied to present-day circumstances. Alfredo Cardinal Ottaviani, Pro-Secretary of the Holy Office, in an article dealing with this precise question made the point that this type of distinction cannot be validly applied to principles on which the teachings of the popes have remained constant. This constancy indicates that the principles so taught pertain to the patrimony of Catholic doctrine.[46]

The final limitation is international law and the international common good. Just as the individual person is a social being and as such is destined to live in a political community and to be bound by its laws, so also is the individual state a social being destined to live in a world community of states and be bound by its laws. International law is both natural and positive. On the natural law level all states are bound by such obligations as truth, honesty, and justice. They, too, lie under the obligation of co-operating with fellow states for the furtherance of the common good of the whole community of nations. On the level of international positive law the society of states, again like the society of individuals, must work out for itself a set of internationally recognized norms under which the universal common good can be pursued. These positive norms trace their origin to a large extent to treaties, conventions, and international organizations.

PRINCIPLE OF SUBSIDIARITY

We approach now a question of political science the correct understanding of which is of crucial importance for our proposed analysis

[44] Pope Leo XIII, "Immortale Dei," *Acta Leonis XIII,* 1885, p. 122.

[45] Among those who have opposed traditional teaching in the United States is Father John C. Murray, S.J. A bibliography of his writings and those of his opponents may be found in *Theology Digest,* I (autumn, 1953), 173–175. Unfortunately, this bibliography does not contain reference to Cardinal Ottaviani's article indicated in the next footnote. In all likelihood it could not have been included, due to the brief time lapse between the two.

[46] "Church and State: Some Present Problems in the Light of the Teaching of Pope Pius XII," *American Ecclesiastical Review,* 130 (May, 1953), 323.

of the state's role in education. That question is the principle of subsidiarity. We have already reached the conclusion that the end of the state is the common good, and this we have defined as the aggregate of those conditions and helps provided by the group's co-operation which aid individuals in the attainment of their proximate and remote ends. It remains for us now to determine the principles that must guide the state in providing those conditions and helps.

The different political philosophies will, of course, offer varying explanations and principles for the guidance of the state in the exercise of its service function. For the collectivist the state is paternal; it is the provider. It is concerned with all facets of the citizen's life and shows that concern by assuming to itself activities that could be discharged easily by the private person himself or at least by some lesser society. At the other extreme lies the individualist's state, the state which sees itself as a mere umpire regulating as little as possible the free competitive forces of society. The individualist state is the *laissez-faire* state. It believes that society flourishes best when individuals are left free to work out their temporal welfare unhampered by any but the most unavoidably needed governmental help. Thus the individualist would not ordinarily favor public housing projects, while the collectivist would like the government not only to aid those projects but to own them as well.

Between these extremes lies the natural law principle of subsidiarity.[47] Although the principle is often stated in its limiting aspect, there are really two elements involved.[48] In its positive aspect subsidiarity means

---

[47] Catholic political science is not, of course, alone in its support of this principle. President Eisenhower has remarked that "the Federal Government should perform an essential task only when it cannot otherwise be adequately performed. . . ." Reported in *Time,* January 17, 1955, p. 22. American courts have likewise upheld the principle of subsidiarity. In the case of *Lawton* v. *Steel,* 152 U.S. 133, 137, we read that "to justify the state in thus interposing its authority on behalf of the public, it must appear: First, that the interests of the public generally, as distinguished from those of a particular class, require such interference; and second, that the means are reasonably necessary for the accomplishment of the purpose, and not unnecessarily oppressive upon individuals. The legislature may not, under the guise of protecting the public interests, arbitrarily interfere with private business, or impose unusual and unnecessary restrictions upon lawful occupations. . . ." See also *Union Fisherman's Co.* v. *Shoemaker,* 98 Ore. 659, 675. *Oregon School Cases* (Baltimore: Belvedere Press, 1925), pp. 331 and 333.

[48] Schmandt refers to these two aspects when he says that "the principle of subsidiarity both requires assistance to men from groups when aid is needed and inhibits interference when men can act alone." Henry J. Schmandt, "State Intervention — When?" *Social Order,* IV (Dec., 1954), 43.

that the state is to help individuals and lesser societies to do what they cannot do efficiently for themselves. Because private persons cannot provide the means for convenient modern transportation, an obligation lies on the state to come to their aid by building and maintaining adequate roads and highways. In its negative aspect subsidiarity requires that the state aid private persons and associations only when they are either unable or unwilling efficiently to execute a needed project. Thus the state may not rightly interfere in an educational enterprise of private citizens as long as that enterprise is being adequately handled.

The principle of subsidiarity applies not only to the sovereign state but to all lesser governmental agencies and societies as well. A national government should not do what a regional government finds possible, nor should the latter undertake what falls within the competency of a local government. It was probably for this reason that the framers of the American constitution left educational matters to the states.

In order to establish a sound basis for our later evaluation of governmental activities in education, it seems imperative that we here discuss the grounds on which the principle of subsidiarity rests. That this principle is in full accord with Catholic social teaching is evidenced by the clear statements on it emanating from the Holy See. Leo XIII touched upon the principle of subsidiarity in his classical encyclical on labor.[49] Pope Pius XI wrote in 1931: "Just as it is gravely wrong to take from individuals what they can accomplish by their own initiative and industry and give it to the community, so also it is an injustice and at the same time a grave evil and disturbance of right order to assign to a greater and higher association what lesser and subordinate organizations can do."[50] Pius XII repeats this teaching and gives one of the reasons for it: "If, in fact, the state lays claim to and directs private enterprises, these, ruled as they are by delicate and complicated internal principles which guarantee and assure the realization of their special aims, may be damaged to the detriment of the public good, by being wrenched from their natural surroundings, that is, from responsible private action."[51]

---

[49] *Great Encyclicals of Leo XIII* (New York: Benziger Bros., 1903), pp. 212, 215–216.
[50] *Quadragesimo Anno* (Washington: N.C.W.C., 1936), No. 79.
[51] *Summi Pontificatus* (New York: America Press, 1939), No. 60.

Aside from authority there are a number of soundly based reasons on which the principle of subsidiarity rests. These for the sake of brevity and clarity we will indicate in numbered order.

1. The full development of the human person demands that he be allowed activity, expression, and freedom in those areas in which he is capable and provided no harm be done to the individual or to the common good. When a man *unnecessarily* depends on others his own growth and personal dignity suffer.

2. Too much state intervention in the affairs of human life can easily result in a lack of equity in the distribution of the community's goods. Somerville made the point that state welfare officials, in order to remove the danger of abuse, are often denied discretionary powers in the dispensing of benefits.[52] Because the law is as a consequence strictly applied, some receive more aid than they need, while others receive less.

3. Closely allied with the preceding reason is the understandably human consideration that governmental services often lack the personal touch usually present in the privately dispensed service. While not as cogent as other reasons here mentioned, this factor merits some attention.

4. The common welfare suffers from too much governmental activity. It is well known that a man will produce much more when he is working with his own property and from his own initiative. The closer a person is to a problem the more clearly does he understand it and the greater is his interest in it. This is one reason local government is, from this point of view, more effective than regional or federal government.

5. A policy running counter to the principle of subsidiarity perverts the very *raison d'être* of the state: the supplementation of man in those things which he cannot do for himself.[53]

6. The state loses in efficiency when it undertakes more problems than it can handle with effectiveness. Aside from the corruption that so readily allies itself with bureaucracy, large scale government tends to a greater sluggishness as it grows. Pope Pius XI took note of the

---

[52] Henry Somerville, "What is the Welfare State?" *Catholic Mind,* LI (Nov., 1953), p. 666.

[53] John F. Kenney, "The Principle of Subsidiarity," *American Catholic Sociological Review,* XVI (Mar., 1955), p. 33.

fact that the state can undertake too much when he wrote that by taking over duties once borne by other associations a state can be over-
whelmed and crushed by almost infinite duties.[54]

7. By undertaking unnecessary tasks the state makes unjust incur-
sions into the citizen's pocketbook. To finance these tasks it must either
raise its tax income without good reason or it will misuse existing tax
revenues. Both possibilities violate distributive justice.[55]

From this list of reasons undergirding the principle of subsidiarity
we must not conclude to the extreme view that the state must be
severely restricted from undertaking the solution of any project hith-
erto administered under private auspices. Modern life with its involved
roots and circumstances is far too complex to admit of the universal
and facile exclusion of the state. Pius XII recognized this fact when he
remarked that "no one of good-will and vision will think of refusing
the state, in the exceptional conditions of the world today correspond-
ingly wider and exceptional rights to meet the popular needs."[56] And
yet great care must be taken before admitting governmental entrance
into a new field. The Pontiff adds the caution that even in present-day
emergencies the lawfulness of the state's entrance into new fields and
the real necessity of such entrance be examined with great rigor.[57]

We can readily agree, therefore, that the criterion of subsidiarity is
not always easy to apply to concrete situations, but because we will
have so to apply it to educational problems, we offer here a few guiding norms.

First of all, diligent consideration of all circumstances should precede
any judgment as to whether the state should or should not assume or
continue to shoulder a particular responsibility. The cry of "creeping
socialism" should not be uttered on the instance of any governmental

---

[54] *Quadragesimo Anno*, No. 78.

[55] Kenney, *op. cit.*, p. 33. John Stuart Mill has appositely observed that "before
making the work their own, governments ought always to consider if there be any
rational probability of its being done on what is called the voluntary principle, and if
so, whether it is likely to be done in a better or more effectual manner by governmental
agency." *Principles of Political Economy* (London: Longmans, Green and Co., 1936),
p. 977.

[56] *Op. cit.*, No. 65.

[57] *Ibid.* While the principle of subsidiarity is admittedly of crucial importance in any
sound political philosophy, its position ought not to be unduly magnified. Ewald Link
in his *Das Subsidiaritatsprinzip: Sein Wesen und Seine Bedeutung fur die Sozialethik*
envisions subsidiarity as the tap root of political philosophy crowding even the common
good into a secondary position. This view is questionable. See Karl Kreilkamp, "The
Principle of Subsidiarity," *Review of Politics*, XIX (Apr., 1957), pp. 240–244.

intervention. A man cannot validly philosophize in a vacuum. And he cannot validly condemn a government project until he knows the facts of the matter, concrete, experimentally verifiable facts. Once he is in possession of these facts he will much more likely be able to judge whether or not private initiative is equal to the task at hand.

Secondly, the advisability of state intervention is to be determined according to the ordinary norms of morality and especially by applying the yardstick of the common good. This latter is, of course, to be viewed in long range perspectus and not in shortsighted pragmatism.

The state, thirdly, once it has entered a field should have to do with it no more than is necessary. If mere subsidy of an industry will enable it to function effectively, the government should not take it over entirely. If mere direction is needed in the administration of an educational system, the state is not thereby justified in operating that system. The burden of proof that the state should assume an activity lies, of course, with the state. The person and the family are prior to the state, and hence any assumption of their activities may not be admitted unless a genuine need is proved.

The state, finally, should periodically examine its service functions to determine whether it need continue in its assumed activities or whether it ought to relinquish them to lesser groups.[58]

Having examined philosophically the state's nature and its functions, we are now prepared to push our investigation further and inquire into the state's functions as educator. This inquiry will furnish us with more particularized principles with which to evaluate governmental practices throughout the world.

---

[58] Kenney, *op. cit.*, p. 35.

PART II

THE STATE AS EDUCATOR

CHAPTER III

INDIVIDUALISM

IT IS not our purpose to offer an analytical treatment and criticism of the varying shades of individualist and statist theories regarding the state as educator. Although comparatively little has been pointedly written on this aspect of political philosophy, yet it is likely that one could deduce as many diverse concepts of state as educator (or non-educator) as there are diverse concepts of individualism and collectivism.[1] Because that task would take us too far afield, we will treat these two poles of political thought in more general terms. Our discussion of individualism will be further delimited by a Spencerian stress, for among individualistic thinkers Herbert Spencer is outstanding for the thoroughness and clarity of his politico-educational writing.

FUNDAMENTAL BASES

Extreme individualism in political thought is almost nonexistent today. Traces of its influence, however, are very much alive. One need only examine the constitutions of modern states and note how many of them ascribe the sovereignty of the people to a kind of social compact whereby individuals give up personal freedom to create a new authority, the state. In a mitigated form individualism seems decidedly much alive in our twentieth century. In the very first issue of *National Review* the new periodical lists its "credenda." Among its convictions we see topping the list the statement that

It is the job of centralized government (in peace-time) to protect its citizens' lives, liberty and property. *All other activities of government*

---

[1] Messner interestingly enough observes that these extreme positions often join hands in their conclusions. *Op. cit.,* p. 5.

tend to diminish freedom and hamper progress. The growth of government — the dominant social feature of this century — must be fought relentlessly. In this great social conflict of the era, we are, without reservations, on the libertarian side.[2]

John Dewey in his "systematic" treatment of his philosophy of the state (*The Public and Its Problems*) describes government in the individualist, police-man-state tradition. Yet in his educational writings he decidedly supposes a governmentally sponsored system of schools. This clash seems nothing but another of Dewey's characteristic self-contradictions.[3] In any event we may not ignore educational individualism on the plea that it has little influence today. That influence is slight, but it is nonetheless worth noting.

The reader will observe likewise, that our investigation of individualist thinking can be extremely valuable in this, that it casts light on the aberrations of the statist position. While Spencer's reasonings, for example, do not justify his rigorous limitation on governmental functions, those reasonings do give the lie to the position that sees in the state a universal provider.

Our analysis of the individualist position will enable us also to help distinguish the genuine Catholic teaching on the state's role in education from false allegations. We will see that this teaching is by no means individualistic or anti-state even though isolated Catholic writers may in the past have gone to excess in the limitations they imposed on state activity in education. It seems that the views of these latter were sometimes not a little influenced by the writings of Mill and Spencer.[4]

To understand the individualist's thinking in the realm of public education we must first grasp something of his underlying philosophy. As the name of his system suggests, the individualist conceives society as a mere collection of human units, if we may so term them. It is not

---

[2] "The Magazine's Credenda," *National Review*, I (Nov. 19, 1955), 6. Italics added.

[3] See Meiklejohn's discussion of Dewey's political philosophy, Alexander Meiklejohn, *Education between Two Worlds* (New York: Harper and Bros., 1942), pp. 169–181. Though he is no friend of natural law political philosophy, Meiklejohn concludes that for "a contemporary world which is entrusting its schools to the control of government, Dewey gives an essentially invalid theory of political institutions. His state is a medley of pressure groups with no guiding principles of belief or action, no common devotion to a common welfare. Such a state cannot possibly teach wisdom" (p. 194).

[4] That influence can be seen in the famous school controversy waged in the last decade of the nineteenth century in the United States.

a body, a whole being that is more than the sum of its constituent parts. Individualism may be described as a social doctrine "which makes the human individual the sole and absolute end of human existence."[5] Society itself is acknowledged to have only a fictitious existence. It is not something new that arises from a union of persons, something founded in their very natures.[6]

The individualist concept of the state denies to government a welfare function. The purpose of the state according to Thomas Hobbes, a typical spokesman, is to protect all against all and for this reason it has been classically called the policeman state or the night watchman state. The system lays great stress on man's freedom and thus envisions the function of government as the mere protector of free play among individuals. For this reason likewise it holds that the less the governing the better the government.

Wilhelm von Humboldt, a German representative of individualism, offered a number of reasons for his denial that the state's function extends to the positive promotion of the general welfare of the community. He argued that the entrance of the state into a welfare role (a) produces a deadening uniformity among the citizenry, (b) hinders self-development by spending energy on making rules for others, (c) weakens a man's powers, and (d) hinders the healthy individualism and idiosyncrasy that so aid progress.[7] John Stuart Mill added the further observation that an increase in the state's functions contributes to the "great evil" of an increase in its power.[8]

At this point an incursion into the political philosophies of Herbert Spencer and J. S. Mill seems in order. As we have pointed out above, the former's reasonings on the functions of government do not always prove his conclusions, but they do offer profitable insights on occasion, insights that often throw into bold relief the extremes of the statist position. Mill is a more moderate individualist and so well represents that shade of political thought.

In his *Social Statics*[9] Spencer has a complete chapter precisely on the

---

[5] Messner, *op. cit.*, p. 4.

[6] *Ibid.*, p. 110.

[7] William Archibald Dunning, *A History of Political Theories* (New York: Macmillan, 1920), Vol. 1, pp. 148–154.

[8] John H. Hallowell, *Main Currents in Modern Political Thought* (New York: Henry Holt and Co., 1950), p. 228. See Mill's own explanation of this reason in his *Principles of Political Economy* (London: Longmans, Green and Co., 1936), p. 944 ff.

[9] This volume offers the advantage of representing Spencer's settled thought on the

individualist position we are examining. This chapter, "The Limit of State-Duty," is followed in a later section by an application of his ideas to the question of the state's relation to education.

Spencer begins his argument supporting the proscription of welfare activities from government competence with the principle that "a function to each organ and each organ to its own function is the law of all organization."[10] He argues that the human body with a nerve for each muscle and gland, an organ for each operation and a channel of food for each fiber exemplifies the truth that every function is performed by a single agent. Specialization in industry and business shows the applicability of the principle even to the sphere of human activities. Why, then, does not this law apply also to the state? "Must we not expect that with a government also, special adaptation to one end implies non-adaptation to other ends?"[11] No one questions the fact that government of its very nature must be protective. The conclusion is apparent. One function to each organ means that government must be protective of rights and nothing else.

In his next line of argumentation Spencer attempts to show that by assuming additional activities the state shifts from its status as a protector of freedom to an aggressor against freedom. As an individualist he of course holds that the function of the state is to guarantee to each citizen the fullest freedom compatible with the freedom of others. By the additional taxes necessary to finance a welfare function the state takes away from the citizen some of his money, that on which he depends for the free exercise of his faculties. These taxes, therefore, are opposed to the very nature of the state, which is supposed to protect freedom, not attack it.

Spencer realizes his opponents' objection to this argument and honestly faces it. "If you argue that taking away a man's property diminishes his freedom to exercise his faculties, because it diminishes his *means* of exercising them, then you must in fairness admit that, by procuring for him certain of the objects he desires, or by taking away the obstacles that lie between him and those objects, or by otherwise helping him to his ends, the State is increasing his power to exercise

state and education. Originally written in 1850, he tells us that "in 1890 at leisure times I went through the work, erasing some portions, abridging others, and subjecting the whole to a careful verbal revision" (New York: D. Appleton and Co., 1892), p. 3.

[10] *Op. cit.*, p. 121.

[11] *Ibid.*, p. 122.

his faculties, and hence is practically increasing his freedom."[12] The answer to the difficulty is readily available. To take away freedom to bestow freedom is at best accompanied by a friction loss due to the "serious waste occurring under official manipulations." What is taken away by taxation does not return to the citizen one hundred per cent. In the operation he suffers a loss, and this loss entails a diminution of his freedom.

Yet this is not all. The idea that the state is not only to protect happiness but also to furnish it defeats the very happiness of the citizen. Each human faculty yields a gratification, a happiness, when it is fully and normally exercised. When men, therefore, are allowed to serve their own needs, they exercise their faculties, each of which yields its peculiar pleasure. A man who exercises all of his faculties and who is rightly constituted cannot be helped.[13] The objection that man is not complete and perfect and able to satisfy all his wants is for Spencer no reason for state interference. He must be inconvenienced by his incompetence into activity with a consequent eventual attainment of perfection and completeness. State interference stifles personal activity, growth, and happiness.[14]

The next argument is based on a practical difficulty. The proponents of a welfare function for the state cannot, says Spencer, set a satisfactory boundary line beyond which the state should not go in providing facilities and helps for the citizenry. For him, to declare that the government should further the common good is to say nothing at all. Definiteness is needed or absurdity results. Ought the state to interfere in determining religious creeds, moderating modes of manufacture, farming, domestic affairs, regulating commerce, establishing public education, caring for public health, setting norms for dress, charity, manners, or amusements? Where is the line to be drawn? "Should the perplexed inquirer seek refuge in authority, he will find precedents

---

[12] *Ibid.,* p. 124.

[13] "To do anything for him by some artificial agency, is to supercede certain of his powers — is to leave them unexercised, and therefore to diminish his happiness" (*ibid.,* p. 125).

[14] "Power is as inevitably lost by inactivity as it is gained by activity. Hence, humanity no longer goes on moulding itself into harmony with the natural requirements of the social state; but begins, instead, to assume a form fitting these artificial requirements. And thus, as before said, not only does a government reverse its function by taking away more property than is needful for protective purposes, but even what it gives, in return for the excess so taken, is in essence a loss" (*ibid.,* p. 126).

not only for these but for many more such interferences."[15] The boundary line for the individualist is clear and definite: the state is the mere protector of the rights of men, nothing more, nothing less. The defender of the welfare state is challenged to offer a like clear demarcation: "Between the one extreme of entire noninterference, and the other extreme in which every citizen is to be transformed into a grown-up baby, there lie innumerable stopping places; and he who would have the State do more than protect, is required to say where he means to draw the line and to give us reasons why it must be just there and nowhere else."[16]

Spencer's additional arguments against state interference are well known in contemporary political life and so we need merely notice them. Governmental inefficiency and waste in the running of its affairs[17] and the huge tax burden which the welfare function makes necessary are for Spencer new motives for limiting the state's role to a mere policeman activity. The manifest conclusion to all of these arguments is that the state is to be nothing but a protector. Any entrance of government into welfare, religious, or educational activities is viewed as an unwarranted intrusion into a field foreign to its *raison d'être*.

John Stuart Mill's individualism is of a much milder variety than is Spencer's. Mill explicitly denies that the state's function may be limited to a mere protective role.[18] To explain his position regarding the welfare function of the state he distinguishes authoritative interference from nonauthoritative interference. The former is a governmental activity that positively commands or negatively forbids something to the citizenry. It consequently limits freedom. The latter is an interference that neither commands nor forbids, but merely offers. Its only limitation on freedom lies in an additional tax burden. Compulsory state education is an authoritative interference, while the mere provision of state schools for those who wish to use them is nonauthoritative. Mill holds it as evident that justified authoritative intervention of

---

[15] *Ibid.*, p. 128.

[16] *Ibid.*, p. 131.

[17] Mill regards this drawback to state interference as due more from bad organization of government than from the mere number and variety of activities undertaken. *Op. cit.*, p. 945. He does hold, however, that for most affairs of life private enterprise is more efficient than public.

[18] *Ibid.*, p. 941. In this section of his book he deals with the grounds and limits of the "non-interference principle" of government.

government enjoys a much more limited sphere than does the nonauthoritative.

Mill lays it down that government should be dissuaded from assuming activities "of any sort which can easily be dispensed with," and this because present civilization strongly tends to minimize individual freedom by making the mass group the only real power in society.[19] This, he asserts, must be remembered especially in a democracy, because in this form of government the individual is not likely to be heard in his appeal against the mass of public opinion as he probably will be heard in a (nondictatorial) monarchy in his opposition to the sovereign.

One of the strongest arguments in Mill's view for limiting state interference in national life is the educational harm done to the populace at large. This is so because "the business of life is an essential part of the practical education of a people."[20] By conducting their own affairs when such is possible natural talents and endowments are developed, judgment and self-control perfected. This educational growth of the body politic is likewise a check on the development of undue power or tyranny in the ruler.

Mill concludes his reasoning in favor of restricting to the narrowest compass governmental intervention with the principle that the burden of proof for the advisability of state interference lies not with the resisters but with the state. He readily grants, however, that contrary reasons of considerable importance can outweigh those opposing state intervention and in such a case that the former should prevail against the latter. We will see below how he justifies state entrance into the field of education by means of this principle.

INDIVIDUALISM AND EDUCATION

Herbert Spencer's position on the relation of the state to education flows logically from his version of individualism as we have explained it above. Because he sees the state as a protector of rights only, he wants it to have nothing to do with education. It may or may not be significant, but it is at least interesting that in his *Social Statics* Spencer devotes more space to his attack on statism in education than to any other phase of governmental interference. His reasons for the attack

---

[19] *Ibid.*, p. 945.   [20] *Ibid.*, p. 942.

are many and varied. We will notice here the more plausible ones only.

1. To take away more of a man's property than is necessary for the maintenance of his rights is an attack on those rights and therefore an injustice. Yet this is what the state does when it taxes a man for the education of his and other men's children, because education is not needed for the exercise of any right. A right for Spencer is a mere portion of an arbitrary subdivision of the general liberty to exercise one's faculties. Even without education a child can exercise its faculties, and so since no freedom is threatened by noneducation, the state is an aggressor against a man's rights when it takes his property in the form of taxes for the purpose of supporting education.[21]

2. If, as the state educationists assert, the state is bound to educate a man's children, where is the line to be drawn regarding the services the state is not to supply? The reasoning that will support the state's duty to educate will likewise support its duty to feed, clothe, and shelter the child.[22]

3. If one grants to the state the right and duty to educate, he is faced with the impossible task of determining at what particular educational level that right and that duty cease. At what point between the "dame-school" and the university the state's financial help may be demanded by the citizens cannot be determined. Neither can the educationist demonstrate the necessity of including certain subjects in the curriculum to the exclusion of others. Each section of the populace will have its preferences and none can be shown to be wrong.[23]

4. The state-education theory is logically realized in its full development by an entire and despotic domination of school life by the government. This is so because the government must of necessity formulate and impose a policy on the schools it operates. The danger of this situation is seen precisely in the fact that there is no higher authority to which the populace can appeal should the policy be objectionable. The authority is absolute and can be despotic.[24]

5. To Mill's justification of state intervention in education for the reason that many private persons are not competent judges of what an adequate education is and how it is to be acquired,[25] Spencer retorts that this is a worn out excuse readily used to justify myriads of governmental interferences. Private persons, he says, do generally know

---

[21] Op. cit., pp. 156–157.   [24] Ibid., pp. 158–160.
[22] Ibid., p. 157.   [25] See below, p. 38.
[23] Ibid., pp. 157–158.

the effects of good teaching even though they themselves lack a good education. They can likewise select well-proved private schools and seek the advice of the better informed when they doubt about the standing of a particular institution. Moreover, ignorance of educational matters where it does occur is slowly being extirpated by advances in education itself.

And if this tardiness is a valid argument for interference in one case, why not in others? Why not have farms superintended by Government, because it may take a century for farmers generally to adopt the plans suggested by modern science.[26]

6. Further, Mill's argument rests on the shaky supposition that the state knows what is best in education both as regards the end and the means. Spencer questions this supposition with his not-too-complimentary opinion of contemporary governmental officials.[27] While he admits that this argument from personnel incompetency is valid only for an unfit government, he argues that in this matter we cannot reason as though government were what it ought to be. This is so because before rulers will become what they ought to be deficiencies of interest and judgment on the part of the citizens must disappear.[28]

7. Government sponsorship of education in Spencer's view is unprogressive both in spirit and in fact. Like all institutions, the state has an instinct of self-perpetuation and so is immersed in the *status quo.* Education, on the other hand, is much interested in changing the *status quo,* and so is incompatible with government.[29]

8. The last of Spencer's philosophical reasons aimed at the exclusion of the state from education is based on an *a pari* argument which he feels excludes religion from state competence. Just as he sees an injustice in the state's preaching of one religion, since all men do not accept that preaching, so also he holds it as unjust for the state to impose one kind of education on all. Even though there is general agreement as to the truths contained in the subject matter offered by

---

[26] Spencer, *op. cit.,* p. 164.

[27] His characterization of state personnel is amusing: "Well-meaning, many of them; thoughtful, some; philosophical, a few; men, however, for the most part, born with silver spoons in their mouths, and prone to regard human affairs as reflected in these — somewhat distortedly" (*ibid.*).

[28] *Ibid.,* p. 165.

[29] Education "is always fitting men for higher things, and *un*fitting them for things as they are." *Ibid.,* p. 166. Italics are Spencer's.

public education, there is wide divergence on educational methodology, curriculum content and disciplinary techniques. Tenable differences of outlook must be respected, and that even as possible matter of conscience.[30]

As we have already shown above, John Stuart Mill's *laissez-faire* individualism is of a more moderate variety than is that of Herbert Spencer.[31] As would be expected, the former does not rigidly exclude the state from the sphere of education as does the latter. Mill is content with limiting governmental intervention to the bare minimum required by necessity.

The fundamental reason that Mill offers for the admission of the state into the field of education is that the populace at large is not a competent judge of matters educational and so must consign that function to the state.[32] The uneducated, he reasons, cannot judge education.[33] We should note, however, that Mill's admittance of the state into education is effected only by way of exception to his general principle of *laissez-faire*.

Mill is willing to push this exception even further in the case of elementary education. All children, he holds, should receive the rudiments of knowledge both for their own sakes and for the common good of society. Government may as a consequence force parents to provide a basic education for their children, but this cannot be done unless the means of education are made available to all, even to the

---

[30] In order to emphasize this last point Spencer places the following words into the mouth of one of his objectors to state-sponsored education: "With me, resistance is a point of conscience. These children of mine I regard as beings with whose welfare, bodily and mental, I stand charged; and I conceive that I am acting unconscientiously if I allow them to be treated in a manner which I believe hurtful. Now to me your scheme of education seems, in many respects, essentially vicious. Would it not, then, be a gross breach of duty in me to put my children under your care? I pity you, if you say no. And if it *would* be a breach of duty, what am I to do but resist? Am I to pay your education-rates and get nothing in return? Perhaps you will answer, yes. I must tell you, however, that my conscience will no more permit me to do this than it will permit me to use your schools. Not only should I be aiding you to mis-educate my neighbor's children, which my desire for human welfare forbids, but I should be submitting to an injustice which I feel bound to oppose." *Ibid.,* pp. 183–184. Italics are Spencer's.

[31] It will be noted that Mill's educational theory is *laissez-faire* more in its reasons than in its conclusions. In other words, he is sometimes right for the wrong reasons.

[32] We have already noted Spencer's reaction to this argument on pages 36 and 37.

[33] "Those who most need to be made wiser and better usually desire it least, and, if they desired it, would be incapable of finding the way to it by their own lights." Mill, *op. cit.,* p. 953.

poor. Hence, the necessity for compulsory education is the second reason Mill advances for the right and duty of the state to enter the field of education.[34]

Mill closes his discussion of the state as educator with a vigorously unmistakable attack on governmental monopoly in any shape or form. The state must be allowed complete control over education on no level, low or high. Nor may it bestow any peculiar advantages on those who have been educated in the public schools. To exercise a monopolistic control over education was, thought Mill, to be despotic, for once a government could mold opinions and ideas, it could do with the citizenry whatever it wished.[35]

Our final (but not in a historical sense) exemplification of a pronounced limitation on state activity in education is found in Adam Smith. We do not advance Smith, however, as a representative of the *laissez-faire* school of political thought, for while he sought freedom from misguided controls, he would not have opposed at least certain types of modern social legislation.[36]

While he seems to have granted the state a role in education, Smith looked with disfavor on the public support of education because he believed that such support had corrupted the diligence of public teachers. He reasoned that if teachers received their pay from the students rather than from the state or "incorporated societies," there would be more healthy, competition-produced diligence and excellence among those teachers. He believed that an assured income independent of what the students think of the quality of the institution produces indolence and neglect. Further, there is, in Smith's mind, less waste of time on useless subjects in a school whose revenue depends on its industry and the results it produces and not on some assured endowment or tax income levied by the state.[37] Even while advocating com-

---

[34] *Ibid.*, pp. 954–956.

[35] "To possess such a (complete) control, and actually exert it, is to be despotic. A government which can mould the opinions and sentiments of the people from their youth upwards, can do with them whatever it pleases. . . Nor ought the power of individuals to set up rival establishments to depend in any degree upon its authorization. It would be justified in requiring from all the people that they shall possess instruction in certain things, but not in prescribing to them how or from whom they shall obtain it." *Ibid.*, p. 956.

[36] John Maurice Clark, "Smith, Adam," *Encyclopedia of the Social Sciences,* XIV, p. 112.

[37] *An Inquiry Into the Nature and Causes of the Wealth of Nations* (Edinburgh: Thomas Nelson, 1840), pp. 326–327.

pulsory education he did not wish the cost of it to be paid principally by the public.[38]

*   *   *   *   *   *   *

While individualism as a political philosophy rather strongly survives in our twentieth century (although in a diluted form), educational individualism has not made much of a ripple on the sea of contemporary thought. Nor does it seem likely, in view of the current and worldwide swing to educational statism, that individualism will exert a great influence on public institutions of instruction in the foreseeable future.

---

[38] *Ibid.*, p. 328.

CHAPTER IV

STATISM IN EDUCATION[39]

RECENT TRENDS

WHILE the individualistic philosophy of the state's function in education is at present a matter of historical interest for the most part, that of the statist combines a long history with a crucial twentieth-century pertinence. And that pertinence is by no means limited to communist-dominated countries. In multiple forms educational statism finds vocal representatives in countries as diverse as socialistically governed Belgium and the traditionally conservative United States. The world-wide movement in the present century toward governmentally sponsored and dominated education is more than a localized and passing phenomenon. It deserves careful and thoughtful attention.

Evidence supporting the existence of a strong statist trend in educational circles is readily available to the student of political philosophy. Because we will refer below to earlier expressions of statism in the course of history, we will here content ourselves with twentieth-century indications.

In the United States the celebrated Oregon case brought to a head the seething statist movement of the first quarter of the present century. In the briefs presented to the Supreme Court of the United States some of the tenets of that movement were crystallized. The attorneys for the governor of the state of Oregon argued that "it is evident that a majority of the voters of Oregon believed that the general welfare of the state would be promoted by compelling all children (with some slight exceptions) to receive a certain amount of education in the

---

[39] It would seem to be explaining the obvious to discuss here the general characteristics of statism. Unlike the philosophy of individualism, that of statism is repeatedly encountered in the literature of the day and is, therefore, well known.

public schools of the state."[40] Statism is not yet extreme; only a *certain* amount of governmentally sponsored education is advocated for all. A bit later the attorney general of Oregon and his assistant argued that "the necessity for any other kind of school than that provided by the state has ceased to exist."[41] In his oral argument before the court Chamberlain, one of the appellant attorneys, stated that "between the church itself and the state, we insist that the state has the prior and paramount right to direct the education of the children in the state."[42]

This trend was not of course confined to the United States. Writing in 1931 against Fascism in Italy, Pope Pius XI said: "We find ourselves confronted by a mass of authentic affirmations and no less authentic facts which reveal beyond the slightest possibility of doubt the resolve . . . to monopolize completely the young, from the tenderest years up to manhood and womanhood, for the exclusive advantage of a party and of a regime based upon an ideology which clearly resolves itself in a true, real, pagan worship of the State — the Statolatria. . . ."[43]

For one contemporary educator the state is a mere sum of services and the school is one of them.[44] A sociologist at the turn of the century criticized the private association that would found a school, for in so doing it usurped the place of society and assumed to act in the latter's behalf.[45] Writing in the thirties an editor and educator stated plainly that in the modern totalitarian state education has become mere propaganda aimed at the regimentation of body and mind.[46]

[40] George E. Chamberlain, Albert H. Putney, and P. Q. Nyce, attorneys for the appellant (no editor), *Oregon School Cases* (Baltimore: Belvedere Press, 1925), p. 130.

[41] I. H. Van Winkle and Willis S. Moore, *ibid.*, p. 200.

[42] *Ibid.*, p. 683.

[43] "Non Abbiamo Bisogno," Cambridge Summer School of Catholic Studies, *Church and State* (London: Burns, Oates and Washbourne, 1936), pp. 229–230.

[44] Jesse B. Sears, "Our Theory of Public School Support," *School and Society*, XLIII (Jan. 18, 1936), 77.

[45] Lester F. Ward, *Pure Sociology* (New York: Macmillan, 1903), p. 575.

[46] I. L. Kandel, "Education in a Changing World," *School and Society*, XLIII (June 27, 1936), 859. Gonzalez, a Spanish philosopher, has collected an interesting array of expressions of the statist view on educational rights: " 'Parents in the education of their children are the delegates and mandatories of the State' (Cousin); 'In educational matters the sole lord is the national will' (Gambeta); 'The nation alone has the right to educate children' (Robespierre); 'Children belong to the nation rather than to the parents' (Danton) . . . 'The total and integral education of the Italian belongs solely to the State as its fundamental and primordial function; it is the principal function of the State' (Mussolini, *Allocution in the Council of Ministers,* March 28, 1928). . . . 'The right of parents to the education of their children lacks a foundation . . . for no one can attain his perfection except in society. . . . Society has the primordial and fundamental right in the education of youth' (Boukarine, *ABC du*

Contemporary nontotalitarian governments are moving in the same direction, although we must in caution note that not all trends are toward statism. A tendency toward statism may be seen in Sweden, for since the time of Gustavus Adolphus education has been moving toward uniformity and a strong government participation. The importance of education for the country's social advancement has not been missed, and so it has been viewed as an immediate object for governmental activity.[47]

In 1955, before the All-India Congress Committee, Jawaharlal Nehru declared that the aim of his government is a welfare state and a socialistic economy.[48] In answer to an inquiry the British Embassy in Washington informed me that it had no literature on the subject of parental influence in the control of English schools especially because the family has far less to say in matters educational than it does in the United States.[49] I was likewise informed by the Turkish educational attaché that in Turkey the church has no rights in education and the parents have no judicial rights.[50]

The trend to governmentally sponsored education in the United States has been unmistakable from the middle of the nineteenth century up to the present day. Aside even from that fact, one can scarcely fail to notice a strong stream of thought supporting a state monopoly in American education. James Francis Cardinal McIntyre has referred to a clearly enunciated policy to eliminate private education in the United States and to replace it by a universal common education, a phrase used by the Educational Policies Commission of the National Education Association, a public school organization.[51] A representative of educational progressivism supports the idea and declares that his position is the most commonly held today: "According to the theory of education most frequently expounded in America the public school

---

Communisme)." Joseph Hellin and Irenaeus Gonzalez, *Philosophiae Scholasticae Summa* (Matriti: Biblioteca de Autores Cristianos, 1952), III, p. 803.

[47] Ingemar During, *The Swedish School-Reform, 1950* (Uppsala: Appelbergs Boktryckeriaktiebolag, 1951), p. 14.

[48] Embassy of India, Washington, D. C., *Indiagram*, mimeo., No. 620, January 19, 1955, p. 1.

[49] Letter from Miss H. B. Lawrance, Nov. 10, 1954.

[50] "The church has no rights in education. Parents have the right to make complaints to the Ministry of Education or to the school about their children but parents have no judicial right in educational affairs." Letter from Mr. Emin Hekimgil, Turkish Embassy, New York City, Nov. 5, 1954.

[51] "Our Educational Heritage," *Facts Forum News*, IV (Dec., 1955), 38–39.

should have no competitor. Into its classroom and shops and play-grounds should come all the children of all the people."[52] This extreme twentieth-century thinking has its nineteenth-century antecedents. Before a committee of the Massachusetts legislature President Eliot of Harvard expressed the opinion that all the members of the legislature would agree that the American school system should be made one for the whole state.[53]

TYPICAL STATIST APPROACHES TO THE PHILOSOPHY OF THE STATE'S ROLE IN EDUCATION

It would be manifestly impossible within the confines of the present study to investigate comprehensively the many shades of statism in educational philosophy. One reason is the sheer number of them. Another is the dearth of comprehensive works on the subject. Most writers who touch upon the subject seem content to voice their educational philosophy of state in a paragraph or two, or at most in a single chapter.[54] In order to get anything like the mere beginnings of a coherent philosophy, we must go to work as on a mosaic, piecing together remarks and deriving conclusions, attempting to be at once fair and accurate. For purposes of convenience we may divide the statist position into three categories: (1) extreme statism; (2) conservative statism; and (3) ordinary secularistic statism. We will consider them in that order.

---

[52] George S. Counts, *The American Road to Culture* (New York: John Day Co., 1932), pp. 79–80. We ought not to suppose, however, that the historical transition from private to public education was based on reasoned theory. Canavan rightly remarks that the American people made this change "not on principle, but for pragmatic reasons and as a matter of expedience, without fully realizing what we were doing or what were the full implications of our deed." Francis P. Canavan, "The State as Educator," *Thought*, XXV (Sept., 1950), 487. We might add that Americans still do not see the implications of their deed. One need read only some of the voluminous literature on the subject to see the scarcity of profound, principle-based thinking on the implications of statist educationalism.

[53] Massachusetts General Court, Committee on Education, a digest of the remarks of the Remonstrants at the hearings of the Legislative Committee on Education in March, 1888, n. pub., n. date, p. 7.

[54] Because he devotes a considerable portion of his book, *Education Between Two Worlds*, to this problem (and hence is an exception to our general statement), we will devote some attention to Alexander Meiklejohn and his philosophy of state in education. Meiklejohn is known in American circles both as a philosopher and as an educator.

Extreme statism

This view of the state's function in education makes of the child the mere property of the state, the rights of which (state) are anterior to those of the parents both in the realm of education and in any other realm. The ancient classical exponent of educational statism was Plato, the modern is Communism.

In Book V of the *Republic* Plato advocated a crude type of statist education for his ideal community. In this community human offspring were to be carefully bred after the manner of select animals by mating the most fit male with the most fit female. Since wives and families were to be had in common, the greatest care was to be taken that no mother would recognize her own child. Rather officers were to take the offspring of the parents to a pen or fold and there deposit them with state nurses. After birth the government was to assume full control of the child and its education.[55] It has been remarked that because this rigoristic system violated man's nature and its law, Sparta (which followed the system) did not produce a single poet, orator, or statesman of superior ability. Even its effectiveness in waging successful war eventually deteriorated.[56]

Revolting though this sort of statism be, it is unfortunately reflected in modern thought. We may rightly term weird the speculations of J. S. Haldane that in the future human life will at the very outset be committed to the care of skillful state-sponsored physicians.[57] Even Soviet statolatria has not progressed that far.

The overwhelmingly dominant exponent of extreme statism in contemporary education is of course Communism. The Communistic philosophy of state presents a curious combination of individualism and ultra statism. This union of extremes is due to the place of government in the varying evolutionary stages through which society must pass. Engels taught that the state is the power established to keep class conflict within the bounds of order.[58] This concept is obviously a mere

---

[55] *The Works of Plato*, ed. Irwin Edman (New York: Tudor Publishing Co., 1934), pp. 390–392.

[56] R. I. Holaind, *The Parent First* (New York: Benziger Bros., 1891), p. 10.

[57] J. J. Findlay, *The Foundations of Education* (New York: Henry Holt, 1925), Vol. 1, p. 98. In the brief of William A. Williams in the Oregon Case we find the A. & A.S.R. School Committee quoted to the effect that "the child is first a national child. He belongs to the nation even before he belongs to himself. His education is first national and after that personal." *Op. cit.*, p. 599.

[58] Hans Kelsen, *The Communist Theory of Law* (New York: Frederick A. Praeger, Inc., 1955), p. 25.

variation on the individualist theme of the protector, policeman state. But as soon as the Communist revolution is complete and classes are abolished, there will be no need for the state; it will wither away and die.[59] During the transitional stage, however, while capitalism is being destroyed, the Communist state is supreme and absolute in its power over the lives, bodies, and souls of men.

Applied to the realm of education the Communistic philosophy of state operates according to the following principles: (1) Youth are the property of the Communist party, which party seeks to control every aspect of their lives. Family and religious influences are to be extirpated as soon as possible.[60] (2) The control of education is to be removed from parents as completely as possible. For example, in Hungary in the kolkhoz, a co-operative, women take their children to a nursery at six in the morning and get them back at eight in the evening in order to be free for work outside the home.[61] (3) Academic freedom is abolished. Despite propaganda about religious freedom, severe restrictions are imposed on church activities. A recent observer reports that in Lithuania through Soviet occupation administrators religious instruction in the schools, operations of the Catholic press and Catholic organizations, and the general functioning of the Church as a spiritual force were all prohibited.[62] On the other hand, a strong antireligious campaign is carried on in the press and in the schools.[63] Even parents are forbidden to influence their own children.[64] (4) Universal education is an aim of Communist policy, for the end cannot be achieved without a bountiful supply of trained personnel.[65] (5) All schools must be state schools.[66] (6) Communist philosophy must be inserted into every subject of the curriculum.[67] (7) The state is to obtain control of extracurricular activities through party-sponsored organizations for

[59] Ibid.

[60] William Juhasz, Blueprint for a Red Generation (New York: Mid-European Studies Center, 1952), p. 12.

[61] Ibid., p. 19.

[62] S. Zymantas, "The Church and Soviet Communism — a Lithuanian Example," East and West, No. 1 (1954), p. 39.

[63] Ibid., p. 40.

[64] Ibid., p. 41.

[65] Juhasz, op. cit., p. 12.

[66] The Communist International tells us that "the working class . . . must take possession of all the schools, from the elementary schools to the universities." Communist International, Blueprint for World Conquest (Washington: Human Events, 1946), p. 206.

[67] Juhasz, op. cit., p. 13.

youth.[68] (8) The Church has no natural or supernatural right to engage in the education of youth.[69]

Conservative statism

What is meant here by conservative statism is an educational philosophy of the state that assigns to the government an excessive educational function even in its theory and yet does not rule out of life the need for religion.[70] Many of those who may be included in this group recognize the validity of and the need for the church, but relegate it to a position of inferiority and subordination to the state — at least in matters of education. Even though he seems to have been a religiously-minded man, Edwin Mead, for example, explicitly declared at the close of the past century that no authority is superior to the state in any respect.[71]

This type of statism is based on the supposition that the secular and religious spheres are disparate and can be treated in disparate ways. The religious is private and its activities are to be conducted chiefly

[68] *Ibid.*

[69] The stark reality of this tenet can perhaps be grasped no more effectively than by a perusal of the following secret document issued by the Lithuanian Socialist Soviet Republic from Kaunas on April 25, 1941: "I, the undersigned clergyman . . . . living at . . . . district . . . . county . . . . village, acknowledge that on April . . . ., 1941, I was informed that I have been strictly forbidden and have no right to teach religion to children of school age, neither in schools, nor in my home, nor any place in general. Thus I have no right whatsoever to talk to them about religious matters. At the same time I have been informed I will be held responsible for failure to comply with this warning, whereto I affix my signature." Baltic States Investigation, House of Representatives, Part I, Washington, 1954, p. 234, cited by Vytautas Vaitiekunas, "Genocide Against the Roman Catholic Church in Lithuania," *The Baltic Review,* June, 1954, p. 58.

Two recent news items show clearly that Communistic educational philosophy is by no means undergoing a change. At a convention in Brussels, Belgium's socialist school teachers passed a motion declaring that "parents do not have a primary right to decide the kind of education their children shall have." In East Germany Education Minister Fritz Lange said that "the alleged right of parents does not exist and is not compatible with the character of our state." Lange must be credited at least with a talent for logic. Both items appeared in the Philadelphia *Catholic Standard and Times* for December 2, 1955, pp. 14 and 11.

[70] By religion here we understand the traditional concept, not Dewey's fuzzy sum of human ideals.

[71] "I do not believe in any institution more divine in its origin and authority, more moral in its true definition and office, than the State. I do not believe in any institutional authority superior in any respect to the authority of the State and what the State creates and sanctions." Edwin D. Mead, *The Roman Catholic Church and the Public Schools* (Boston: George H. Ellis, 1890), p. 61.

in the home and in the church. The secular is public and influences everything. Education, being a preparation for civic life, is viewed as a public, secular affair and hence is to be conducted in one common system of schools.

This philosophy of education has in the course of history offered several arguments in support of its contention that the common good is best served by one, state-operated system of education. One spokesman (Benjamin Rush in 1786) observed that a uniform system of instruction would render the masses more homogeneous.[72] Just a few years later another (Robert Coram) remarked that unless equal education was offered to all, the sons of farmers could not eventually work themselves into positions of leadership in the community, and even if they got into the legislature, they would not be able to speak with propriety and hence represent their constituency adequately.[73] The latter likewise supported a national system of education as against mere state systems because he felt that otherwise opportunity could not be diffused among all.[74]

Perhaps the most frequently recurring argument in behalf of a state monopoly in education is the alleged devisiveness of private schools. This charge was urged as far back as 1799 by Samuel Knox in his *Essay on Education.*[75] A century later before the Nashville convention of the National Education Association in July, 1889, Edwin Mead declared that the private school creates and encourages "class distinctions" and that "it does not make for public spirit."[76] The charge is periodically repeated up to the present day.[77]

A nonmonopolistic variety of statism acknowledges the right of citizens to establish private schools at their own expense, but then proceeds to ignore private education as seemingly unworthy of attention. The National Education Association, for example, has gone on record

---

[72] Allen Oscar Hansen, *Liberalism and American Education* (New York: Macmillan 1926), p. 49.

[73] *Ibid.*, p. 75.

[74] *Ibid.*, pp. 71–74.

[75] *Ibid.*, p. 119.

[76] *Op. cit.*, p. 46.

[77] Although the reason does not appear in reputable publications, the impartial observer cannot deny that simple dislike for the Catholic Church is the real root of many attacks on private education. One need merely think, for example, of the selective targets chosen by the Protestants and Other Americans United for the Separation of Church and State.

as favoring the "appointment of qualified representatives of *public* education by the Department of State to the United States delegations to UNESCO."[78] This type of statism tends to favor a monopoly on governmental finance and favor.

Ordinary secularistic statism

The dividing line between what we have called conservative statism in education and this present characterization is admittedly not always crystal clear. For one thing, however, we mean to include in the present category all materialistic philosophies other than the extremist we treated first. Second, we envision those theories that make the state the source of human rights, although, unlike Communism, they do not *intend* to enslave the citizen. The third leading characteristic is the substitution of the state for the church, supernatural religion, and God.

As has been suggested above, systematic secularistic studies of the philosophy of state as educator are extremely rare. For this reason we have chosen to consider Alexander Meiklejohn as a representative of secularistic political philosophy. He has set for himself the explicit purpose of giving to modern education a churchless, nontheological philosophical basis. More precisely, he has tried to devise a coherent secularistic foundation for state participation in education. He is acutely aware that democratic secularism does not have one.

In building his secularistic philosophy of the state's role in education Meiklejohn begins with an acceptance of Rousseau's general will theory of social authority. Having rejected God as the source of governmental power (as Locke had rejected Him), Rousseau goes further and rejects Him as the source of human nature and man's individual dignity (as Locke did not do). Manifestly, then, any explanation of society and state in the realm of education must be entirely naturalistic, secularistic.

Having adopted Rousseau's social contract theory to explain the origin of society and its authority, Meiklejohn gives the Frenchman's general will theory a modern explanation and name, the "pattern of culture."[79] Since authority is manifestly necessary for the operation of society and the school, and since God is not the source of that author-

---

[78] National Education Association, "The Platform of the National Education Association," IX, "International Relations," C, *NEA Handbook,* 1956–57 (Washington: National Education Association, 1956), p. 100. Italics added.

[79] Alexander Meiklejohn, *op. cit.,* p. 86 ff.

ity, Meiklejohn finds it in the pattern of culture. A particular culture approves or disapproves of it. We have here nothing but the custom theory of morality in a new dress.[80]

But what of the morality of international relationships between sovereign states? Because all morality derives from the state, Meiklejohn can see that unless there be set up some universal state with authority over member nations there can be no question of right and wrong in international relationships.[81] Without some international authority, Japan cannot logically be accused of treachery at Pearl Harbor. Thus an international government becomes necessary to found a total morality.

Applied to education we find that the purpose of teaching is to express the "cultural authority" of the community that is conducting the school. Society has values and aims and it is up to the school to form the pupil according to those values and aims. "In a word, education is the agent of a social, cultural intention."[82]

These cultural intentions, however, are many and the educations they sponsor are also many. Scholars make their code and their "education," and so do doctors, and football teams, and sects.[83] And these various codes and educations cross one another and conflict in the ordinary life of a person and a nation. There must, therefore, be an arbiter, an outside factor that can judge cultural patterns and their educations. That arbiter is reason, critical intelligence.[84]

We may ask who is the possessor of this reason, this intelligence that is to judge all others? In Meiklejohn's atheistic world it can be nothing but the state. "In the field of education, control of the development of intelligence should fall into the hands of the state as it slips from the hands of the church."[85] If there is to be any unity of belief in the secularized world, it can be achieved by the state alone. "The state has the task of bringing into reasonable relation with one another all the activities, all the associations, which fall within its scope. In a secular world, the state replaces the church."[86]

Meiklejohn nicely sums up his political philosophy of the state's participation in education in the following paragraph. His two fundamental premises can be seen as pure Rousseauianism.

---

[80] See Thomas English Hill, *Contemporary Ethical Theories* (New York: Macmillan Co., 1950), for a description of the custom theory of morality.

[81] *Op. cit.,* pp. 241–242.   [84] *Ibid.,* p. 104 ff.

[82] *Ibid.,* p. 92.   [85] *Ibid.,* p. 258.

[83] *Ibid.,* p. 96 ff.   [86] *Ibid.,* p. 259.

The first statement (of Rousseau) had said that, when men form a state, they give everything into its hands. The second statement corrects this by saying that men have nothing to give, except as the state has already given it to them. Men have no rights: they have no property: they are not men, except as they are citizens of a politically organized community. That assertion seems to me to go to the very roots of a public system of education. If it is true, then we may be able to see how a government can plan and administer a teaching enterprise suitable to the life of a democratic community. *The agency which creates the community may well undertake to teach what it is and does. The agency which is human reason in action may teach its members how to live reasonably.*[87]

It logically follows that if lesser associations are to be criticized by the higher, the greatest of all of them must be the world-state. "The control of education, its planning and basic administration should be in the hands of the world-state."[88] Thus Meiklejohn.

Perhaps we can best indicate the educational political philosophy of other secularistic writers by a mere summary listing of typical tenets they have proposed.

1. Man has no natural, inherent, inalienable rights, but only those granted by the state. "There is no such thing as right outside the state."[89] Any right in education, therefore, is given and withdrawn at the discretion of the government.

2. Being merely material, man has no personal dignity transcending earthly society.

3. Marriage and the family are purely civil institutions with no moral bonds other than those given by the state.

4. The child belongs to the state before he belongs to the parents. The former has sole rights of education, and if the parent educates at all, it is only as the delegate of the community.[90] One of America's first educational writers, Samuel H. Smith, in his *Remarks on Education,* published in 1798, declared that "society must establish the right to educate, and acknowledge the duty of having educated, all children. . . . It is proper to remind parents, that their children belong to the

---

[87] *Ibid.,* p. 219. Italics added. We would not wish to suggest that all or even most secularistic writers would subscribe to Meiklejohn's exposition *in toto.*

[88] *Ibid.,* p. 287.

[89] Ward, *op. cit.,* p. 550.

[90] See the opinion of La Chalotais in the *Encyclopedia of Social Sciences,* Vol. V, p. 415.

state."[91] He spoke of the public educational system as "independent of, and superior to, parental authority."[92] Smith would have begun public education at birth because he thought parental authority hindered progress and the child's right to develop the habit of independent thinking.[93]

5. Morality and law are positive only. Right, therefore, is only what the state says is right, wrong only what it says is wrong. A sociologist has affirmed that the state cannot perform a wrong act; it can only err.[94] Trendelenburg argued that the state is by its very nature an educator because it has the right to see that the same principles of morality sway all minds.[95]

6. Supernatural religion is either ignored or explicitly denied with the consequence that there is no objective check on state action. By a denial of a personal God, the state becomes the object of a new religion, and patriotism the master virtue. Our own civilization has witnessed the truth that the "laic State sought to obtain from its citizens not merely formal and outward assent (which would suffice for a certain conformism) but a convinced and entire support, which is best expressed by the word, 'confessionalism.' Instead of a confession of faith in God and in the Church, there was a kind of confession of faith in the laic state."[96]

7. The state must be the sole educator. It is on this principle in particular that our line of demarcation between the various brands of secularism necessarily becomes somewhat blurred. All statists desire some sort of state monopoly in education. For that reason we will add here only those arguments and comments bearing on this point that were not made when we discussed the other two statist philosophies.

A recent writer argued that the aim of an unbiased education cannot be left safely to any private group. If a religion, a philosophy, or a business engage in education, they will likely be influenced by their

---

[91] Hansen, *op. cit.*, p. 149.

[92] *Ibid.*, p. 163.

[93] *Ibid.*, pp. 156–157.

[94] Ward, *op. cit.*, p. 552.

[95] Cited by Holaind from Hammerstein, *De Ecclesia et Statu. Op. cit.*, appendix.

[96] Luigi Sturzo, *Church and State* (New York: Longmans, Green and Co., 1939), pp. 526–527. We might observe in passing that this is one reason the public schools cannot be religiously neutral. Man must have some supreme allegiance and so must the school.

own interests to the possible damaging of the common good. Only the state in its universality of outlook and aim can serve the purposes of democracy and the needs of all the citizens.[97] Another offered a related argument when he said that education is so important for the common good that it cannot be left to the uncertainties of private endeavor.[98] A third saw more than a mere incapacity in nongovernmental agencies. For him the state alone is capable of educating adequately, other agencies being at best mere assisters. The inadequate agencies are the home, the church, and the press.[99]

The attorneys for the State in the celebrated Oregon case offered some novel arguments in behalf of a state monopoly of at least a part of the child's education. They looked upon a common system of education as a means of reducing religious suspicions and internal dissensions among the citizens of their state.[100] That system was likewise to afford children the "privilege and right" to receive a part of their education in an atmosphere free from class or religious bias.[101] There was the further danger that if Oregon did not compel all children to attend state schools "religious denominations may, without constitutional restrictions, develop a system of educational training which will result in doing away with public schools."[102] The counsel for the appellant likewise suggested that at least in some counties public authorities cannot effectively supervise schools not under their control.[103]

If one looks for the logical, rockbottom basis of state supremacy in education, he will find that it is nothing but materialistic monism. In the materialist's universe the present life is everything. There are no values, and there is no reality unperceivable by the senses. Everything is temporal. In this worldview the state manifestly becomes the supreme society to which all others are subject. It is both the most universal and the most powerful of societies. Man must have a god.

---

[97] Sears, *op. cit.,* p. 78.

[98] Counts, *op. cit.,* p. 27.

[99] Harold Rugg, *Culture and Education in America* (New York: Harcourt, Brace and Co., 1931), p. 72.

[100] *Op. cit.,* pp. 97–98.

[101] *Ibid.,* p. 122.

[102] *Ibid.,* p. 202. If this argument were valid, one would seem justified in questioning the value of a venture that could not cope with competition. He might also wonder whether this same fear lies behind the stanch contemporary opposition to state aid for private schools.

[103] *Ibid.,* p. 219.

Because the materialist has rejected a transcendent, personal God, he understandably turns to the tangible order for an object that will merit his unswerving allegiance. For many materialistic monists that object is the powerful, universal state. It is supreme. It is the primary if not the only educator, for there is none above it, none equal to it. Thus in the statist's school the great ideal inculcated is patriotism and the exemplary saints are national heroes. The statist position becomes a religion as well as a philosophy of education.

CHAPTER V

THE CATHOLIC POSITION

A THOROUGH appreciation of the state's role in education cannot be had without a prior understanding of the functions to be played by the Church and the family. Any attempt to isolate the educational philosophy of the state from the other two agencies of education would result in a grotesque system of thought and practice.[104] For this reason we must preface our study of the state as educator with a brief analysis of the roles played by the Church and the family.

THE CHURCH AS EDUCATOR

In the very nature of reality any agency or person that is directly commissioned to perform a function takes precedence, *caeteris paribus,* over one that is indirectly commissioned. Likewise, a superior agency or person takes precedence over an inferior. We may deduce from the first principle the fact that if an organization or agency should receive directly from God a commission to teach, it would, all else being equal, be the primary and supreme educator of men. From the second principle we may infer that a supernatural educator enjoys a more basic educational function than a merely natural one. Because the Catholic Church has received from God a direct commission to teach and because her function is a supernatural one, it follows that she is the primary and supreme educator of men.[105]

---

[104] Strictly speaking, we can envision a fourth educational agency, private groups representing neither Church nor family. Gonzalez hints at this fourth agency, *op. cit.,* pp. 811 and 817. Writers commonly, however, do not consider a fourth agency, nor do we consider it necessary to construct another category. In most cases, as a matter of fact, this fourth agency would represent Church and/or family and would therefore share the rights of these primary educators.

[105] This truth, we are well aware, is immensely distasteful to some non-Catholics.

This supremacy in the field of education is founded on a twofold title. Pope Pius XI tells us that education "belongs pre-eminently to the Church, by reason of a double title in the supernatural order, conferred exclusively upon her by God Himself, absolutely superior therefore to any other title in the natural order."[106] The first title is, of course, the direct commission given to her by Christ to teach all men: "Go, therefore, and make disciples of all nations . . . teaching them to observe all that I have commanded you. . . ."[107] The second title is the "supernatural motherhood, in virtue of which the Church, spotless spouse of Christ, generates, nurtures and educates souls in the divine life of grace, with her Sacraments and her doctrine."[108] Nature intends the complete perfection of the offspring. Since in the present order this perfection must be supernatural, and supernatural perfection can be attained only through the Church, nature indirectly founds the Church's right.

From her divinely given duty to lead men to their last end several derivative rights accrue to the Church. (1) In the exercise of her teaching mission she is independent of any earthly power. (2) She may make use of the means that are necessary and useful in the attainment of her end. (3) Because all types of education have some connection with man's final destiny, none can be entirely immune from the divine law and of this the Church is the guardian and infallible

---

It is more than distasteful; it is unthinkable, so unthinkable that they are prone to cast it aside without a second thought. Such a rejection, nonetheless, is tragic — and decidedly unscientific. It is a glaring example of *a priorism*. This study, manifestly, is not the place in which to present the mass of irrefragable evidence supporting the divine mission of Christ and the Catholic Church He founded. However, since our whole statement of the Church's role in education rests upon it, we think it well to suggest a minute part of the extensive literature available on the point. In English there are Hilarin Felder, *Christ and the Critics* (London: Burns, Oates and Washbourne, 1933), 2 vols.; Joseph Baierl, *The Theory of Revelation* (Rochester, N. Y.: Seminary Press, 1933), 2 vols.; and John Brunsmann, *Fundamental Theology* (St. Louis: Herder, 1928), 4 vols. The Latin offers A. C. Cotter, *Theologia Fundamentalis* (Weston, Mass.: Weston College, 1940); Michael Nicolau and Joachim Salaverri, *Sacrae Theologiae Summa* (Matriti: Biblioteca de Autores Cristianos, 1952); and Reginald Garrigou-Lagrange, *De Revelatione* (Rome: F. Ferrari, 1929), 2 vols. Two comprehensive French works are A. D'Ales, ed., *Dictionnaire Apologetique de la Foi Catholique* (Paris: Gabriel Beauchesne, 1911–1922), 4 vols.; and A. Vacant, E. Mangenot, E. Amann et al., ed., *Dictionnaire de Theologie Catholique* (Paris: Librarie Letouzey et Ane, 1903–1950), 15 vols.

[106] *Christian Education of Youth* (Washington: National Catholic Welfare Conference, 1936), p. 6.

[107] Mt. 28:19–20.

[108] Pope Pius XI, *op. cit.,* p. 7.

interpreter.[109] (4) The Church may participate in all kinds of education dealing with the various branches of learning. This right includes that of founding schools in which these branches may be taught.[110] (5) Finally, the Church has the right to watch over the entire education of her children in all institutions, both public and private. She may oversee both their religious instruction and other branches of learning in so far as these latter are related to religion and morality. We need scarcely mention that this right neither does nor is meant to interfere with the state's administration of its public schools.[111] It merely protects a field in which the Church alone is competent, the field of religion and morals.

It has been rightly remarked that the Catholic Church's right to educate is neither to be confused with nor derived from the right Catholic parents have over the education of their children.[112] They are two distinct rights. It is thus perfectly true to say that Catholic schools exist as a result of two fundamental rights in education: the Church's divine commission to teach and the Catholic parents' right to procure the religious formation of their offspring.

THE FAMILY AS EDUCATOR

While philosophers treating the agencies of education often equate the terms, "family" and "parents" when discussing the home as an educational institution, there is a difference between the two. The family is a broader expression and seems to be the preferable, since parents are not the only educators in the home. They themselves are influenced and educated by their duties toward each other and toward their children, and it is undeniable that brothers and sisters have a decided formative influence on one another.[113] Moreover, in the event of the death of one or both parents their duties and rights by natural law fall to a large extent on capable brothers and sisters.

At the very heart of the natural-law philosophy of education lies the position of the family. Just as the being of the child cannot be effected

---

109 *Ibid.*, p. 8.

110 See the Code of Canon Law, canon 1375.

111 Pope Pius XI, *op. cit.*, p. 9.

112 Richard J. Gabel, *Public Funds for Church and Private Schools* (Washington: Catholic University Press, 1937), pp. 733–734.

113 Messner, *op. cit.*, pp. 299–300.

without parents, neither can its proper formation be conceived or rightly executed without them. The proper education of the child by the parents flows just as naturally from their procreation of that child as the finished bloom and fruit of the plant flow from the seed and twig. One is merely the perfected state of the other. St. Thomas remarks that a child is naturally something of the father and that even after birth it remains in a kind of spiritual womb to be formed by both parents. Hence he concludes that there is an offense against natural justice "if the child before attaining the use of reason is taken from the care of the parents or if any disposition is made concerning him against the will of the parents."[114]

The statist argument that the child is born first a citizen and then an individual misses the mark. Pius XI forcefully reminded the statist that "before being a citizen man must exist; and existence does not come from the state, but from the parents."[115]

A nineteenth-century educator discussed this same parental right to educate from a slightly different angle, that of the nature and conse- quences of the marriage act. He observed that every free creature is accountable for the consequences of its actions in so far as it can foresee them, and that as a result of this responsibility, it is bound to take care that those consequences be beneficial rather than harmful. Parents in the procreation of new life are certainly free and hence bound to see to it that the consequences of that procreation be bene- ficial to all concerned.[116] It follows, therefore, that the fundamental duty of education lies with the parents.

This same conclusion can be seen in the very educational equipment with which the Author of human nature has endowed the family. This fundamental unit in the community's life is wonderfully fitted with two educational requisites that no other natural society possesses:

---

[114] *Summa Theologica,* II, II, q. 10, a. 12. The Saint suggests that after the attain- ment of reason the child is susceptible to outside interference. Cappello remarks that if parents refuse to see to the religious education of their offspring the Church can see to it against their will: *Summa Iuris Publici Ecclesiastici* (Rome: Universitas Gregoriana, 1943), p. 398. Victor Cathrein holds the same. Cf. *Philosophia Moralis* (Friburgi Bris- goviae: B. Herder, 1911), No. 656.

[115] *Op. cit.,* p. 13. Cappello remarks that society is formed not from individuals but from families, and that children consequently belong to society only mediately through their membership in a family. Felix M. Cappello, *Summa Iuris Publici Ecclesiastici* (Rome: Gregorian University, 1943), p. 400.

[116] Holaind, *op. cit.,* pp. 8–9,

a special authority and love.[117] The child is naturally disposed to accept the authority of its parents, and through love to receive willingly their teaching. And on their part the love parents bear toward their off-spring is an effective assurance of diligent care. We may rightly lay great emphasis on the lasting imprint imposed on the child by family formation or malformation.[118] Any experienced teacher will readily grant that the school's influence on the moral character and develop-ment of the child is decidedly less than that of the home. This un-deniable fact of itself points to the natural and primary educator.

Messner reminds parents that their aspirations to see themselves in their children indicates not only a right to educate but the very privi-lege involved in forming their offspring. With Aristotle he notes that education, which alone can fully form this image, must be both the duty and the privilege of parents.[119]

Because the parents' right to educate flows from the very natures of all concerned, it is an inalienable right. Parents may delegate some of the actual teaching to private and public institutions, but they can in no wise divest themselves of the responsibility for their children's proper formation. The school is, consequently, an extension or instru-ment of the home and the Church. From this vantage point it is easy to see the narrowness of the statist's references to the state's "toleration" of private enterprise in education.[120] In the United States one has even spoken of an American *policy* of tolerating private educational endeavor.[121]

We must finally note that while the family's rights in education are basic and inalienable, they are not despotic and absolute. An Italian canonist refers to the parents as mandataries and organs of the Church in the religious formation of their children. This relationship he traces to the sacramental nature of Christian marriage, which, as Christian,

---

[117] Messner, *op. cit.,* pp. 301–302. Findlay finds a basis for the family's right to educate in the intimacy and sympathy present in that circle alone. The younger mem-bers are aided in their growth precisely because of this close relationship, a factor easily lacking in a public effort. *Op. cit.,* I, 97.

[118] A. Castelein, *Droit Naturel* (Bruxelles: Albert Dewit, 1912), pp. 645–646.

[119] Messner, *op. cit.,* p. 301.

[120] See, for example, Counts, *op. cit.,* pp. 34–38.

[121] *Ibid.,* p. 57. Two other writers likewise missed the basic root from which the school springs when they said that "the social order is the source of authority from which the schools issue . . ." Calvin Grieder and Stephen Romine, *American Public Education* (New York: Ronald Press, 1955), p. 50.

is subject to the exclusive jurisdiction of the Church. In the celebration of a sacramental marriage husband and wife receive from the Church their mandate to educate their children for a supernatural end, a mandate stemming from the primary purpose of that marriage.[122]

Pope Pius XI has stated that parents' rights are "necessarily subordinated to the last end and to natural and divine law."[123] This is, of course, true of any right that man enjoys. A man has a right to drive a car, but that right must be subordinated to the public welfare and his own good. No parent, therefore, is morally free to neglect the religious formation of his child any more than he is free to neglect provision for food and shelter.

One of the most common misunderstandings of the Catholic position on Church and parental rights in education revolves about this very point. When the non-Catholic hears the Catholic insistence on the inalienable and basic rights of the family to determine the education of the child, he often suspects something less than honesty in that insistence. One thought Cardinal Manning glib and dishonest when the prelate spoke of parental rights.[124] He held that the Church's policy of establishing parochial schools interferes with the family's liberty of conscience and that it is "in truth the capital sin of the Roman Church."[125] He argued that the refusal of the sacraments and the threat of eternal damnation deprive the Catholic parent of liberty to send his child to a public school.[126] An appellant attorney in the Oregon Case asserted that the Canon Law of the Catholic Church in forbidding parents to send their children to neutral schools did away with parents' liberty and denied them their rights.[127]

As we have remarked above, the rights of parents are not absolute but rather may be conditioned in specific cases by any legitimate authority, civil or ecclesiastical. Catholic parents, therefore, may not send their children to schools precluded by duly established ecclesiastical authority any more than they may reject a just disposition of a duly established civil authority. It is clear that if the state can forbid parents, without depriving them of their liberty or their rights to send their children to schools that will undermine their loyalty to their country, the Church can forbid them in the same way to send those children to schools that will undermine their faith. In answer to this

---

[122] Cappello, *op. cit.*, p. 398.
[123] *Op. cit.*, p. 14.
[124] Mead, *op. cit.*, p. 65.

[125] *Ibid.*, p. 67.
[126] *Ibid.*, pp. 71–73.
[127] *Oregon School Cases*, p. 683.

same objection a contemporary American has remarked that "all parents have the moral obligation to see that their children receive religious instruction. The Catholic hierarchy, realizing the divine mission of the Church to care for the spiritual needs of its children, provides the parochial school system to aid the Catholic parent in fulfilling this obligation. This is no more authoritarian in nature than the obligation of every one to obey the Commandments of God.[128]

There is, consequently, no clash whatsoever between the Church's divine commission to teach all men and the family's right to teach flowing from the fecundity of procreation. The one protects, perfects, and elevates the other in much the same way that the whole supernatural order protects, perfects, and elevates the natural. The Church and the family go together; they are basic. In the words of Pius XI "the mission of education regards before all, above all, primarily the Church and the family, and this by natural and divine law, and . . . therefore it cannot be slighted, cannot be evaded, cannot be supplanted."[129]

THE STATE AS EDUCATOR

We have already analyzed the two extreme philosophies regarding the state's function in education. The individualist holds that the state has no role (or at most an extremely limited one) to play; the statist declares that it alone has any competency. Catholic truth rejects both views as extreme and unrealistic. Against the individualist we will show that the state does have a role to play in education and a role that surpasses a mere police protection. Against the statist we have already shown that the state is not the only educator, that it is not even the primary educator. On this latter point there remains for us the task to explain positively in what precise way the state is an educator. We will leave to later chapters a detailed analysis of the state's educational functions.

---

[128] John E. O'Malley, letter to the editor, *Washington Post and Times Herald*, Dec. 22, 1955, p. 22. While the Church's law and moral decisions bind her members, we may note with the 1957 statement of the American hierarchy that "her sanctions upon them (the people) are only spiritual and moral." *U. S. News and World Report*, XLIII (Nov. 22, 1957), p. 77.

[129] *Op. cit.*, p. 16. Cappello, *op. cit.*, pp. 397–398, gives a clear treatment of this question. See also Alfredo Ottaviani, *Institutiones Juris Publici Ecclesiastici* (Typis Polyglottis Vaticanis, 1936), II, pp. 234–235.

The state is an educator

We may remind the reader that we are here taking the term, "state," in its strict meaning of government, and therefore as distinguished from "society" or "body politic" or "political community." Society (or the body politic or the political community) surely has an essential role to play in education, since it makes possible both a full sufficiency of material goods and a life of full intellectual and moral virtue, two ends the family in itself cannot attain. We are now, however, concerned precisely with the state, "that part of the body politic especially concerned with the maintenance of law, the promotion of the common welfare and public order, and the administration of public affairs."[130]

We must be clear at the outset that the state's role in education is quite different from that of the Church and the family. The state is not of its nature, natively, directly, an educator as are the Church and family.[131] Its direct function is the promotion of the common good, not education, as some would seem to make it. This truth can be seen from the fact that the Author of nature and supernature has already committed the direct function in education to two other societies, the Church and the family. There remains, consequently, only an indirect function. We will later develop this point at greater length.

If we are going to find a basis for the state's participation in education we must, manifestly, find it in a principle distinct from the fundaments of the Church's and the family's role.[132] The state, unlike the Catholic Church, has not received a direct divine commission to teach, and, unlike the parent, it does not communicate life. It is reasonable, therefore, to look for the foundation of the state's educational function in the end or purpose of the state. In Chapter I we have shown that the end of society and the state is the common good and thus in its obligation to promote the common good we will find the basis for the state's role in education.

The state cares for the common good by two general functions: protective and promotive. It must enable the citizen to obtain his temporal and eternal ends by warding off unjust interferences with the

---

[130] Maritain, *op. cit.,* p. 11.

[131] Cappello, *op. cit.,* p. 399. He points out that the state usurps a direct role if it *alone* selects and approves teachers, if it positively or negatively determines subject matter or methodology, and if it denies to others the permission to teach.

[132] Pius XI, *op. cit.,* p. 16.

fulfillment of his duties. This is the protective function. The state must also positively help the citizen to do what he cannot do for himself. This is the promotive function.[133]

The state's participation in education is founded both on its protective function and on its promotive function. This Pope Pius XI has clearly stated: "The function therefore of the civil authority residing in the State is twofold, to protect and to foster, but by no means to absorb the family and the individual, or to substitute itself for them."[134]

a) The state's protective function.

The state's first and most basic function in education is so to dispose and regulate the factors operating in society that the primary educators may do the work God and nature itself have assigned to them. It must protect the educational rights of the Church and the family.[135] Even though the Catholic Church is a perfect society and hence possesses all the means she needs to attain her supernatural end, she does need the assistance of the state to ward off temporal hindrances to the accomplishment of her mission. This assistance is not essentially different from that which the state is bound to offer any person or group within its sphere of jurisdiction.

The family is not a perfect society[136] and hence all the more needs the protective aid of the state in its attempts to exercise its primary educational rights. The state must protect the parents from any unwarranted outside interference in the education and formation of their children. It must likewise protect the child in its right to a proper training. The state may enter the sanctuary of the home on behalf of the child "when the parents are found wanting either physically or morally in this respect, whether by default, incapacity or misconduct."[137]

---

[133] For a more complete explanation see Chapter II. Aside from extreme individualists of the Spencerian cast, most political philosophers hold this doctrine of the two functions. They differ, however, on the limits of its application.

[134] Op. cit., p. 16.

[135] Ibid., p. 17.

[136] This is so because the end of the family community is included in the end of the political community, namely, the common good. The end of the political community is the perfection of human life. The family, as a natural society, does have all the necessary means to achieve its end for nature does nothing in vain. But the family of itself cannot attain the perfection of human life. This is the achievement of the community.

[137] Pope Pius XI, op. cit., p. 17.

Ottaviani adds that it falls within the competence of the government to watch lest anything in private schools be harmful to the good of society. He singles out for special notice care that health regulations be observed.[138] We will discuss in a later chapter just how detailed this sort of state vigilance may be.

b) The state's promotive function.[139]

Besides enabling the Church and the family to attain their educational ends by warding off unjust interference, the state must also aid the citizen in a positive way to do what he cannot do for himself. The state must *promote* his educational welfare. The first way in which the state fosters and promotes education is to assist the "initiative and activity of the Church and the family."[140] Since these latter are the primary educational agencies, the state's first positive duty must be to aid them in the fulfillment of their basic educational functions. The amount of governmental assistance necessary will vary according to the conditions of the society in which the school finds itself. Citizens of a backward country would manifestly need much more assistance than would those in a land where private schools flourish in both quality and number.[141]

To this promotive function of assisting the Church and the family is to be added that of supplementing these two primary agencies by the founding of state schools when they are needed. Even before his encyclical, Catholic writers taught, in the words of Pius XI, that the state should "supplement their (the Church and the family) work whenever this falls short of what is necessary, even by means of its own schools and institutions."[142] Although in some places Conway, writing in the last decade of the past century, seemed unduly to limit the state's function in education, yet it is clear that in his theory he allowed the state to maintain educational facilities and institutions if private enterprise failed to do so.[143] Likewise at the close of the nine-

---

[138] *Op. cit.,* p. 247.

[139] We propose to discuss here only general principles. Applications to individual questions will be made in later chapters.

[140] Pope Pius XI, *op. cit.,* p. 17.

[141] Felix Cavagnis, *Institutiones Juris Publici Ecclesiastici* (Romae: Typis Societatis Catholicae Instructivae, 1889), pp. 198–199.

[142] *Op. cit.,* p. 17.

[143] James Conway, *The Respective Rights and Duties of Family, State and Church in Regard to Education* (New York: Fr. Pustet, 1890), pp. 32–33. Reilly states that before Bouquillon's famous pamphlet appeared in 1891, no American Catholic had

teenth century the *American Ecclesiastical Review* stated in an unsigned article that although the state has no direct right in education, it should erect schools, appoint teachers, and prescribe the program to be followed.[144] And the position of Catholic writers has not changed. Cappello explicitly recognizes the fact that the state sponsorship of schools in the conditions of modern society can be both an ordinary and a stable practice.[145]

A caution regarding this last point is in order. The human mind is prone to identify the primary with the ordinary and the secondary with the extraordinary, and yet the combinations may easily be reversed in unusual circumstances. In times of depression large segments of a population may depend somewhat stably on government for food, shelter, and clothing, but even after the passage of years the growing ordinariness of the situation does not alter the fundamental truth that government is not meant to be the primary feeder, shelter, or clothier of men. Changing situations do not change fundamental principles, but they do call for the application of other pertinent ones. For this reason, in a country of extreme poverty or illiteracy state-sponsored education may be much more common than the privately sponsored, and yet the philosophical principles and natural rights involved remain exactly the same. The family and Church remain primary educators; the state remains secondary.

The third promotive educational function of the state is the right and duty to exact a minimum amount of education from the generality of its citizens. Pius XI was clear: "The state can exact, and take measures to secure that all its citizens have the necessary knowledge of their civic and political duties, and a certain degree of physical,

---

publicly defended the state's rights in education. We question that statement. On pages 114 and 115 of his dissertation he himself notes the Catholic periodicals which approved Bouquillon's teaching as the *common* opinion among Catholics. Hence it must have been at least an opinion. Archbishop Ireland himself had asserted the state's right in July, 1890, before the National Education Association convention in St. Paul. See Daniel F. Reilly, *The School Controversy* (Washington: Catholic University Press, 1943), pp. 106–108, 114–115, and 237.

[144] "State Control and Relative Rights in the School," VI (Apr., 1892), 300.

[145] *Op. cit.,* p. 401. So well founded is this Catholic position that Cavagnis was able to say that "no one has ever denied to the civil state the right to establish schools." *Op. cit.,* p. 187. It can be seen how grievously Counts misrepresents — unintentionally we suppose — Catholic teaching when he asserts that the Catholic Church "has never conceded to the state the right to educate." *Op. cit.,* p. 30. Such is not, as he thinks, the reason she establishes schools of her own.

intellectual, and moral culture, which, considering the conditions of our times, is really necessary for the common good."[146] It may be difficult to determine just how much knowledge is usually required in the citizen to secure the common good, but that the state may exact a minimum educational standard for its citizens is now beyond dispute.

The fourth way in which the state may engage in the work of education is its maintenance of institutions necessary for the training of its own personnel.[147] Besides the academies and training programs established for the benefit of the armed forces, under this category would fall those educational enterprises that equip candidates for employment in the various and sundry governmental offices and services. The right of the state to train its own personnel would seem to be similar to, if not identical with, the ordinary right any private association has to instruct its own members in its own particular aims and methodology.

The final promotive educational function of a government is one that is involved in almost every activity sponsored by public authority. Pope Pius remarks that this civic education "consists in the practice of presenting publicly to groups of individuals information having an intellectual, imaginative and emotional appeal, calculated to draw their wills to what is upright and honest, and to urge its practice by a sort of moral compulsion, positively by disseminating such knowledge, and negatively, by suppressing what is opposed to it."[148] Aimed as it is at all ages and classes and by no means to be confined to the school environment, we might style this activity a governmental program of informal education. Under such a program we might place bulletins or lectures dealing with soil conservation, youth activities, political rights, home building, etc. An American theologian seems to have been thinking of a somewhat related educational function when he observed that the state in the very exercise of its normal functions is a teacher. When it promulgates a law or hands down a judicial decision, it necessarily instructs the citizenry in the area of information with which the document deals.[149]

---

[146] Op. cit., p. 17.

[147] Ibid., p. 18.

[148] Ibid., pp. 18–19.

[149] Thomas Bouquillon, Education: To Whom Does It Belong? (Baltimore: John Murphy and Co., 1891), pp. 12–13.

Critique of individualism

We are now in a position to evaluate the views of those philosophers who would deny that the state has any but a mere protective function to play in the work of education. We will consider only those aspects of individualism that are not clearly confronted by the foregoing discussion.

Spencer's argument based on "a function to each organ and each organ to its own function" does not prove that because government does admittedly have a protective function it cannot have also a promotive one. If his principle were applied strictly, the state could have only one protective function, say from external aggressors. It would have to leave other protective activities to private groups. Moreover, modern life embraces any number of associations that offer more than one kind of service and offer them effectively. Spencer's principle cannot, therefore, be used logically to exclude the state from fostering education positively as well as protecting it negatively.

The objection that taxation takes away a man's freedom because the taxes paid do not return to the citizen completely in the services he receives, proves only that government is not always as efficient as it ought to be. And yet one may not condemn a good thing merely because it sometimes does not measure up to all of its possibilities. It should be further remembered that even with a certain amount of graft and inefficiency mixed in with state services the citizen often benefits more from his tax contribution than he could possibly benefit from a like expenditure for his private endeavor. One need think only of taxes paid for the construction of streets and highways. We cannot deny, however, that this objection does prove that government ought to tax for its service function only when private initiative is insufficient. Spencer does, consequently, point out a weak kink in the statist's armor.[150]

One of Spencer's favorite arguments against the promotive function is the alleged impossibility of drawing a line of demarcation at which that function ought to begin. He sees an impossibility in the effort to determine exactly what services the government ought to offer and why it ought to offer them. Applied to education he cannot see how

---

[150] His argument that the promotive function of the state stifles individual growth and activity is valid as demonstrating the principle of subsidiarity, but it cannot be urged further. Much individual growth would be stifled without state aid.

his opponent can decide at exactly what point the citizen would be able to demand governmental help for the education of his child. The principle of subsidiarity readily solves this problem in general outline. The state is to intervene precisely at the point at which the private person cannot adequately help himself. While it may be difficult in the abstract to decide at what exact point this situation will be reached, like all such matters a satisfactory solution can be worked out in the concrete.

Spencer's objection that his adversary cannot demonstrate the necessity of including certain subjects in the curriculum to the exclusion of others and that, as a consequence, sections of the populace will feel wronged when their preferences are not honored, at best proves that schools must be sensitive to the will of parents. It does not prove that such schools should not exist. A practical difficulty does not require the abolishment of that in which the difficulty is found.

The alleged unprogressiveness of state-sponsored education is, like a number of Spencer's other arguments, based on defect and possible abuse. If government tends to canonize the *status quo* in order to preserve itself, the solution lies not in the abolition of government but in its improvement. The same must be said of governmental schools.[151]

Spencer's final argument is based on conscience. Just as the state may not force one religion on all, so also it may not force one "education" on all. Honest differences of opinion on educational methodology, curriculum content, and disciplinary techniques must be respected, and even as possible matters of conscience. Again we must observe that while this argument possesses much truth, it does not demonstrate all that Spencer would like it to demonstrate. Since parents are the primary educators in the natural order, their wishes on the points mentioned must certainly be respected, *in so far as right reason and the common good allow*. The methodology and curriculum cannot manifestly be so exactly cut out that they will suit all the desires of all the patrons of any school, be it public or private. However, we may not lose sight of the fact that the school must represent the *reasonable* wishes of parents. That this is more difficult for the state school to

---

[151] Spencer's fear that state entrance into the field of education leads logically to despotism is not entirely unfounded. But the fear ought not to be exaggerated. It ought rather to occasion extreme vigilance that the state assume no more responsibility in education than is actually necessary.

accomplish than it is for the private is undeniable; yet it is possible, especially when the state system is decentralized. And so Spencer does show that governmentally sponsored schools must remain close to the home (and, we must add, to the Church) and in their administration develop a sensitivity to the just wishes of the primary educators. More than that he does not prove.

As we have noted, Adam Smith opposed state schools for the practical reason that an assured source of income independent of the quality of the teaching produces indolence and inefficiency in the teacher. Human nature being what it is, the alleged danger cannot be said to lack all foundation. And yet there are ways of assuring a high quality of teaching in state schools, ways that experience has proved to be both adequate and just.

In a positive vein we must criticize individualism (at least of the Spencerian variety) in that it does not fully grasp reality. The family is often simply not able to meet its modern educational obligations. One need think only of the great numbers of the poor spread throughout the world. Private enterprise and private charity, excellent though they may be, are not adequately endowed to cope with the needs of these poor. And sometimes the inertia of private endeavor would not cope with those needs even if it could.

Individualism fails also to recognize (or at least to state that it recognizes) that government must carry on some educational activities in behalf of its own efficient operation. This is unmistakably true in regard to the gigantic promotive functions of modern governments, but these, the individualist would assert, ought not to exist. But *ad hominem* we may point out that even the protective function of the state demands considerable governmental educational activity in its own behalf.

The state is a subsidiary educator

Having shown that the state does have a genuine role in education, it remains for us to examine more closely the precise relationship of that role to the function of the Church and the family. Much of what we will say here will be a mere clarification of the principles discussed in the immediately preceding section dealing with the state as educator.

Our first clarification is the principle stated above: the state is a *subsidiary* educator. In Chapter II we went to considerable lengths in explaining and demonstrating the validity of the principle of subsidiarity as a factor in political philosophy. Here we will apply the fruits of that investigation.

We have seen that the principle of subsidiarity involves both a positive and a negative aspect. Positively, subsidiarity indicates that a government should do for the citizenry whatever it (the latter) cannot do for itself. Negatively, it means that government should not do what can be done by private initiative. The positive aspect is opposed to the *laissez-faire* principle of individualism, the negative, to statist paternalism. Subsidiarity, therefore, means that the state is to enter the field of education *only when that entrance is necessary or at least beneficial to the common welfare.* It means that the state's function in education is essentially a supplementary one. It is to supplement the work of the primary educators, Church and family, whenever and wherever they are unable adequately to carry out the full mission entrusted to them.

The subsidiary function of the state as educator is, consequently, firmly set against the notion that the state is the first and *de iure* the ordinary educator of children. It is no more such an educator than it is the first and *de iure* farmer or manufacturer. If private enterprise fails to farm or manufacture adequately, the state must step in and supply *what is wanting,* but it may go no further. So also, if private effort is unequal to the entire educational task, the state may and must supply what is lacking, but nothing more.

Many of the reasons lying behind the principle of subsidiarity as applied to the state's function in education are substantially the same as those supporting that principle as applied to other state functions. And to these we can add others peculiar to the educational function.

1. An educational policy of the state that does more than supplement private initiative runs contrary to the very *raison d'être* of the state: the supplementation of the citizen in those things which he cannot do for himself.

2. When a man depends unnecessarily on government, his own growth and dignity suffer. If the work of education is done for him, when he could very well do it himself, his development, initiative, and freedom are unreasonably curtailed. One of the reasons for the lack of imagination in Communist-dominated countries is an all-embracing paternalism. Applied to education the same deadening effect cannot be escaped.

3. The work of education itself suffers from unnecessary governmental interference and activity. A man operates more effectively and

more efficiently when he deals with his own property and under his own initiative. The closer he is to the school the more clearly does he see and understand its problems, the more interest does he show in them. It is common knowledge that the dollar buys much more education today in the private school than it does in the public. A contemporary educator was referring to this fact when he remarked before the 41st annual convention of the Association of American Colleges that "an exceedingly tax-conscious generation will not indefinitely overlook the fact that gift dollars purchase substantially more education than tax dollars. In my state (Minnesota) the tax dollar purchases about $1.25 of higher education and the gift dollar purchases $4 worth of education."[152] This phenomenon and the truth underlying it are not to be confined to education. They apply with equal validity to other enterprises in which government is in competition with private initiative.

4. When the state assumes a greater role in education than necessity or utility requires, it either weakens or totally destroys competition and the healthy results that flow from it. An institution does not have to compete with itself, and so if the state dominates education it has only itself to contend with. On the other hand, when the state assumes only a supplementary role, it is able to strengthen all education, both private and public. In this way a fair and keen competition results with obvious benefit to all concerned.[153]

5. A neglect of the principle of subsidiarity in any field of government leads by its very nature to a loss of freedom in the citizen. In the field of education this is especially true. Dealing as it does with the minds of men, education can bind them more effectively and lastingly than any other activity. The ruthlessness of contemporary Communism bears out the truth of John Stuart Mill's observation that "a government which can mould the opinions and sentiments of the people from their youth upwards, can do with them whatever it pleases."[154] Although this danger is full-blown only in a state monopoly of education, it is proportionately present in any unnecessary interference with or injustice toward the primary educators.

---

[152] Edgar M. Carlson, "Responsive and Responsible Christian Education," *Association of American Colleges Bulletin,* XLI (Mar., 1955), 76.

[153] Needless to say, the use of tax money paid by all parents for state schools alone is neither fair nor contributory to keen competition. This we will discuss in a later chapter.

[154] *Op. cit.,* p. 956.

6. Unwarranted entrance of the state into education can easily result in an intrusion into the rights of conscience. A parent has a conscientious right to give his child the kind of education God and his conscience indicate, and as long as that parent may choose the school to which he may send the child, that right is likely to be honored. But if the state *establishes* public schools where mere *assistance* is needed to establish and maintain private schools, the parent may be forced by economic pressure to patronize a school of which he does not approve. And we may observe in a practical vein that it is no secret that many parents do patronize public education only by reason of the subtle coercion of economic pressure. The very fact that millions are willing to pay twice for the benefits of private education indicates in what esteem it is held.

The advisability of the state's assumption of an educational work in determined and concrete circumstances is not always easily decided. Guiding norms, however, are both possible and helpful in reaching a correct decision. These norms we have suggested at the close of Chapter II.[155]

The complexity of modern society, however, demands that those guiding norms be supplemented by all available data. One cannot apply norms in a vacuum. As an example of the need for serious study of the concrete situation we may cite the activities of the Commission on Intergovernmental Relations, established in the United States as a result of Public Law 109, 83rd Congress, and approved July 10, 1953. This commission was authorized to investigate all of the activities in which federal aid was being given to state and local governments and to analyze the financial arrangements involved in that aid. Section 3 of the act declared that the "Commission shall determine and report whether there is justification for Federal aid in the various fields in which Federal aid is extended; whether Federal control with respect to these activities should be limited, and, if so, to what extent; whether Federal aid should be limited to cases of need; and all other matters incident to such Federal aid, including the ability of the Federal Government and the States to finance activities of this nature."[156]

---

[155] For the sake of completeness we must note that the state does have a minor nonsubsidiary educational function: the maintenance of institutions to train candidates for governmental duties and services.

[156] "Report of the Commission on Intergovernmental Relations, Its Significance to Education," *Higher Education,* XII (Sept., 1955), 7.

Critique of statism

We may now proceed to an evaluation of the views of those whom we have described as "statist" in their educational thinking. As in our critique of individualism, we will discuss here only those aspects of statism that we have not already considered. Practically, this means that we need touch chiefly on the statist's attacks on the adequacy of private education, since the inadequacy of his own substructure is sufficiently shown by theodicy, soundly based ethics, and our own discussion.[157]

The first argument in favor of state-sponsored education as opposed to private education is that the former offers an equal opportunity to all, whereas the latter does not. In reply we must note that private education would come much closer to offering equal opportunity to all children if it were given the supplementary assistance the state by its very nature is bound to give.[158] However, as we have already observed above, it may easily happen that private enterprise in a given situation and even with governmental aid is unequal to the task of educating all children in a given locale. The Catholic philosophy of state is by no means embarrassed by this possibility, for it explicitly allows the state to step in when a lesser society cannot meet its obligations. Hence, all the objection proves is that the state should aid those children who do not enjoy an equal opportunity. Such is precisely our position.

The second difficulty brought against private education is the charge that it is "interested," biased toward its own class or religion and that it consequently ill serves the universal good of the nation. This difficulty is somewhat surprising for, if pushed to its logical conclusion, it would require a man to be indifferent to his own class, business, or religion. A special concern for one's own affairs in no way injures the

---

[157] For theodicy the reader may consult Bernard Boedder, *Natural Theology* (New York: Longmans, Green and Co., 1927), Henri Renard, *The Philosophy of God* (Milwaukee: The Bruce Publishing Co., 1952), Reginald Garrigou-Lagrange, *God: His Existence and His Nature* (St. Louis: B. Herder Book Co., 1934 and 1936), 2 vols., Paul J. Glenn, *Theodicy* (St. Louis: B. Herder Book Co., 1938). Available in the field of natural ethics are Michael Cronin, *The Science of Ethics* (Dublin: M. H. Gill and Son, 1920 and 1929), 2 vols., Paul J. Glenn, *Ethics* (St. Louis: B. Herder Book Co., 1939), Victor Cathrein, *Philosophia Moralis* (Friburgi Brisgoviae: B. Herder, 1911), and Henri Renard, *The Philosophy of Morality* (Milwaukee: The Bruce Publishing Co., 1953).

[158] The truth of this assertion can be seen in countries in which the state does assist private educational initiative. The Provinces of Quebec and Ontario in Canada are cases in point.

common welfare. On the contrary, the common welfare profits from individual interests in as much as a man does better that for which he has a special concern. The unexpressed premise in the objection, namely, that a special concern is incompatible with concern for the common welfare, is of course untenable and merits no comment. The same may be said for the charge of bias, which is not only unverifiable, but actually disproved by thousands of private schools eminently successful in their scholarly competition with public education.

Closely allied with the preceding objection to private education is the charge of devisiveness. Whereas a common system of schools tends to knit the nation together, so the argument goes, a variety of private institutions tends to fragment that nation on class and/or religious lines. This objection, if logically developed, would eventually seek the very abolition of classes and religions. There would be in the nation of its proposers no room for different political theories, fraternal organizations, or kinds of education. Rigid conformism would be the guiding norm of government policy and practice. One need not be astute to see that this sort of political philosophy has no place in a democratic society. It is thoroughly totalitarian. It is of the very genius of democracy that unity thrives in a healthy diversity. The Catholic Bishops of the United States pointed out in their statement of 1955 that religion, as a matter of fact, is the strongest unifying force a nation can have.

> It is true that in the case of the religious schools there is a difference, inasmuch as they exist to teach positive religion as the integrating element of the curriculum. But surely, religion itself is not a discordant factor in American life. Surely, Christianity, with its primary inculcation of love of God and love of neighbor is not divisive. *Only those who teach hatred teach division: those who teach love teach unity.*
>
> How can it be, then, that religion in the school should be accused of sowing the seeds of national discord? Rather, is it not obvious that positive Christian training, with its emphasis on the sanctions of divine law, of the natural law, and of civil law, on the social nature of the virtues of justice and charity, on the moral obligations of patriotism and public service, *provides the strongest cement that can possibly bind a nation together.*[159]

The secularist in his attempts to abolish the religious school some-

---

[159] "The Place of the Private and Church-related Schools in American Education," *Washington Post and Times Herald,* Nov. 20, 1955, p. B5. Italics the present writer's.

times argues that religion is a private matter and that it is, therefore, to be taught in the church and the home only. Since, on this premise, education is entirely secular, it ought to be conducted in one religionless universal system of schools. The immediately obvious answer to this line of reasoning is the simple but flat denial that religion is a mere private affair and that education is secular. Man is a unit and he must be educated as a unit, whole and entire. He must also operate in the same way. To attempt to sever his religion and his eternal destiny from either his education or his life is to rend him asunder in a most unnatural and tragic way. But this is not the only flaw in the objection. Even if education and public life were secular, the principle of subsidiarity would still apply and for the same reasons we have given above. Public education may in no circumstance monopolize the field.[160]

In addition to the observations we have already made in its regard the concept of state educational monopoly merits a cursory but direct critique. The general deficiencies running through a general state absolutism are patent to all. The educational deficiencies infecting an educational absolutism are sometimes latent. These latter we wish here to indicate. (1) A state educational monopoly cripples all educational effort in a country. After it has quashed private enterprise, it tends to occasion its own decay by the removal of all competition with itself. (2) The very existence of private schools is a powerful check on the growth of a general state absolutism. History is a witness to the tendency of absolutists to assume control of education as soon as their power permits. (3) State monopoly hinders a healthy experimentation in matters educational. Public educators themselves readily admit that private institutions have been historically characterized by innumerable instances of experimentation.[161] And undeniable are the diverse kinds of benefits that have accrued to education as a whole from these experiments.[162] (4) One sole system of education tends to cast all citizens into the same intellectual mold, a situation hardly conducive to a

---

[160] We may note that Rugg's objection proves only that *some* kind of school is necessary — which no one denies. Counts' fear of the "uncertainties of private enterprise" is belied by the historical stability of private institutions, many of them far outdating public ones. At best his point indicates that the state should assist private schools that they may not fail and supply for them if and when they do.

[161] Counts, *op. cit.*, p. 36.

[162] Paul Klapper, "Social Control of Education," *School and Society*, XLIX (Feb. 11, 1939), 177.

vigorous national life. (5) Governmental monopoly in higher education easily impedes the progress of culture and science by subjecting scholarly endeavor to political factions.[163] That academic freedom may suffer in these circumstances has been demonstrated by contemporary reports from Communist countries.[164]

The state is a delegated subsidiary educator

In this section our investigation proceeds a step further. We have shown first that the state is an educator, and then that it is a supplementary educator. We wish now to inquire in whose name the state educates. Does it act in its own name and with a direct right? Or does it act as a representative, a delegate of another and consequently with an indirect right? It does not appear that these questions are superfluous for the mere reason that we have demonstrated the subsidiary character of the state's function in education, since it is conceivable that an educational agency be subsidiary and yet teach with a direct right and in its own name.

We have shown in our philosophical analysis of the nature of the state that the *raison d'être* of the state is the protection and promotion of the common good. The state by nature is a procurer of the common welfare. It follows, therefore, that it is not by nature an educator. Both the Church and the family, however, *are* by nature educators; such is their very *raison d'être*. The state's right to educate is indirect: *if* the common good requires intervention, *then* the state may and must educate. In the same way, the state is not by nature a farmer, or a railroader. It may enter these fields only if the common good requires that entrance. Directly the state is bound to care for the general welfare and only for this reason does it enter any field. The educational duty of both Church and family, on the other hand, does not spring from some inadequacy elsewhere; that duty in their case is native and direct.

From this indirect, derived, secondary duty to educate we must conclude that the state teaches, not in its own name but in the name and

---

[163] Cathrein, *op. cit.*, No. 663 and Cronin, *op. cit.*, II, p. 490.

[164] Even from the nonreligious point of view Marxist statism is, of course, vulnerable in many of its doctrines. Vysheslavtsev (who considers himself a neo-liberal) has vigorously attacked Marxism on mere philosophical grounds. See George L. Kline's review of his study, *The Crisis of Industrial Civilization: Marxism, Neo-Socialism, Neo-Liberalism* in "A Philosophical Critique of Soviet Marxism," *Review of Metaphysics*, IX (Sept., 1955), pp. 90–105. Kline writes from Columbia University.

as the delegate of another. That other can be of course no one but an agency with a direct, underived, primary duty to educate: either the Church or the family.

Such has been the common opinion of Catholic authorities. As far as I can ascertain, only Cavagnis dissents, and even then he is not treating the question as such but mentions his opinion in passing as he discusses another matter. Cavagnis held that the state does not teach with the delegated authority of the father but rather in its own right, and that even though it is supplying the insufficiency of the father.[165]

Catholic writers have expressed their views on this question with a number of diverse expressions. Cathrein calls the school an extension of and supplementary institution to the family ("extensio quaedam et institutum subsidiarium familiae"). He also uses the word, vicarious, to describe the school's relationship to the family.[166] An anonymous writer in the *American Ecclesiastical Review* spoke of the school as a substitute for the family and an annex to the Church. He concluded that the state has no *direct* authority over the school.[167] Cappello, denying to the state a proper and native right to educate, speaks of its function as supplementary, delegated, derived, and resulting from a commission and free consent of the parents or due to their physical or moral incapacity. He likewise speaks of the state as taking the place of parents.[168] Messner says that the state acts merely in the name of parents.[169] Gonzales styles the state's educational role as supplementary and auxiliary, and the state itself as being a natural substitute for the family and other private associations.[170] Though these writers use different expressions, it will be seen that they hold the same substantial view.[171]

---

[165] "Aiebant enim auctoritatem civilem in scholis instituendis repraesentare auctoritatem paternam; sed non est verum; aliud enim est ipsam supplere insufficientiam patrum, aliud est eorum auctoritatem representare . . . Verum in supplenda hac familiarum insufficientia, non procedit auctoritate patrum delegata, sed sua, idest publica." *Op. cit.,* pp. 169–170.

[166] Cathrein, *op. cit.,* No. 659–660.

[167] "State Control in the School," VI (Apr., 1892), 300.

[168] "Excluso jure *proprio* et *nativo,* palam est politicae potestati competere non posse nisi ius *suppletorium, delegatum, devolutivum,* scil. ex *commissione* quadam et libero consensu parentum eorumve *impossibilitate* physica aut morali. . . . Status *vices parentum christianorum gerat. . . .*" (italics Cappello's). *Op. cit.,* p. 399.

[169] *Op. cit.,* p. 303.

[170] *Op. cit.,* p. 810.

[171] Catholic philosophers are not alone in holding this opinion. The Supreme Court of Alabama in *Boyd* v. *State,* 88 Ala. 169, 7 So. 268 (1890) declared that "the

We will now examine the reasoning behind these assertions. We may note that the writers we now advance approach the problem from somewhat different vantage points than the one we explained above. One argued that no one has the right to educate children unless the parents grant him that right, because to teach jurisdiction is needed. Now the state cannot have the peculiar jurisdiction belonging to parents because the peculiar relation on which parents' jurisdiction is founded is present only in them. Therefore, unless parents delegate their teaching jurisdiction, no other can possess it.[172] A second writer pointed out that parents alone in the natural order have a direct right to educate, because if any other natural agent also possessed such a direct right, there would be lacking the unity necessary for a proper education.[173]

A third begins his treatment of the question by indicating the function of public law: the ordering and directing of public affairs. Civil law has nothing to do with private and personal matters. Since human procreation is obviously a personal and private affair, the infant's early development and formation are also personal and private. There is an unbroken continuity between the child's early life and its education because the latter is merely a complement of the former. Just as mother and father do not procreate at a command of the state, so also they do not educate at a command of the state or as its delegate. Consequently, parents educate in their own name; all others educate only in the name of the parents.[174]

Messmer, an American writing at the close of the past century, anticipated this last argument for he, too, approached the question from the private and personal nature of the formation of the child. The state, he pointed out, has no direct right over the child and hence can-

---

teacher is, within reasonable bounds, the substitute for the parent, exercising his delegated authority." As we will see later in Part III, the public educational systems of many nations are based on the supposition that the school is the extension of the home. Notable even among these, the Federal Republic of Germany states in its constitution that "the natural right of the parents to determine the education and training of their children is the foundation of the educational and school system." *Constitution of North-Rhine-Westphalia,* June 28, 1950, article 8. United Nations, *Yearbook on Human Rights for 1950* (New York: United Nations, 1952), p. 101. This work will hereafter be cited as U.N.Y. with the appropriate date.

[172] Holaind, *op. cit.,* p. 7. Holaind notes that "this argument does not exclude a jurisdiction founded on another relation than paternity . . . such as a divine command."

[173] Cathrein, *op. cit.,* No. 652.

[174] Lino A. Ciarlantini, *The Liberty of the School and Family Education* (New York: Educational Publishers, 1954), pp. 96–97.

not legislate for the inner operation of the family. Just as it does not prescribe the mother's nursing of the infant nor the father's clothing of it, so also it may not control their instructional duties toward the child.[175]

The statist objection to the position we have taken above revolves about the necessity of education for the procurement of the common welfare of society. Since the state has a direct duty and right to secure the common good, and since in modern society especially education is an indispensable condition for the attainment of the common good, they argue that the state has a direct right to educate and that it educates in its own name and not as the delegate of another.

Though this sequence of reasoning may seem cogent, it does not stand up under analysis. First of all, the very progress of the argument belies a direct right. The statist must proceed from the end of government, the common good, to another entity, education. The argumentation obviously appeals from one thing to another, from the direct to the indirect. Because the state can justify its entrance into education only on the basis of its duty to secure the common good, it may enter that field only when that common good is threatened. Its right to educate, therefore, is patently conditional, based on something else.

Second, the mere necessity of a function for the common good in no way demonstrates a direct right in the state for the exercise of that function. Manifestly untenable conclusions flow from the contrary assertion of the statist. The flourishing condition and practice of medicine is necessary for the common good, and yet no one but the radical will claim that the state is natively and properly a healer, that it has a direct duty and right to practice medicine. If the state had a direct right to dispose of anything which is necessary for the common good, it could determine the citizen's food, clothing, and marriage in order, for example, to insure a healthier army.[176]

Third, the statist must face the fact that there can be only one *direct* and *basic* right to educate in the natural order. That right must belong either to the parent or to the state. Now if the statist wishes to assign

---

[175] S. G. Messmer, "Compulsory Education," *American Ecclesiastical Review*, VI (Apr., 1892), 285–286. This writer is not to be confused with Messner, which latter we have on occasion cited above.

[176] Cathrein, *op. cit.*, No. 654. Thus it can be seen that Communism is the logical consequence of the ordinary statist's basic principles. Communism merits at least this commendation that it pushes principles to their implied conclusions. Ordinary statism does not.

that right to the state, he should honestly tell us that he means to deny it to the parent. Few secularists, however, are willing to draw this conclusion. Most seem to prefer the hazardous task of sitting on both sides of the fence and to allow parents to think that secularism does not oppose what those parents very well know to be their natural and inalienable rights.

It may be well to point out in conclusion that in discussing the delegated character of the state's educational right we have been thinking of the usual work of education conducted by the ordinary school. We do not mean to deny that the state has a direct right to conduct schools for civic duty, i.e., the training of personnel necessary for governmental work and the armed services. In this case the educational work is really a mere part of the over-all governmental service and hence participates in the direct right the state has to conduct such a service.

CHAPTER VI

THE STATE IN LARGER PERSPECTIVE

EDUCATIONAL PHILOSOPHIES OF MODERN STATES

WE ARE now in a position to apply our basic philosophical principles of the state as educator to the concepts modern nations entertain regarding their function in education. This concretization of the principles we have established will serve a double purpose. It will enable us to illustrate those principles and thus see how eminently pertinent they are to contemporary problems. It will also serve as an evaluation of modern worldwide educational trends in the light of sound moral and political norms. In order to effect this evaluation, it will not be necessary to indicate what is praiseworthy or defective in every statement of policy. The reader, we trust, will readily make his own evaluation with the help of our foregoing discussion.

For the sake of clarity we will group the nations into more or less homogeneous categories beginning with the extreme statists and finishing with those which recognize both the natural law and the supernatural order.[177]

1. *Nations which deny both parent and Church rights in education either explicitly or implicitly.*
Albania

> The schools belong to the State. Private schools can be opened only by special permission. All their activities are supervised by the State. . . . Schools are separated from the church.[178]

---

[177] As we indicated at the outset of this study, no nation today actually advocates individualism as a philosophy of state in education.
[178] *Constitution of the People's Republic of Albania,* Mar. 15, 1946, article 28. Amos J. Peaslee, *Constitutions of Nations* (Concord, N. H.: Rumford Press, 1950), I, p. 42.

It will be noted that this statement gives the state a practical monopoly in education, since private schools may open only by exception to general policy. Both parent and Church rights in education are violated by the exclusion of the latter from the work of education.

Bulgaria

Education is secular, with a democratic and progressive spirit. . . . Schools are run by the State. The establishment of private schools may be allowed only by a special law, in which case the school in question is under state supervision.[179]

Thailand

This nation stipulates in its constitution that it is the exclusive duty of the state to erect an educational system. All educational institutions are "under the control and supervision of the State."[180]

Romania

No religious denomination, congregation, or community can open or maintain institutions of general education, but may only run special schools for training personnel necessary to the cult under state control.[181]

Romania places an exception to the state sponsorship of education, namely, the maintenance of seminaries. This, however, is not much of a concession for even the seminary is under governmental control. Whether the state has any rights over seminaries we will discuss in a later chapter.

Czechoslovakia

All schools shall be State schools.[182]

Mexico

Private persons may engage in education of all kinds and grades. But as regards primary, secondary and normal education (and that of any

[179] *Constitution of the People's Republic of Bulgaria*, Dec. 4, 1947, article 79. Peaslee, I, p. 242.

[180] *Constitution of the Kingdom of Thailand of December 10, 1932 as amended up to and including March 12, 1952*, section 42, U.N.Y. for 1952, p. 269.

[181] *Constitution of the People's Republic of Rumania*, Apr. 13, 1948, article 27, Peaslee, III, p. 39.

[182] *Constitution of the Czechoslovak Republic*, June 9, 1948, Section 13. Peaslee, I, p. 607.

kind or grade designed for laborers and field workers) they must obtain previously, in every case, the express authorization of the public power. The said authorization may be refused or revoked by decisions against which there shall be no judicial proceedings or recourse.

Private institutions devoted to education of the kinds and grades specified in the preceding section must be without exception in conformity with the provisions of sections I (which states: "standard which shall guide the said education shall be maintained entirely apart from any religious doctrine . . .") and II of the first paragraph of this article and must also be in harmony with the official plans and programs. Religious corporations, ministers of religion, stock companies which exclusively or predominantly engage in educational activities and associations or companies devoted to propagation of any religious creed shall not in any way participate in institutions giving primary, secondary and normal education and education for laborers or field workers.

The State may in its discretion withdraw at any time the recognition of official validity of studies conducted in private institutions.[183]

Although it proceeds in a more roundabout way, Mexico's official attitude toward its position in education is not significantly different from the usual Communist country. While it allows some scope for restricted private initiative in education, it reserves to itself an absolute power to wipe out a school or a system of schools. Against that power there is no recourse. The Church's legal rights are, of course, almost nil.

Turkey

In modern Turkey education is considered to be a prerogative of the government. Although private schools are allowed, the official attitude toward them is usually cool. The Ministry of Education exercises direct control over all schools and no institution may be opened without its authorization. Secularism and nationalism are twin characteristics of the Turkish approach to education.[184] "The church has no rights in education. Parents have the right to make complaints . . . but (they) have no judicial right in educational affairs."[185]

---

[183] *Political Constitution of the United States of Mexico,* Jan. 31, 1917, article 3, numbers II to V. Peaslee, II, pp. 415–416.

[184] Abul H. K. Sassani, *Education in Turkey,* U. S. Office of Education, Federal Security Agency Bulletin 1952, No. 10 (Washington: Government Printing Office, 1952), pp. 13 and 81.

[185] Letter to the writer from Mr. Emin Hekimgil, Turkish Embassy, New York City, Nov. 5, 1954.

Ukrainian Soviet Socialist Republic

> To insure the citizens freedom of conscience, the Church in the UkSSR is separated from the State and the School from the Church.[186]

This republic, and Soviet Russia likewise, add to their devastating abolishment of private rights the humorous reason, "to insure the citizens freedom of conscience." The latter's stipulations in education are the same as the above.

Yugoslavia

> Schools are state-owned. The founding of private schools may be permitted only by law, and their work is controlled by the state. Elementary education is compulsory and free. The school is separate from the Church.[187]

2. Nations which unduly limit Church rights.

Norway

Norway has a provision in its constitution unlike any other the present writer was able to find: binding parents to bring up their children in their own religion. Interesting though this provision may be, it is not our chief purpose here. The last sentence quoted below is educationally both pertinent and telling.

> The Evangelical-Lutheran religion shall remain the public religion of the State. The inhabitants professing it shall be bound to bring up their children in the same. Jesuits shall not be tolerated.[188]

At the same time Norway operates on what its citizens call the "common school principle." All children in the age group from six to fourteen are required to attend one school system of the same type. University level institutions of higher education are also state institutions.[189]

---

[186] *Constitution of the Ukrainian Soviet Socialist Republic,* Jan. 30, 1937, article 104. Peaslee, III, p. 217. Russia's provision can be found in its constitution, article 124, Peaslee, III, p. 280.

[187] *Constitution of the Federal Peoples' Republic of Yugoslavia,* Jan. 30, 1946, article 38. Peaslee, III, p. 527.

[188] *The Constitution of Norway,* May 17, 1814, article 2. Peaslee, II, p. 675.

[189] Olaf Devik, "Norway," *Educational Yearbook,* 1944, ed. I. L. Kandel, pp. 249–251.

Switzerland

The cantons shall make provision for elementary education, which must be adequate, and be exclusively under the control of the civil authorities. It is compulsory and, in the public schools, free. Ecclesiastical jurisdiction is abolished.[190]

3. *Nations which unduly stress state rights to the detriment of Church and family rights.*

Chile

Public education is preferentially an affair of the State.[191]

Bolivia

Education in all its degrees shall be subject to the State's guardianship, to be exercised through the ministry of education.
    Education is the highest function of the State.[192]

While these statements of Chile and Bolivia can be interpreted in a nonstatist sense, their obvious meaning indicates that the state is the primary educator in society and that, as a consequence, Church and family become secondary.

4. *A nation which partially recognizes Church and family rights.*

Italy

It is the duty and right of parents to support, teach, and educate their children, even if born out of wedlock. In cases of inability of the parents, the law provides for the fulfillment of such obligations. The Republic prescribes general rules on education and establishes state schools of all types and grades. Private groups and individuals have the right to establish schools and educational institutes without state support. The law, in specifying the rights and obligations of non-state schools requesting parity of status, provides for their complete freedom and assures to their pupils a treatment equivalent in every way to that of pupils of the state schools.[193]

---

[190] *Federal Constitution of the Swiss Confederation,* Sept. 12, 1848, articles 27 and 58. Peaslee, III, pp. 127 and 137.

[191] *Political Constitution of the Republic of Chile,* Sept. 18, 1925, article 10, No. 7. Peaslee, I, p. 414.

[192] *Political Constitution of the Bolivian State,* Nov. 23, 1945, articles 162 and 154. Peaslee, I, pp. 174 and 173.

[193] *Constitution of the Italian Republic,* Dec. 22, 1947, articles 30 and 33. Peaslee, II, pp. 282–283.

It will be noted that while Italy recognizes the right of private persons to establish and maintain schools, it does not allow them a share of the tax money they contribute to the state for the work of education. This, of course, involves a denial of parent and Church rights in that the violation of distributive justice morally forces many parents to patronize schools of which they may not approve. This question of distributive justice we will consider in detail in Chapter VIII.

5. *Nations which explicitly recognize family rights in education.*

Philippines

The natural right and duty of parents in the rearing of the youth for civic efficiency should receive the aid and support of the government.[194]

Argentina

The responsibility for education and instruction rests upon the family and upon the private and official establishments which collaborate with the family in conformity with the laws. For this purpose the State shall establish primary, secondary and technical-professional schools, and universities and academies.[195]

Nicaragua

The education of children is the primary duty and natural right of the parents.

Parents without economic resources are entitled to solicit the aid of the State for the education of their children.[196]

Besides their recognition of the family's position in education, the constitutions of the Philippines and Nicaragua likewise acknowledge the principle of subsidiarity as governing the state's function.

Denmark

Children whose parents have no means to see to their education have a right to free instruction in the elementary school. Parents or guardians who themselves undertake that their children or wards receive an instruction that is up to the standard of the elementary school shall not

---

[194] *Constitution of the Philippines*, Feb. 8, 1935, article II, section 4. Peaslee, II, p. 793.

[195] *Constitution of the Argentine Republic*, Mar. 16, 1949, Chapter III, article 37. Peaslee, I, p. 70. At the time of writing Argentina is in a state of transition and may eventually adopt a new constitution.

[196] *Constitution of the Republic of Nicaragua*, Jan. 21, 1948, articles 69 and 70. Peaslee, II, p. 642.

be compelled to have their children or wards taught in the elementary school.[197]

England

In the exercise and performance of all powers and duties conferred and imposed on them by this Act the Minister and local education authorities shall have regard to the general principle that, so far as is compatible with the provision of efficient instruction and training and the avoidance of unreasonable public expenditure, pupils are to be educated in accordance with the wishes of their parents.[198]

Portugal

The State shall ensure the constitution and protection of the family as the source of the maintenance and development of the race, the primary basis of education, discipline, and social harmony. The constitution of the family is based upon . . . equality of the rights and duties of husband and wife in regard to the maintenance and education of their legitimate children.

With the object of protecting the family it appertains to the State and local bodies . . . to assist parents in the discharge of their duty of instructing and educating their children, and to co-operate with them by means of public institutions for education and correction, or by encouraging private establishments destined for the same purpose.

Elementary, primary instruction is obligatory and may be given at home, or in private or State schools.[199]

Portugal is extremely clear in its recognition of the state's supplementary function in education. It lays it down that the state must "assist parents" and "co-operate" with them in the work of education either by providing public schools or by "encouraging private establishments." Only Venezuela, as we shall note presently, is clearer in concretizing the principle of subsidiarity in education.

Ecuador

Education of children is primarily the duty and right of the parents or those who stand in their place. The State shall watch over the compliance with this duty and facilitate the exercise of this right.[200]

---

[197] *Act of Constitution of the Kingdom of Denmark,* June 5, 1915, article 83. Peaslee, I, p. 652.

[198] Her Majesty's Stationery Office, *Education Act, 1944,* Part IV, sec. 76.

[199] *Political Constitution of the Portuguese Republic,* Aug. 1, 1935, articles 12, 13, 14, and 43. Peaslee, III, pp. 7 and 10.

[200] *Constitution of the Republic of Ecuador,* Dec. 31, 1946, article 171. Peaslee, I, p. 707.

Uruguay

The care and education of children, so that they may attain their fullest physical, intellectual and social capacity, is the duty and the right of parents. Those who have large families are entitled to compensatory aid if they need it.[201]

Venezuela

The State shall share with the parents, in a subsidiary manner and within the economic possibilities of the parents, the responsibility incumbent on them for the rearing of their children. Private initiative in educational matters shall deserve the encouragement of the State, provided that it is in accordance with the principles contained in this Constitution and in the laws.[202]

It will be noted that Venezuela explicitly describes its educational function as subsidiary and that it aims at encouraging private initiative.

6. *Nations which explicitly recognize both Church and family rights.*

We do not suggest by the above caption that other nations are lacking in their recognition of Church rights in education, but we wish merely to indicate in the present category explicit and official recognitions to that effect found in primary governmental documents.

Canada

In and for each Province the Legislature may exclusively make laws in relation to Education, subject and according to the following Provisions: (1) Nothing in any such Law shall prejudicially affect any Right or Privilege with respect to Denominational Schools which any Class of Persons have by Law in the Province at the Union.[203]

Spain

The Spanish State guarantees the teaching of the Catholic religion as an ordinary and compulsory subject in all teaching establishments whether or not belonging to the State, and of whatever kind or grade. The children of non-Catholic parents shall be dispensed from such lessons at the request of their parents or guardians.

---

[201] *Constitution of the Oriental Republic of Uruguay,* Mar. 24, 1934, article 40. Peaslee, III, p. 394.

[202] *Constitution of Venezuela,* July 5, 1947, articles 49 and 56. Peaslee, III, pp. 476–477.

[203] *The British North American Act,* 1867, No. 93. Peaslee, I, p. 337. This stipulation does not mean that in practice all Canadian provinces fully recognize Church rights.

The Church shall be allowed freely to exercise the right pertaining to it, under canon 1375 of the Code of Canon Law, to organize and direct public schools of any kind and grade, even for laymen.[204] All Spaniards have a right to receive education and instruction and the duty of acquiring them either in the family circle or in private or public centers of their own free election. The State will see that no talent is wasted because of lack of economic means. Parents are obliged to provide for, educate, and instruct their children.[205]

It will be noted that Spain is extremely clear in its recognition of both Church and parent rights in education. Worthy of note also is the concordat recognition by the Holy See of the practice of excusing from Catholic instruction children of non-Catholic parents who so indicate their will.

Liechtenstein

The whole system of education and instruction, without prejudice to the inviolability of the doctrine of the Church, is subject to the control of the State.[206]

Ireland

1. The State acknowledges that the primary and natural educator of the child is the Family and guarantees to respect the inalienable right and duty of parents to provide, according to their means, for the religious and moral, intellectual, physical and social education of their children.

2. Parents shall be free to provide this education in their homes or in private schools or in schools recognized or established by the State.

3. (1) The State shall not oblige parents in violation of their conscience and lawful preference to send their children to schools established by the State, or to any particular type of school designated by the State. (2) The State shall, however, as guardian of the common good, require in view of actual conditions that the children receive a certain minimum education, moral, intellectual, and social.

4. The State shall provide for free primary education and shall endeavour to supplement and give reasonable aid to private and corporate educational initiative, and, when the public good requires it, provide

---

[204] *The Concordat Between Spain and the Holy See,* Aug. 27, 1953 (Madrid: Diplomatic Information Office, 1953), articles XXVII and XXXI, pp. 14 and 17.

[205] *Charter of the Spanish People,* July 16, 1945, articles 5 and 23. Peaslee, III, pp. 77 and 79.

[206] *Constitution of the Principality of Liechtenstein,* Oct. 5, 1921. Peaslee, II, p. 378.

other educational facilities or institutions with due regard, however, for the rights of parents, especially in the matter of religious and moral formation.

5. In exceptional cases, where the parents for physical or moral reasons fail in their duty towards their children, the State as guardian of the common good, by appropriate means shall endeavour to supply the place of the parents, but always with due regard to the natural and imprescriptible rights of the child.[207]

This section of the Irish constitution is outstanding in its treatment of the family-state educational relationship. So true is this that it might stand as a remarkably complete but concise statement of Catholic thought on the state's function in education.

THE STATE'S ULTIMATE END IN EDUCATION

We come now to a problem that seems not to have presented itself — at least in philosophical terms — to Catholic writers on the state's educational role. And yet it seems to lie at the very heart of any complete consideration of that role.

Every agent acts for an end. It must act for an end or it would not act at all.[208] And what is more, whenever an agent acts, it acts for an ultimate end, an end that it treats as the supreme good. St. Thomas gives two reasons for the truth of this last statement. Whatever a man seeks, he seeks as good in some way or other. If he seeks it not as his supreme good, he does so at least as tending toward that supreme good. This is so because any beginning is ordered to its consummation.[209] In explaining his second reason the Angelic Doctor observes that the last end as the mover of the will is like the first mover in other motions. Just as second causes do not move except in so far as they are moved by the first mover, so also intermediate final causes move the will only in so far as they are ordered to the supreme final cause, the ultimate end.[210]

---

[207] *Constitution of Ireland*, Dec. 29, 1937, article 42. Peaslee, II, p. 260.

[208] "Manifestum est autem, quod omnes actiones, quae procedunt ab aliqua potentia, causantur ab ea secundum rationem sui objecti; objectum autem voluntatis est finis, et bonum; unde oportet, quod actiones humanae propter finem sint." St. Thomas, I, II, q. 1, a. 1.

[209] "Quidquid homo appetit, appetit sub ratione boni; quod quidem si non appetitur ut bonum perfectum, quod est ultimus finis, necesse est ut appetatur ut tendens in bonum perfectum: quia semper inchoatio alicujus ordinatur ad consummationem ipsius." *Ibid.*, a. 6.

[210] "Causae secundae moventes non movent, nisi secundum quod moventur a primo

The state, because it is made up of and acts through human beings, is no exception to this principle. In every one of its activities it acts for an end, and indeed an ultimate end. When the state, therefore, opens and operates a school, it opens and operates that school not only for some intermediate end (e.g., the teaching of reading or arithmetic), nor merely for its own proper end, the common good. It opens and operates that school also for some supreme, ultimate end; it cannot do otherwise. This fact is especially significant in the state's educational function. When it accepts a child for formation, the state has an ultimate end in that formation. In its educational activity the state *must* intend more than good citizenship and the furtherance of the common good. Like any ordinary human being the state also necessarily intends something ultimate, something supreme.

Now all of this raises some weighty questions. The supreme, ultimate end intended by the state in its work of education is either true or false; it either measures up to objective reality or it does not so measure up. What will prevent the state from falling into errors, errors conceivably both grave and egregious? Can a secular state in its neglect of the supernatural possibly have a true philosophy of education? Can it really prepare its children for the objective reality of the supernatural order in which the entire human race willy-nilly now exists? If it does not prepare them for objective reality, does it have any right to prepare them at all? If the answer to the last question is no, who will prepare those children? If it is yes, on what does the right rest?

It seems that to answer these questions adequately we must distinguish three distinct kinds of states.

1. For the state that accepts the supernatural order and achieves its end of the common good in the framework of that supernatural order there is no philosophical problem. In its concrete operation of the school such a state does *de facto* intend the true ultimate end, the students' possession of God in the beatific vision.

2. If a state *positively* teaches a false last end in its schools, it is simply wrong and illegitimate in so teaching. The state has no more right to teach error than any private individual has that right. The existence of such a school is morally unjustifiable. Parents patronizing

---

movente; unde secunda appetibilia non movent appetitum, nisi in ordine ad primum appetibile, quod est ultimus finis." *Ibid.* A more complete treatment of this question can be found in Joseph Gredt, *Elementa Philosophiae* (Friburgi Brisgoviae: Herder, 1953), II, No. 881–889.

this type of school are ordinarily bound to withdraw their children from the school and provide for their education in some other way.[211]

3. If the state is officially negative or neutral in that it neither acknowledges nor denies the true last end of man, it may conduct schools even though those schools are necessarily deficient. Several observations must be kept in mind in judging this problem.

a) The state itself is objectively wrong in failing to choose the true ultimate end. But this is not to say that it thereby forces a false ultimate end on the child. A man can give five dollars to a pauper for an evil reason, but it does not follow that the pauper is going to be harmed by the five dollars. So also the state may be wrong in its choice of a last end, but that does not prevent its influence on the child from being at least partially beneficent, if not totally so.

b) The operation of a school religiously neutral (if such be possible) is not a positive evil but the mere omission of a good. This school teaches arithmetic, geography, and reading; and these are good. It does not teach religion; that is an omission of a good and to be distinguished from the positive teaching of error.[212]

c) Even though a religiously neutral school is not practically possible, we may still argue that the slight religious harm that may be done to the child can be balanced by a great deal of secular good that itself may redound to the religious benefit of the child. Learning to read, for example, may well aid the child later to grasp better the significance and import of his religion.

d) If a state were compelled to discontinue its educational function merely because it is failing to operate for a genuine ultimate end, any number of secular states would be forced to cease all activity. Such is manifestly untenable, for its operation even for a false last end is a lesser evil than its non-operation.[213]

---

[211] See canon 1372.

[212] Cavagnis holds this opinion: "Etenim nunquam liceat nisi per accidens ex erronea conscientia malum facere, ut esset constituere scholam acatholico spiritu imbutam, tamen licet aliquando a bono alias obligatorio abstinere, cum nempe id sive physice sive moraliter impossibile est, seu praestari nequit absque gravioribus malis. Schola autem negative se habens quoad religionem, est per se tantum omissio boni et non mali positio." *Op. cit.*, pp. 211–212. Bouquillon is of the same opinion. See his *Education: to Whom Does It Belong? — A Rejoinder to Critics* (Baltimore: J. Murphy & Co., 1892), p. 34.

[213] That our conclusion is correct is borne out by the statement of canon 1374 assigning to the ordinary the judgment of the circumstances that would justify the toleration of a religiously neutral school.

These distinctions and observations, when applied to the problems we posed above, readily enable one to formulate pertinent solutions.

Among the nations of the world that have rendered explicit their aims in education, Syria is outstanding. This predominantly Islamic country in its constitution of September, 1950, declares that "education shall be directed at creating a generation strong physically and mentally, believing in God, morality and virtue, proud of the Arab legacy, equipped with knowledge, conscious of its duties and rights, working for the public interest and full of the spirit of solidarity and brotherhood that should prevail among all citizens."[214]

---

[214] *Constitution of Syria*, Sept. 5, 1950, article 28, U.N.Y. for 1950, p. 282.

PART III

THE STATE AND THE PRIMARY
EDUCATORS

CHAPTER VII

PROTECTIVE FUNCTION OF THE STATE
TOWARD THE CHURCH

AS WE have already intimated in the course of our study, the state has a considerable number of duties toward and relationships to the primary agents of education, the Church and the family. These duties and relationships we are now prepared to discuss in some considerable detail.

The first protective duty of the state toward the primary educators is merely one facet of its general protective function toward the whole of its citizenry. A government must preserve society in such a condition of peace and harmony and confidence that the Church and the family may be able to carry out their educational missions freely and without undue interference from other members of society. It is particularly in reference to the Church that this function of the state will have pertinence. The latter must see to it that organizations hostile to the welfare of religion be prevented from obstructing the Church's educational work by fraud or physical violence. The state must likewise suppress, where such is feasible and conducive to the greatest good, vigorous antireligious crusades, since these militate against the very life of society. In this connection Pope Pius XI remarked that "all diligence should be exercised by states to prevent within their territories the ravages of an anti-God campaign which shakes society to its very foundations."[1]

Closely allied to this first protective duty of the state toward the Church is the obligation of allowing the Church to carry out her divine teaching commission freely and without undue interference from governmental agencies. This obligation is a mere derivative of

---

[1] *Atheistic Communism* (Washington: National Catholic Welfare Conference, 1937), p. 31.

what we said in Chapter V regarding the primary agents of education. We may note, however, that John S. Mill's withering denunciation of state monopoly in education is again pertinent here.

> To possess such a (complete) control, and actually to exert it, is to be despotic. A government which can mould the opinions and sentiments of the people from their youth upwards, can do with them whatever it pleases. . . . *Nor ought the power of individuals to set up rival establishments to depend in any degree upon its authorization.* It would be justified in requiring from all the people that they shall possess instruction in certain things, but not in prescribing to them how or from whom they shall obtain it.[2]

What this freedom for the Church involves in the concrete order is nicely outlined in that section of the Code of Canon Law which deals with the Church's work of education.[3] The state must, in the first place, honor the Church's right to establish and operate schools of all kinds and grades.[4] Since the latter has her teaching commission directly from God,[5] no human authority may interfere with or obstruct the fulfillment of that commission. From this it follows that the state does not have the right to give or deny permission to the Church to open and operate schools, whether they be on primary, secondary, higher or seminary levels.[6] If at times the Catholic Church conforms to the requiring of such a permission she is by no means acknowledging a right in the state but merely tolerating an evil for the sake of attaining a greater good.[7]

Instances in contemporary history of the fulfillment and the non-fulfillment of this duty on the part of modern states are abundant. First, are those nations which do not fulfill this obligation. The Government of Syria prohibits the establishment of a private school with-

---

[2] *Op. cit.,* p. 956. Italics added.

[3] The section, "De Scholis," is made up of canons 1372–1383.

[4] "Ecclesiae est ius scholas cuiusvis disciplinae non solum elementarias, sed etiam medias et superiores condendi." Canon 1375.

[5] See above, Chapter V.

[6] The canonist Coronata points out that the right to found a school in the strict sense includes the right to arrange the curriculum and appoint teachers independently of civil interference. *Institutiones Iuris Canonici* (4th ed. rev.; Taurini: Marietti, 1951), II, p. 316.

[7] Catholics in Colorado recently objected to a proposed educational law for the reason that it aimed to give the state the authority to "authorize, approve or license non-public schools." The proposal died with the adjournment of the Assembly. "News from the Field," *Catholic Educational Review,* LIV (Feb., 1956), 130–131.

out previous authorization by the Minister of Education.[8] In the Dominican Republic any private person or society may establish any type of school without governmental authorization or regulation. Primary schools, however, are an exception in that they do fall under regulation.[9] Lebanon requires previous approval by the Minister of National Education and Fine Arts,[10] while Albania allows the establishment of no private school except "by virtue of a law."[11] Egypt recently legislated to the effect that "no private school may be opened without a permit from the district education board."[12] Typical of the severity of Communist-dominated countries, Romania does not permit religiously sponsored "institutions of general education, but only special schools for training the personnel of the cult."[13] In Sweden permission to private initiative for the opening of a school for school-age pupils is granted "on condition that the head of the school is a member of the Swedish Lutheran State Church, that he leads a moral life and has the necessary teaching qualifications." Under an older law requiring merely that the head of the school be "a God-fearing person of good reputation" a Catholic school was established and still exists, but without state subsidy. Churches are permitted to open schools for pupils who are past school age.[14]

Among nations recognizing the right of private groups and the Church to found educational institutions without the previous approval of the state is Portugal, whose constitution permits the free establishment of private schools, but, like many nations, requires their submission to state inspection.[15] The Constitution of India seems likewise to recognize this right in its statement that "all minorities, whether based on religion or language shall have the right to establish and administer educational institutions of their choice."[16] According to Act. No. 214 of June 7, 1952 Denmark no longer requires prior gov-

[8] Decree No. 175, art. 5, of Mar., 1952, U.N.Y. for 1952, p. 265.

[9] *Organic Education Act,* June 5, 1951, art. 6, U.N.Y. for 1951, p. 70.

[10] Decree of May 23, 1950, U.N.Y. for 1950, p. 187.

[11] *Constitution of the People's Republic of Albania,* July 4, 1950, article 31, U.N.Y. for 1950, p. 14.

[12] Denver *Register,* Jan. 8, 1956, p. 5.

[13] *Constitution of the Romanian People's Republic,* Sept. 24, 1952, article 84, U.N.Y. for 1952, p. 240.

[14] B. J:son Bergqvist, "Sweden," *Educational Yearbook, 1932,* ed. I. L. Kandel (New York: Teachers College, Columbia University, 1933), pp. 400–401.

[15] Article 44, U.N.Y. for 1951, p. 299.

[16] Article 30, typed document sent to the writer from the Indian Embassy, Washington, D. C., n.d.

ernmental authorization for the opening of any private school.[17] The Netherlands likewise requires the consent of no one for the establishment of an elementary school.[18] The Concordat between Spain and the Holy See makes explicit reference to the former's duty regarding the point under discussion:

> The Church shall be allowed to exercise the right pertaining to it, under canon 1375 of the Code of Canon Law, to organize and direct public schools of any kind and grade, even for laymen.
>
> As regards the civil ordinances relating to the recognition, for civil purposes, of the studies carried out in them, the State shall proceed in agreement with the competent ecclesiastical authority.[19]

The United States, finally, may be cited as an example of a country in which no previous approval of the state is required for the opening of a private or Church school. There have been indirect attempts, however, to prevent the establishment of private schools through zoning laws. The courts thus far have not been of one mind in their interpretation of these laws. The Wisconsin State Supreme Court upheld a ban on a Lutheran high school in a residential district of Wauwatosa, Wisconsin.[20] The New York State Supreme Court has declared that the banning of a private school from a residential district where public schools are permitted is not an unjust discrimination.[21] The New York Court of Appeals, however, reversed this decision in a 5–1 judgment. The State District Court of California ordered the city of Piedmont to grant an originally denied building permit to a Catholic school.[22]

The second duty incumbent on the state and concerned with the Church's teaching mission as such is the co-operation the former is to afford to the latter in her work of supervising the religious instruction of her children. In countries, therefore, in which religion is taught in the public schools the government must allow the Church to inspect the religious teaching given to her children and to preserve it free from error.[23] She must likewise be permitted to approve or reject individuals

---

[17] U.N.Y. for 1952, p. 47.

[18] Philip J. Idenburg, *Education in the Netherlands* (The Hague: Netherlands Government Information Service, 1954), p. 18.

[19] Art. 31, *op. cit.*, p. 17.

[20] Denver *Register*, May 15, 1955, p. 1.

[21] *Ibid.*

[22] *Ibid.*

[23] "Religiosa institutio in scholis quibuslibet auctoritati et inspectioni Ecclesiae subiicitur."

selected for the teaching of religion.[24] This religious supervision does not, of course, give the Church grounds to interfere in the teaching of secular subjects or to enter into the administration of the schools.

In those countries in which the teaching of religion is a part of the public school curriculum some sort of supervisory function is often allowed the representatives of the various religious groups. Even Communist Romania allows some religious sponsorship of the religion program in state schools,[25] although it also reverses the procedure by requiring state approval in the field of religious instruction for syllabuses used and teachers employed by the church group. The Ministry of Religion "may cancel appointments on grounds of public interest or the security of the State."[26]

The Principality of Liechtenstein cares for this problem by the simple statement that "the instruction in religious matters shall be given by ecclesiastical authorities."[27] The Federal Republic of Germany is outstandingly clear and specific in its guarantees to the churches:

> Teachers imparting religious instruction (in the public schools) must be authorized to do so by either the church or the religious society concerned. No teacher may be compelled to impart religious instruction.
>
> Syllabuses and textbooks for religious instruction shall be determined by agreement with the church or religious society concerned.
>
> Without prejudice to the State's right of supervision, the churches or religious societies shall be entitled, in a manner to be agreed upon with the education authorities, to inspect schools for the purpose of ensuring that religious instruction is being imparted in accordance with their teachings and requirements.[28]

"Ordinariis locorum ius et officium est vigilandi ne in quibusvis scholis sui territorii quidquam contra fidem vel bonos mores tradatur aut fiat." Canon 1381, 1 and 2.

"Ordinarii locorum sive ipsi per se sive per alios possunt quoque scholas quaslibet, oratoria, recreatoria, patronatus, etc. in iis quae religiosam et moralem institutionem spectant, visitare. . . ." Canon 1382.

[24] "Eisdem similiter ius est approbandi religionis magistros et libros; itemque, religionis morumque causa, exigendi ut tum magistri tum libri removeantur." Canon 1381, 3.

[25] Many of these "state" schools are nothing but confiscated private institutions. Romania's *Education Reform Act* of August 3, 1948 simply stated that "all sectarian or private schools of whatever nature become State schools." U.N.Y. for 1948, p. 181.

[26] Decree No. 177 *Concerning the General Regulations Governing Religious Denominations,* August 3, 1948, chap. VI, articles 44 and 45, U.N.Y. for 1951, p. 306.

[27] *Constitution of the Principality of Liechtenstein,* October 5, 1921, article 16. Peaslee, II, p. 378.

[28] *Constitution of North-Rhine-Westphalia,* June 28, 1950, article 14, U.N.Y. for 1950, p. 102.

The German states of Brandenburg and Mecklenburg (both in the Soviet occupation zone at time of writing) allow religious groups to give doctrinal instruction on school premises and by teachers selected by the churches.[29] Portugal stipulates that although "the State and the Catholic Church shall be separate," yet that Church "shall be free to organize its activities in accordance with Canon Law."[30] Spain provides that

> The Ordinaries shall freely exercise their mission of supervising the said educational establishments in matters concerning the purity of the faith, morals, and religious education.
> The Ordinaries may demand the banning or withdrawal of books, publications, and teaching material opposed to Catholic Dogma and Morals.
>
> . . . .
>
> In State primary schools, the religion lessons shall be given by the school teachers, except in the event of an objection to any of them being raised by the Ordinary for the reasons stated in canon 1381, paragraph three, of the Code of Canon Law. Such teaching shall also be given, periodically, by the parish priest or his deputy, by means of catechism lessons.
> In State Secondary Schools, the religious teaching shall be given by masters, priests or religious, and, subsidiarily, by lay masters appointed by the competent civil authority, at the proposal of the diocesan Ordinary. . . .
> The Civil and ecclesiastical authorities, in common accord, shall organize, throughout the nation's territory, special tests of pedagogical competence for those to whom the teaching of religion in Universities and State Secondary Schools is to be entrusted.[31]

In Sweden Protestant bishops may visit public schools in order to inspect religious instruction, but if they "discover practices of which they disapprove, they are not permitted to interfere in instruction but must submit their criticisms to the Central Board [a lay board of education]."[32] In the Canadian province of Quebec public education

. . . comes under two committees, one Catholic, the other Protestant.

---

[29] *Constitution of Mark Brandenburg*, Feb. 6, 1947, article 66. *Constitution of Mecklenburg*, Jan. 15, 1947, article 93. Both in U.N.Y. for 1948, pp. 76 and 79.

[30] *Political Constitution of the Portuguese Republic*, Mar. 19, 1933, article 45 (as amended in 1951), U.N.Y. for 1951, p. 299.

[31] Concordat, *op. cit.*, articles 26 and 27, pp. 14 and 15.

[32] B. J:son Bergqvist, *op. cit.*, p. 410.

Each committee has jurisdiction over the schools of its faith. The Catholic committee is constituted by all the bishops of the province ex officio and an equal number of lay members appointed by the government. These committees plan the curriculum, approve textbooks, draw regulations for their schools, and make recommendations to the government on school policy. A Department of Education supervises the working of the whole system.[33]

We could, while treating of the protective duties of the state, consider those toward the child and the family; but, since these latter are for the most part bound up with other questions, we have chosen to discuss them in other places. One of these duties toward the child, for example, is that of supplying the lack or neglect of parents who fail to provide education for their offspring. This question, however, is intimately bound up with the larger one of compulsory education and so we have determined to consider both in one place.

---

[33] Charles Bilodeau, "Canada," *The Year Book of Education 1951,* ed. J. A. Lauwerys and N. Hans (London: University of London, 1951), p. 397.

CHAPTER VIII

POSITIVE ASSISTANCE TO PRIVATE INITIATIVE IN EDUCATION

IN CHAPTER II we dwelt at some length on the subsidiary character of the state's function as a state and in Chapter V we showed how the state's role in education is essentially a supplementary one. An immediate derivative of a supplementary function on the part of a secondary agent (the state) in the field of education is manifestly the assistance rendered to the primary agents (Church and family) when they need it.[34] And among the ways in which the modern state must assist the initiative of primary educators the chief by far is that of financial aid. For the most part financial aid is nothing but a question of distributive justice, and so we will here discuss the problem from that point of view.[35]

DISTRIBUTIVE JUSTICE — A GENERAL CONCEPT

The virtue of justice is commonly defined by Catholic moralists as the constant and perpetual will to give to each one his due.[36] Like all virtues justice is a habit, a principle of right action, but, unlike other virtues, justice deals with the rights and properties of others as belong-

---

[34] "It is the duty of the Christian State to concur actively in this spiritual enterprise of the Church, aiding her with the means at its command, which although they be external devices, have none the less for their prime object the good of souls." Pope Pius XI, *Atheistic Communism*, p. 31.

[35] What we say here applies, of course, not only to Church schools but to any bona fide private educational enterprise. As a matter of fact, the Church does not directly enter into the question at all. The distributive justice is directly due to the parents who pay the taxes.

[36] St. Thomas, II, II, q. 58, a. 1; Benedict Henry Merkelbach, *Summa Theologiae Moralis* (Paris: Desclee, 1938), II, p. 145; E. F. Regatillo and M. Zalba, *op. cit.*, II, pp. 443–444.

ing in some way to these others. Moralists distinguish three kinds of justice: commutative, legal, and distributive. Commutative justice is that by which a private individual (physical or moral) renders to another private person what is strictly due to him. The "otherness" element is clearly present in commutative justice, for the two persons are clearly distinct from each other. For this reason and also because the person to whom the debt is owed has an exact (neither more nor less) right to the good, commutative justice is justice in the most strict sense and an infraction of it entails the obligation of restitution.

Legal justice is that by which the individual renders to society what is due to it (society). The otherness element is partially absent here since the individual is a part of the society to which he owes some good. Nor is the debt owed strictly the community's property before it is paid, but only after payment.[37] A violation of legal justice does not usually involve the obligation of restitution.[38]

Distributive justice is that virtue by which the rulers of a society apportion the burdens and the benefits of that society among the citizens according to a proportionate equality. Examples of the burdens would be military service and, of course, taxes. Among the benefits are offices and appointments, protection and security, services and grants from public funds. These burdens and goods are to be distributed, not according to an exact arithmetical equality as is the case with commutative justice, but according to the gifts, abilities, resources, merits, and needs of the citizens.[39]

According to the common opinion of Catholic moral theologians, violations of distributive justice do not of themselves entail the obligation of restitution.[40] This is so because the citizen does not own the benefits or have a strict right to them before they are distributed. Even though the state acts iniquitously in an unjust distribution, yet it is disposing of its own property, not another's.[41]

---

[37] Regatillo and Zalba, *op. cit.*, II, pp. 448–449.

[38] *Ibid.*, pp. 461–463.

[39] Merkelbach, *op. cit.*, pp. 253–255.

[40] However, Regatillo and Zalba cite Faidherbe and Hering as holding it to be more probable that infractions of distributive justice bind to restitution just as those of commutative justice do. *Op. cit.*, pp. 462–463.

[41] "Bona scil. communia non simpliciter et immediate sunt bona membrorum, ac si essent ipsis appropriata aut debita, velut sua propria et sua possessio (sunt enim bona communitatis), sed tantum sub aliquo respectu et mediate ad eos pertinent scil. destinatione, quatenus in hisce est dignitas aut indigentia ad ea obtinenda." Merkelbach, *op. cit.*, p. 255.

Responsibility for the execution of distributive justice in the name of the community rests with officials in the various branches of government. "In particular, distributive justice has to direct the sovereign, the legislative, executive, and administrative authorities, the judiciary (with regard to the apportionment of punishments it is called vindictive justice)."[42]

DISTRIBUTIVE JUSTICE — APPLIED TO EDUCATION

According to the principles we have discussed above — principles that even the secularist will accept until, perhaps, they are applied to the question of education — the state is bound to dispense its benefits to all groups in society in proportion to their abilities, merits, and needs. We take the position, therefore, that the state is bound to dispense educational tax money according to the reasonable needs of the primary educators, who happen to be, of course, the payers of the tax money. We do not hold that the state must build and maintain a school for *any* group that may demand it, no matter how small or how ill equipped to educate that group may be.[43] We do hold, on the other hand, that when a group of parents large enough to sponsor an efficient school demands a certain type of education for their children, they have as primary educators every right to exact from the state the educational taxes they have contributed for the payment of that education. If the state refuses to accede to that reasonable demand it is obviously violating a basic principle of simple justice. It is not dispensing the community's benefits to all members of that community.

[42] Messner, *op. cit.*, p. 218.

[43] We make this exception for two reasons. First, the state is not bound to the impossible task of multiplying schools to an absurd extent. Second, these extremely small minorities can have their rights protected by some proportionate state *aid* or special accommodation in the public school. That our position is not unknown to Catholic writers may be seen in Cronin's statement: "Nobody would, of course, expect the State to provide schools for every handful of children whose parents entertain conscientious objection to the system that is actually provided by the State. But wherever a multiplicity of schools has to be provided, the State is bound to make special provision for any large and important body of parents making common appeal to the State, and resting their appeal on the same group of conscientious principles or difficulties." *Op. cit.*, II, p. 489. This element of reasonableness is reflected in England's educational legislation. Section 76 of the law of 1944 states that authorities "shall have regard to the general principle that, so far as is compatible with the provision of efficient instruction and training and the avoidance of unreasonable public expenditure, pupils are to be educated in accordance with the wishes of their parents." Her Majesty's Stationery Office, *Education Act, 1944*, Part IV, sec. 76.

Catholic writers are of one mind in seeing a violation of distributive justice in the state's denial of funds to private education.[44] At the head of the list is Pope Pius XI.

Let no one say that in a nation where there are different religious beliefs, it is impossible to provide for public instruction otherwise than by neutral or mixed schools.[45] In such a case it becomes the duty of the State, indeed it is the easier and more reasonable method of procedure, to leave free scope to the initiative of the Church and the family, while giving them such assistance as *justice* demands. That this can be done to the full satisfaction of families, and to the advantage of education and of public peace and tranquility, is clear from the actual experience of some countries comprising different religious denominations. There the school legislation respects the rights of the family, and Catholics are free to follow their own system of teaching in schools that are entirely Catholic. Nor is distributive justice lost sight of, as is evidenced by the financial aid granted by the State to the several schools demanded by the families.[46]

An Italian canonist writes that a proportionate distribution of educational tax money is a matter of justice. "A state," he observes, "which supports only public schools helps only a part of its citizens, while it deprives the other part (those namely who educate their children in private schools) of the aid to which they have a right because of their payment of taxes."[47] Another canonist writes in a similar vein, but makes explicit the exception which we mentioned above.[48] A Spanish philosopher, Gonzalez, points out that if the state does not use tax

[44] The unanimity to which we refer concerns principles. We readily grant that some Catholics (at least in the United States) would refuse state aid if it were offered. Their reason is chiefly a fear of governmental control.

[45] We will see below this possibility exemplified by the actual practice of many nations.

[46] *Christian Education of Youth*, p. 31. Italics added. Speaking of the fact that Sisters' schools fall far short (in number) of the demands for them on the part of parents, Pope Pius XII remarked that "from those who have a part in drawing up school legislation we must expect that determination for justice, that democratic sense, so to speak, which corresponds to the will of the parents, in such a way that the schools founded and directed by religious institutes be not placed in a worse condition than the State schools, and that they be given the freedom which is necessary for their development." An apostolic exhortation to the first International Congress of Teaching Sisters, Sept. 15, 1951, *Catholic Mind*, L (June, 1952), 378. Recently Bishop Matthew F. Brady asserted that some support is due to parochial schools in "equity and justice." Neil G. McCluskey, "Public and Private Schools Talk It Out," *America*, XCV (May 26, 1956), p. 222.

[47] Ottaviani, *op. cit.*, p. 245.

[48] Cavagnis, *op. cit.*, p. 211.

money for both systems and according to the proportion of pupils in each, patrons of private schools are either unjustly burdened financially or are morally forced to use the public school.[49] An Austrian philosopher argues from the natural right of parents to establish private schools if they wish. And once they provide their own institutions, the state cannot justly require them to pay again for state schools they do not use. For this reason he points out that the state is bound by distributive justice to allot subsidies to private schools equal to the money it provides for its own schools of similar size.[50]

Few persons, even among those opposed to natural law ethics, are prepared to deny that parents who feel obliged to send their children to private schools carry a double tax burden.[51] Though certainly no lover of things Catholic,[52] Herbert Spencer could see the fundamental injustice involved in being forced to pay for schooling one cannot use in good conscience. In his *Social Statics* he declares that he would be lacking as a father if he put his children into schools he considered essentially vicious. By refusing to do so, he asks

> Am I to pay your education-rates (taxes) and get nothing in return? Perhaps you will answer, yes. I must tell you, however, that my conscience will no more permit me to do this than it will permit me to use your schools. Not only should I be aiding you to miseducate my neighbor's children, which my desire for human welfare forbids, but I should be submitting to an injustice which I feel bound to oppose.[53]

The failure of a government to observe the dictates of distributive justice in the use of educational tax money is highly objectionable on the further count that it morally forces the parents in many cases to use schools of which they do not approve. No one but the extremely radical statist denies to parents the right to determine the education of their children. And yet if through financial pressure they are pre-

---

[49] *Op. cit.*, p. 811.

[50] Messner, *op. cit.*, p. 602. Ciarlantini argues from the point of view of discrimination. "Protestant, Jewish, Catholic, and non-denominational families should be legally equal before the State. As there is no rank of civil rights between denominational and non-denominational families, so, no legal and financial discrimination should exist between public and private schools. . . . Any aid or preference given to public schools and denied to the schools founded by private citizens is contrary to justice." *Op. cit.*, p. 102.

[51] How the secularist approaches this problem we will consider below.

[52] This fact indicates clearly enough that the present problem is by no means an essentially religious one.

[53] *Op. cit.*, pp. 183–184.

vented from sending their offspring to the school they desire, their right is useless. By compulsory education laws their children are compelled to attend an unsatisfactory school. No other choice is open to them.

This fact is obvious, and has been widely recognized. A firm advocate of public education has insisted on "the right of every parent of a public school child to decide whether he likes this philosophy (Deweyism) as the determining influence upon his child's education."[54] From the point of view of religious freedom a priest has remarked that "Catholics do not forget for one moment that the refusal of the State to permit them to use the money they contribute through taxes for education to provide for their children a schooling that accords with the dictates of their conscience, is a limitation imposed on their religious freedom."[55] The Frenchman, Marcel Martin, noted the incomplete notion of freedom espoused by those who deny tax money to private education. "Freedom is, in fact, sometimes a mere word and is confined to 'freedom of enjoyment' without reaching the fullness of 'freedom of exercise,' if, in order to be exercised, it calls for pecuniary sacrifices which many individuals are economically and socially unable to make."[56] In England, Gladstone saw clearly enough that there is a suppression of freedom in the denial of governmental subsidy to one or another school system. "Consequently, you may well believe that I contemplate with satisfaction the state of feeling that prevails in England, and that has led all governments [sic] to adopt the system of separate and independent subsidies to the various religious denominations."[57] Speaking of man's God-given natural rights, Pius XI declared that society cannot "systematically void these rights by making their use impossible."[58]

---

[54] Albert Lynd, *Quackery in the Public Schools* (Boston: Little, Brown and Co., 1953), p. 216.

[55] George Johnson, "The Catholic School and American Democracy," National Catholic Education Association *Proceedings,* 1936, p. 79.

[56] "Note on the Development of Human Rights (in France)," U.N.Y. for 1951, p. 92.

[57] Quoted from Morley's *Life of Gladstone* in S. J. Gosling, "The State and Religious Education — The English Way," *Catholic Educational Review,* XXXIII (June, 1935), pp. 321–322.

[58] "Atheistic Communism," *op. cit.,* p. 13. See also Aloisius J. Muench, "Religion in Education," *Social Justice Review,* XLVIII (Apr., 1955), 21. In a recent letter to the editor of *Newsweek,* Donald Vives referred to one ill effect of financial pressuring of Catholic parents to use public schools: "It might also be well to remember that because the money they pay in school taxes cannot be used to educate their children in schools of their choice, they are the recipients of an intellectual heritage at variance with their

The policy adopted in some modern nations of excluding denominational schools from State aid merely enthrones the secularistic religion of a minority as the official attitude of the public system. No school any more than an individual can be neutral toward the question of religion. Who is the teacher that can avoid by glance, word, or inflection expressing an opinion on the religious matters that are bound to arise in a typical classroom?[59] Even perfect silence — if such were possible — would weigh the balance against religion as not worth mentioning. A professor of law put the matter succinctly when he observed that "a state school cannot escape being, in some measure at least, a state church."[60]

We might note in conclusion that the refusal of subsidy to the private school hurts the state school in the long run. Excellent though they usually are, it is undeniable that a lack of funds often prevents private institutions from reaching their full potentialities. When they are aided by governmental subsidy they can, as Ottaviani points out,[61] provide more vigorous competition to the public schools and thus force the latter to a higher level of achievement. As a consequence patrons of both private and public institutions reap the benefits of more efficient education.[62]

We may turn now to the secularist's viewpoint on the matter under discussion. No secular writer that I have read treats the problems of state aid to private education from the viewpoint of distributive justice. How an honest confrontation with this principle can be avoided seems unintelligible to me, but avoided it seems to be. In all fairness, however, we must note that the secularist discusses points that touch issues

religious heritage, and consequently cannot make the best of either." *Newsweek*, XLVI (Oct. 31, 1955), p. 2.

[59] That many professors in state universities openly espouse secularism and materialism is a secret to no informed observer. It has been well said that this "secularism is a religion of its kind, and usually a very loud-spoken and intolerant religion." Archbishop John Ireland cited in Richard J. Gabel, *Public Funds for Church and Private Schools* (Washington: Catholic University of America, 1937), p. 494.

[60] George K. Gardner, from *Law and Contemporary Problems* (Durham, N. C.: Duke University, 1955), reprinted as an article, "Liberty, the State, and the School," in *The Catholic Lawyer*, I (Oct., 1955), 295. The author is a professor of law at Harvard University.

[61] *Op. cit.,* p. 245.

[62] That the state has no right to tax private education is, in view of distributive justice, too obvious to bear demonstration. And yet the Coquitlam Municipal Council of British Columbia, Canada, recently seized three Catholic schools for the nonpayment of taxes. See the Denver *Register,* Dec. 11, 1955, p. 1.

related to distributive justice, even though he does not get down to the basic principles undergirding the question. These related issues we will review below as we discuss the opposition case positively presented. The secularist does confront our second argument, that of double taxation for the patrons of private schools. One recent answer, however, can hardly be taken seriously, for its author seems to deny that there is really any noteworthy financial difficulty for these patrons. He points out that public education costs only two per cent of the national income and that parents who wish private education for their children could presumably finance it by another mere two per cent levy on their collective income. He does not feel that a total four per cent of income is an impossible figure for an item as important as education.[63] Aside from an apparent lack of contact with the financial pressures of the lower and middle classes, this argument violates basic statistics. The base of support for public schools is much broader than that for the support of private institutions. An entire populace (even nonusers) supports public education, whereas only a small segment (chiefly users) supports private education. The total cost percentage for many of the latter would consequently be much higher than four per cent.

Thayer, an American editor and educator, is more realistic. He argues that parents are not forced to pay twice for the education of their children, since there is no legal compulsion involved in the choice of a private school. That choice is entirely voluntary and the consequent expense freely undertaken. The government could not without drastic effect grant a remission of tax money when a private service is preferred to a public one. Such a remission would involve commitment to a principle that would be suicidal both for education and for all services administered at public expense.[64]

The argument is specious: there is no legal compulsion; therefore, there is no compulsion. Thayer evidently supposes that there is no such thing as a well-based obligation stemming from conscience, an obligation that has objective and cogent value. His position betrays a positivistic philosophy of law and ethics. He makes the further mistake of placing all government services on the same level as that of education.

---

[63] John K. Norton, "Church, State, and Education," *National Education Association Journal,* 38 (Jan., 1949), p. 23.

[64] V. T. Thayer, *The Attack Upon the American Secular School* (Boston: Beacon Press, 1951), p. 131.

At this point the secularist invariably makes the comparison between the governmental service of education and its other services. The citizen is not exempted "from helping to pay for the maintenance of a health department because he employs a private physician, the fire department because he lives in a fire-proof house, the park department because he has ample private grounds about his house, or the city or county library because he buys his own books." And these services are to be equated with education: "There is no difference between these and the school department, except that the charge is a little larger" and the organized opposition more determined.[65]

We might suggest, first of all, that if one thinks education costs just a little more than the other services this observer mentions, he might with profit consult any reliable set of statistics on government expenditures. But there are other fallacies in this line of argumentation. Extremely few people avail themselves of the private services and possess the facilities compared above with education, while large numbers of persons in any country desire private education for their children when public institutions do not satisfy religious or other needs. As we pointed out above, a state is obligated to use tax money according to the reasonable needs of the citizenry and according to a due proportion. Our objector's examples would betray both unreasonable demands and a lack of proportion, while private education shows neither.

We may further note that even the few persons enjoying the private advantages mentioned in the above quotation still profit much from public facilities and hence should pay taxes for them. A health department, for example, protects the citizen in many more ways than does a private physician, and the fire department protects much more than a man's fireproof home. Parents, however, who send their children to private schools receive no direct return for their tax money. The indirect benefit they receive through the public school's contribution to the general welfare is doubly balanced off by their tax money and the same contribution to the general welfare by the private school.

The basic fallacy in the secularist position, however, lies in a failure to recognize the vast difference between a citizen's right to choose a

---

[65] Elwood P. Cubberley, *State School Administration* (Boston: Houghton Mifflin Co., 1927), p. 717, footnote I. Broudy also employs the very same argument and refers it to the taxes paid by nonowners of automobiles. Harry S. Broudy, *Building a Philosophy of Education* (New York: Prentice-Hall, 1954), p. 120. See Thayer, *op. cit.*, pp. 128–129.

private physician (or any of the other facilities mentioned) and the right of parents to choose a type of education for their children. Ordinarily a man has no imaginable obligation to supply himself with any of the advantages the secularists pose in their comparisons. He is patently free from any point of view, moral or legal. While parents are in many countries legally free to choose among kinds of education, they often are not morally free.[66]

Occurring frequently in secularistic writings on education is an expression of fear that the organization of education on denominational lines would be a divisive factor in the life of a nation. The public school is viewed as a reconciling agency among the different groups that make up a community.[67] The obvious and logical issue of this argument against state aid to private education is an absolute governmental monopoly in education, but most secularists do not wish to be pushed that far. Perhaps the most effective answer to the difficulty, however, is the successful practice of many modern nations that sponsor a multi-differentiated system of educational finance. Some of these we will note below. Preconceived theories must fall before facts.

When the private school to be aided by state funds is also a religious school, the common objection is made that one man is being taxed to support another man's religion.[68] If a man were to take this observation seriously, he would be led to believe that the religiously minded man does not pay taxes at all but rather depends on the funds furnished by the nonreligious. If the argument were valid, it could be turned against the secularist, public school which is financed by the nonsecularist's tax money.

The remaining objections brought against our position lie not in the realm of principle, but in that of difficulties, i.e., "what would happen if public funds were used for private education?" Lest our discussion be extended beyond due measure, we will merely give an outline of the alleged problems and their solutions.

1. Giving public funds to private enterprise in education "would place education under agencies which for centuries have tended to

---

[66] This absence of moral freedom in some cases is not, of course, to be restricted to Catholics as some might think. Herbert Spencer felt it. See above, p. 108.

[67] Norton, *op. cit.,* p. 22. See also Thayer, *op. cit.,* p. 130, and Aalbert Boogaard, "Tax Money for Church Schools?" *Phi Delta Kappan,* XXXVI (Apr., 1955), p. 270.

[68] Thayer, *op. cit.,* p. 115. Norton, *op. cit.,* p. 22, asks, "What is a combination of church and state, if the compelling of all men by the state to pay taxes for denominational instruction is not?"

indoctrinate rather than to release the human mind."[69] This objection is nothing but a prejudice. What the secularist objects to is not indoctrination (for he himself indoctrinates), but indoctrination that does not suit his point of view. This mode of thinking is a mere intellectual denial of academic freedom.

2. Religious and moral values can be communicated by nonreligious public schools.[70] It is interesting to note that this sort of approach convinces almost no one but the secularist himself. But even supposing the impossible, the parent still has the right to decide (in accordance with divine and ecclesiastical law) what kind of religious and moral values he wants communicated to his child and to use the schools he judges will communicate them.

3. If public money is used for private education, the death knell would sound for public schools. Educational money would have to be spread thin, standards would fall, and many inferior schools would result.[71] Judge Dunne's reply to this difficulty in 1875 holds good today. If, as is commonly urged, the public schools are desired by the majority of the people, no such fear (the destruction of the public school system) ought to be entertained. "But even should the majority prefer church schools to teach their distinctive beliefs and philosophy instead of the secular philosophy of the 'experts,' the public school is, after all, a means and not an end in itself."[72] That the fear of inferiority in standards is unfounded is proved by the experience of many nations. One may not argue with facts.[73]

4. Public aid would likely result in an infringement of freedom in that grants of tax money usually carry with them a generous portion of political control.[74] We readily acknowledge the probability that this difficulty offers, and in a given country the danger may well be reduced to actual fact. But at the same time this danger can be forestalled. A provision such as is carried in the Constitution of the Netherlands seems nicely to care for the matter: "The standards of efficiency to be prescribed for education to be defrayed wholly or in part from public

[69] Norton, *op. cit.*, p. 22.

[70] *Ibid.*, p. 23.

[71] Thayer, *op. cit.*, pp. 133–134; Boogaard, *op. cit.*, p. 269.

[72] Gabel, *op. cit.*, pp. 776–777.

[73] Nor are we supporting the thesis that any group of parents, no matter how small, may demand a separate school. See above, p. 106.

[74] Norton, *op. cit.*, p. 23; Thayer, *op. cit.*, p. 139.

funds shall be regulated by law, with due observance in so far as private education is concerned, of freedom of direction."[75]

We do not consider worthy of serious attention some of the remaining secularistic arguments against public aid to private education. Such are, for example, one writer's dislike of the government's money going to "monks and nuns"[76] or another's contention that American religious growth in numerical strength suggests that present educational arrangements in that country promote healthy growth among the churches.[77]

We may note in conclusion that the position we have proposed on distributive justice in education is in our mid-century receiving more vocal support even in non-Catholic circles. Philosopher-psychologist Robert F. Creegan in an address before the 1958 meeting of the American Psychological Association criticized governmental subsidy of public schools only as monopolistic and containing some threat to educational liberty. He remarked that "a monopolistic public philosophy of education which is designed to serve all groups serves none of them well. A system which must be religiously neutral because serving persons from a variety of religious backgrounds becomes in effect an opponent of every religious way of life and a proponent of secularism . . . a system which serves every ethnic and racial group becomes in effect amalgamationist."[78] And Gardner observed recently that "the doctrine that the state may, and ought to, regard all school children as equally worthy of its assistance, regardless of how the schools which they attend are staffed and governed, and regardless of the religious instruction which they may offer, is not just now very popular; but it is the only doctrine which wholly succeeds in reconciling the state support of compulsory education with freedom, and the arguments which can be offered against it will not bear examination in the light of the principles which we (Americans) profess."[79]

DISTRIBUTIVE JUSTICE — INTERNATIONAL PRACTICES

We are prepared now to examine representative practices of the nations of the world in the matter of public aid to private initiative

---

[75] *Constitution of the Kingdom of the Netherlands,* Aug. 24, 1815, reissued Jan. 22, 1947, article 200. Peaslee, *op. cit.,* II, p. 538.

[76] Boogaard, *op. cit.,* p. 270.

[77] Norton, *op. cit.,* p. 23.

[78] Associated Press report in the New Orleans *Times-Picayune,* Sept. 2, 1958, p. 13.

[79] *Op. cit.,* p. 295.

in the work of education. Since this question is recognized as being of pivotal importance and since operating policies are illustrative of active possibilities, a somewhat detailed account of these contemporary practices follows. Attention will first be directed to those states which deny financial aid to private schools.

In many cases it is impossible to know whether a given nation aids or does not aid private education from public tax money. This difficulty arises when no mention is made in that country's constitution or in any other available source of its financial relationship to the private school.[80] We may be sure, of course, that Communist countries which have abolished the private school do not aid it. There is nothing to aid.

Two countries in their constitutional provisions for education imply that state funds are not used for private schools. Cuba stipulates that "financial provision for all *public* instruction shall be made in the budgets of the Nation, the province, or the municipality. . . ."[81] El Salvador suggests that at least some of its educational institutions are not governmentally supported: "The instruction given in establishments supported by the government shall be gratuitous and subject to proper regulations."[82]

In three non-Communist nations the writer did find an explicit constitutional denial of state aid to private enterprise in education: Italy, Honduras, and the United States. The first declares that "private groups and individuals have the right to establish schools and educational institutions without state support."[83] Honduras states that "subsidies for cults for religious education are prohibited."[84] The Federal Constitution of the United States makes no statement to the effect that public funds may not be used for private or religious education. Nor was the nonestablishment clause so interpreted at the time it was written.[85] Gardner is clear on this point.

---

[80] Among nations which in their constitutions bypass the problem of aid to private education we can mention Haiti, Colombia, Korea, Jordan, Turkey, Mongol People's Republic, Thailand, and the Dominican Republic. See Peaslee, *op. cit., passim.*

[81] *Constitution of the Republic of Cuba,* July 5, 1940, article 52. Peaslee, I, p. 536. Italics added.

[82] *Constitution of El Salvador,* Aug. 13, 1886, article 33. Peaslee, I, p. 743.

[83] *Constitution of the Italian Republic,* Dec. 22, 1947, article 33. Peaslee, II, p. 283. This provision, however, is not as harsh as it first appears since room is made for religious instruction in the public schools.

[84] *Political Constitution of the Republic of Honduras,* Mar. 28, 1936, article 57. Peaslee, II, p. 140.

[85] See the historical account of this question in Wilfrid Parsons' *The First Freedom* (New York: Declan X. McMullen Co., Inc., 1948). Gabel in his outstandingly thorough

The Constitution does not forbid Congress, nor does it forbid any state, to subsidize religion. It forbids Congress to "establish" religion, or "prohibit the free exercise thereof." If we read "prohibit" to include "place burdens upon" and "discourage," it will, I submit, be apparent that a system under which all school children receive the same measure of support from the taxpayers comes closer to reflecting the spirit of the Declaration of Independence and the First Amendment than a system under which the right to receive any measure of support from the taxpayers is conditioned upon attendance at a municipally controlled school.[86]

Individual state constitutions, however, almost without exception explicitly forbid the use of tax money for private and religious education. The state of Kentucky can serve as an example: "No portion of any fund or tax now existing, or that may hereafter be raised or levied for educational purposes, shall be appropriated to, or used by, or in aid of, any church, sectarian or denominational fund."[87] While illustrative evidence for the denial of public aid to private schools in non-Communist nations is scarce, it is abundant for the granting of that aid by other governments.[88] We shall divide our discussion into three sections. First we shall consider those nations that give partial aid; second, those whose provisions are not perfectly clear

---

dissertation (xiv + 858 pp.) shows conclusively how Parsons' account of the original understanding of the Federal Constitution is an accurate account. The use of governmental money for private education was extremely common in the early years of the union. It is being so used to the present day in Indian schools and for the higher education of ex-servicemen. Writing in 1937 Gabel was able to give a list including "seventeen states and the District of Columbia in which private colleges received either federal, state, or local public aid within the past eight years. Eight states granted subsidies to one or several church-controlled or affiliated institutions." Even though the amounts received were comparatively small, "six Methodist schools (of different branches), three Baptist, four Presbyterian, two Congregationalist, one Brethren, and one Catholic are recorded." *Op. cit.,* p. 759. For another approach to the American problem of achieving distributive justice in the field of education see William E. McManus and Thomas O. Martin, "Distributive Justice and Aid to Education," Catholic Theological Society of America *Proceedings,* 1953, pp. 157–173.

[86] In a footnote commenting on his interpretation of "prohibit" Gardner appositely observes that "there is, it seems to me, really no other way to read it. Neither Congress nor anyone else has any way of prohibiting anyone from doing anything except by placing discouraging burdens on the activity which it attempts to forbid." *Op. cit.,* p. 295.

[87] Wendell Huston, *School Laws of the Forty-Eight States,* "Constitutional Provisions, State of Kentucky," Sec. 189 (Seattle: Wendell Huston Co.), Vol. I, "Kentucky," p. 1.

[88] This is true regarding both constitutional provisions and the responses I received from the various embassies in Washington, D. C.

as to how much aid is given; and third those which clearly offer complete support.

a) *Nations which grant partial aid to private schools*

Denmark. This country contributes to the support of private schools of all types providing they accept governmental inspection aimed at ordinary pedagogical requirements.[89] The Royal Ministry for Foreign Affairs observes that private institutions are financed chiefly by fees paid by parents but that both the state and the local governments contribute large grants to their support.[90]

Chile. Chile bases its partial grant on the cost of education in public schools. Primary, secondary, vocational, and teacher training institutions that are free and private receive an average allotment equivalent to half the cost of educating an equal number of pupils in similar public institutions.[91] A free private institution is one which does not charge tuition.[92]

Japan. In its Private School Law of 1949 Japan authorized state and local bodies to aid private education in a financial way. Further, the Private School Improvement Law enacted in 1951 opened the way for private institutions to receive aid from state and local autonomous bodies.[93]

Ecuador. This nation permits municipalities to subsidize private education provided the financial aid thus given does not exceed twenty per cent of the money set aside for educational purposes.[94]

England. Aside from the special agreement schools, England offers all other voluntary institutions on the primary level (and these are usually denominational) the choice of the following alternatives. (1) If the managers of the institution do not pay half the cost of the improvements necessary to bring buildings up to standard and to maintain them in that condition, the L.E.A. shoulders all financial obligations but also assumes considerable control of the school.[95] (2)

---

[89] U.N.Y. for 1952, p. 47. We may note that the danger of extreme governmental control seems avoided here by the inspection clause.

[90] Royal Danish Ministry for Foreign Affairs and the Danish Statistical Department, *Denmark* (Copenhagen: Bianco Luno, 1952), p. 80.

[91] Act No. 9864, article 1, Jan. 15, 1951. U.N.Y. for 1951, p. 45.

[92] *Ibid*. Other stipulations for receiving the grant are given in this same place.

[93] Ministry of Foreign Affairs, *Japan's Problems* (Tokyo: Public Information and Cultural Affairs Bureau, Ministry of Foreign Affairs, 1954), p. 37.

[94] *Constitution of the Republic of Ecuador,* Dec. 31, 1946, article 171. Peaslee, I, p. 707.

[95] The Local Education Authority is a local governmental body which is concerned

If the managers meet one half of the above costs, the L.E.A. meets the other half and assumes notably less control than under the first alternative.[96] England offers the same choices to voluntary secondary schools but excepts direct grant institutions.[97] Besides the above types of private schools there were in England in 1957 approximately 4700 independent schools which receive no grant of public money.[98] As a result of the English system of private school support Catholics in England and Wales receive from public funds approximately 90 per cent of the money they need to finance their primary and secondary schools.[99] Other religious groups likewise benefit from this arrangement, but I do not have available an exact figure for them.

Spain. This nation pays the teachers' salaries for its nonstate schools and in addition usually offers a 50 per cent subsidy for the erection and maintenance of buildings. In the case of religious schools the sponsoring group must pay the remaining costs.[100]

---

with many governing duties besides education. In England and Wales there are 146 L.E.A.'s under terms of the Education Act of 1944. See British Information Services, *Education in Great Britain* (rev.), 1958, p. 8.

[96] "(1) Where the managers of the school are unable or unwilling to pay half the cost of alterations and improvements necessary to bring the buildings up to the required standards, and to keep them to those standards, all financial obligations pass to the L.E.A. Two-thirds of the managers are then appointed by the L.E.A. and the remaining third by the school foundation. The L.E.A. also assumes the power to appoint and dismiss teachers, but the foundation managers have the right both to a voice in the appointment of a headmaster or headmistress, and to be satisfied concerning the appointment of a proportion of the teachers (not more than one-fifth of the teaching staff), who, as 'reserved' teachers, may give denominational instruction for not more than two periods a week for those children whose parents desire it. Apart from this denominational teaching, the religious instruction given in the school is according to an 'Agreed Syllabus.' Schools in this category are now known as 'Controlled Schools.'

"(2) Where the managers of a Voluntary School are able and willing to meet half the cost of necessary alterations and improvements, the remaining half is met by direct grant from the Ministry. The school foundation then appoints two-thirds of the managers and the L.E.A. one-third. The powers and duties of the managers in the appointment and dismissal of teachers and the giving of denominational instruction remain substantially as they were before the Act, but religious instruction according to an Agreed Syllabus must be given to children whose parents so desire it. Schools in this category are known as 'Aided Schools.'" *Ibid.*, pp. 10–11.

[97] *Ibid.*, p. 12.

[98] *Ibid.*, p. 19. Northern Ireland provides public funds for private schools in somewhat the same way as England. See this same booklet, pp. 27–28.

[99] A. C. F. Beales, "The Organization of Catholic Schools in Britain," release of the British Information Services, ME 513, Apr. 7, 1955, p. 1.

[100] Spanish Diplomatic Information Office, *Fifteen Years of Spanish Culture* (Madrid: Diplomatic Information Office, 1952), p. 94.

France. In 1951 France created a special treasury fund from which the head of each family having children in attendance at an elementary school is allowed one thousand francs per child per term. The allowance is paid to the educational system patronized by the child, whether it be public or private. In the case of the private school, the money is remitted to its parents' association which may apply to educational purposes specified by the parents a sum not exceeding 10 per cent of the money allotted to the association.[101]

Belgium. In Belgium the salaries of teachers in free (private) schools are assured by state subsidies.[102]

b) *Nations which do not specify in available documents whether or not their aid to private education is partial or full*

Portugal. The constitution of Portugal contains a simple statement to the effect that the government may subsidize private schools.[103]

Finland. A member of the state board for Finnish education tells us that the private school's greatest source of income is the state grant, although the community also offers some support. The state grant is based to a large extent on the number of qualified teachers a school has and the number of classes it sponsors.[104]

China. The Nationalist constitution of China declares that the state will encourage or subsidize privately operated educational enterprises that have a good record.[105]

Ireland. This country stipulates that in dispensing its aid to private institutions the government may not discriminate between the various

---

[101] Marcel Martin, "A Note on the Development of Human Rights," U.N.Y. for 1951, p. 92.

[102] Julius Hoste, "Belgium," *Educational Yearbook, 1944,* ed. I. L. Kandel (New York: Teachers College, Columbia University, 1944), p. 24.

[103] *Political Constitution of the Portuguese Republic,* Mar. 19, 1933, article 44, U.N.Y. for 1951, p. 299.

[104] "The State aids private schools which satisfy certain conditions by paying them each term for each regular class and each parallel class a state grant prescribed by law; besides, a contribution for each qualified teacher, as well as for the sides of the gymnasium. Moreover, private schools receive from the State 40–60 per cent, from the interest of loans, the rents of school premises, and the expenses caused by heating, lighting and wages of servants. The state grant is the greatest income of private schools. The support of the community is relatively small. On the other hand, the State Council settles the minimum salaries of private school teachers." Niilo Kallio, *The School System of Finland,* 3rd ed. (Helsinki: Soumalaisen Kirjallisuuden Seuran Kirjapainon Oy, 1952), p. 36.

[105] *The Constitution of the Republic of China,* Dec. 25, 1947, article 167. Peaslee, I, p. 461.

religious denominations, but must treat all alike. It also requires that children attending a school receiving public money be free to take part in religious instruction or not.[106]

Brazil. The state of Piaui provides that a private person who establishes a rural elementary school for ten or more children is entitled to a governmental grant.[107]

Indonesia. This nation has determined that pupils of private schools which meet state standards "have the same rights as accorded to pupils of public schools,"[108] and that any state aid given to religious denominations or organizations "shall be rendered on the basis of equality."[109] Slightly more explicitly we learn from a secondary source that in order "to safeguard sectional interest especially in the matter of religion, full opportunity is provided to open private-schools which, provided they meet certain requirements, are subsidized by the Government."[110] At the moment Christians and Moslems, Chinese and Dutch groups operate a considerable number of private schools.[111]

India. Bombay State in its Primary Education Act of 1947 makes provision for the recognition of private schools as approved schools when they meet prescribed conditions. The act states further that "the manner in which grant-in-aid is to be given to such approved school shall be as prescribed."[112] The Government of Mysore declared that it follows a liberal and common policy in grants to church schools.[113]

---

[106] *Constitution of Ireland,* Dec. 29, 1937, article 44, No. 2, No. 4. Peaslee, II, p. 261. The religious instruction clause is not perfectly clear to me: "Legislation providing State aid for schools shall not . . . be such as to affect prejudicially the right of any child to attend a school receiving public money without attending religious instruction at that school."

[107] *Constitution of the State of Piaui,* Aug. 22, 1947, article 142, U.N.Y. for 1948, p. 20.

[108] *Provisional Constitution of the Republic of Indonesia,* Aug. 15, 1950, article 41, U.N.Y. for 1950, p. 155.

[109] *Ibid.,* article 43, p. 155.

[110] Indonesian Ministry of Information, *Basic Information on Indonesia* (Djakarta: Ministry of Information, Republic of Indonesia, 1953), p. 159.

[111] *Ibid.* A recent report issuing from Djakarta indicated that seventy-five per cent of the Catholic schools in Indonesia were benefiting from state subsidies. Denver *Register,* May 6, 1956, p. 10.

[112] Detached sheet entitled "Replacement Series No. VII — p. 83," and sent to me by Mr. M. S. Sundaram, Embassy of India, Washington, D. C., under date of Feb. 24, 1955.

[113] Typed memorandum from the Mysore Government Secretariat, Bangalore, Feb. 25, 1955 and forwarded by M. S. Sundaram.

Ceylon. From Asia issues another report that Ceylon aids in a financial manner all denominational schools in the nation.[114]

c) *Nations which clearly indicate in available documents that tax money is used on an equal basis for public and private schools*

Canada. The Canadian provinces of Ontario, Quebec, Saskatchewan, and Alberta make provision for separate or dissentient schools meant to serve minority groups (whether Catholic or Protestant) which do not wish to patronize the ordinary public school. These separate institutions are financed from public funds, offer a curriculum similar to that of the public schools, and are under governmental supervision. Yet at the same time they are under the church's control and are taught by teachers belonging to the religion of the controlling body. "In Quebec a satisfactory dual system of education has been worked out, giving the Roman Catholics and Protestants control of their own schools but keeping them all under central supervision."[115]

Germany. The Federal Republic of Germany recently determined that private schools shall be entitled to public grants "necessary for the performance of their functions and the fulfillment of their duties." Private institutions may waive their right to charge tuition and may claim due compensation from the state. There is no distinction between public and private schools regarding the provision of "free equipment for teachers and pupils."[116]

Scotland. We may sum up the situation prevailing in Scotland with the statement that since 1918 "every school (Catholic and Protestant alike) has been entirely financed by the local government authorities, who appoint the teachers in such a way that a Catholic school is staffed by Catholic teachers. . . ."[117]

Netherlands. Perhaps the best known instance of state support for systems of private schools is the policy and practice prevailing in the Netherlands. The constitutional basis for that policy and practice is found in article 201:

> The cost of private institutions for general primary education which satisfy the statutory conditions shall be defrayed by the public treasury

---

[114] K. Nesiah, "Ceylon," *The Year Book of Education, 1951,* ed. J. A. Lauwerys and N. Hans (London: University of London, 1951), p. 587.

[115] K. M. Glazier, "Canada, Part I," *The Year Book of Education, 1951,* J. A. Lauwerys and N. Hans (London: University of London, 1951), pp. 376–377.

[116] *Constitution of North-Rhine-Westphalia,* June 28, 1950, articles 8 and 9, U.N.Y. for 1950, p. 101.

[117] Beales, *op. cit.,* p. 2.

to the same extent as in the case of public education. The law shall lay down the conditions for the making of grants from the public treasury to private institutions for general intermediate education and to institutions for preparatory higher education.[118]

In actual practice civil authorities are bound to assist in providing a school when an organization representing a specified minimum number of parents asks for it. In cities of more than 100,000 population, 125 children are required for an elementary school, 91 for a continuing elementary school, and 61 for an advanced elementary school. As the size of the city decreases the minimum number is proportionately diminished until in small towns the minimums are fifty, thirty-one, and twenty-four.[119] These minimums are not absolutely rigid and allow for the eventuality of a school's temporarily falling below the exact figure.[120] The city has the duty of supplying the expense of the building or of furnishing an already existing one. It must likewise reimburse the sponsoring organization for the expenses entailed in furnishing the school.[121] For the maintenance of the institution

> . . . the municipality pays to the management, for the running of the school, the same sum per pupil as is paid to the public schools of a corresponding type. Every five years the management submits its accounts for the expenses incurred during that period. The surplus, if any, is paid back into the municipal treasury. If a municipality incurs expenses entailed by the appointment of "super-numerary" teachers or specialists, the "free" schools are treated in that regard in the same manner as the public schools. The managements of the "free" schools are of course entitled to appoint "supernumerary" teachers or specialists at their own expense, but in most cases they have not the necessary funds at their disposal.
>
> The State reimburses to the managements the salaries of the compulsory number of teachers and pays the half-pay salaries and the pension fund contributions of the teachers, in the same manner as in the case of the public schools.

. . . .

In this way our system of education provides any somewhat important group of parents with the opportunity of giving their children the

---

[118] *Constitution of the Kingdom of the Netherlands,* Aug. 24, 1815 with amendments and additions up to Sept. 3, 1948, article 201, U.N.Y. for 1948, p. 150.

[119] Philip J. Idenburg, *Education in the Netherlands,* 3rd ed. rev. (The Hague: Netherlands Government Information Service, 1954), p. 23.

[120] *Ibid.,* p. 25.

[121] *Ibid.,* p. 24.

desired education. If necessary, the municipalities pay part of the expenses incurred by parents for the transportation of their children to the school they have chosen.[122]

Although public money is not given to any private school that fails to measure up to stipulated standards, the degree of governmental interference is kept down to a minimum. Required subjects, length of the school year, and number of class periods per week on the various educational levels are some of the state regulations to which the school must conform. On the other hand, the institution is free to deviate and experiment in teaching methodology and to include in the curriculum subjects and activities related to the religious character of the school. State inspectors do not examine the religious aspect of a private school's curriculum.[123]

The reader will note as a consequence of this brief investigation of international practices regarding state aid to private education that many of the secularists' objections are proved by actual practice to be ill-founded. That there are difficulties no one will deny, for there are difficulties in any system of education be it public merely or public and private together. But that those difficulties are by no means unsurmountable is readily shown by the many countries that are actually surmounting them. These nations are both protecting the primary educational rights of family and Church and at the same time efficiently providing for the common good of the nation at large. As a matter of fact the promotion of the common good itself is a consequence of the protection of the rights of the primary educators.

AUXILIARY SERVICES

We may note as a corollary to the above discussion that if the state is bound by distributive justice to provide equal financial aid to all justifiable forms of education, public and private, it is also bound by this same justice to provide auxiliary services to all children attending these same schools. The reason is simply that the greater includes the

---

[122] *Ibid.*, p. 25.

[123] *Ibid.*, p. 26. The parents' preference for the private school (when they are not penalized for its use) seems indicated by the fact that as of Jan., 1953 "free" schools in the Netherlands enrolled 72 per cent of the lower elementary school population and 68 per cent of the advanced elementary group, while the public schools enrolled 28 per cent and 32 per cent respectively. *Ibid.*, pp. 26, 28.

lesser. The greater in this case is the substance of an education, the lesser, all of the services that accompany the full care and development of the children in and about the school. Among these auxiliary services and supplies are to be included necessary transportation to and from the place of instruction, textbooks, school lunches, medical examinations, and health precautions.

Understandably enough, the nations of the world rarely make provision in their constitutions for auxiliary services in education. Ecuador, however, does stipulate that "social services shall be furnished without distinction to the students who need them in the free, official, or private schools."[124] Regarding the medical examination and care of pupils the English Education Act of 1944 provides that "a local education authority may give direction to the managers or governors of any voluntary[125] school requiring them to provide such reasonable facilities as may be specified in the directions for the purpose of enabling the authority to carry out their functions under this section so, however, that the managers or governors of a voluntary school shall not be required by any such directions to incur expenditure."[126] Although many states in the United States do not provide textbooks to private school children, the state of West Virginia does have a law to the effect that "the board of education of every county, upon application of the proper authorities of any private school, may likewise provide state adopted textbooks for use of the pupils enrolled therein, whose parents, in the judgment of the board, are unable to provide same."[127]

*   *   *   *   *   *   *

Although the state's positive assistance to the primary educators does, from the philosophical point of view, embrace more than mere

---

[124] *Constitution of the Republic of Ecuador*, Dec. 31, 1946, article 171. Peaslee, I, p. 707.

[125] In English law a voluntary school is a private one.

[126] English Government, *Education Act, 1944* (London: Her Majesty's Stationery Office, n.d.), section 48.

[127] Huston, *op. cit.*, Vol. I, "West Virginia," Chapter 18, article 5, sec. 21-a., p. 20. In declaring the right of church schools to receive textbooks from the state a Mississippi court stated that "there is no requirement that the church should be a liability to those of its citizenship who are at the same time citizens of the state and entitled to privileges and benefits as such." *Chance* v. *Mississippi State Textbook Rating and Purchasing Board et al.*, 190 Miss. 453, 2005.706 (Miss. 1941), cited in Sister M. Bernard Francis Loughery, *Parental Rights in American Educational Law: Their Bases and Implementation* (Washington: Catholic University Press, 1952), p. 152.

financial aid, yet it can be seen that from the practical point of view distributive justice in education is largely a money matter. The workability of the philosophical position we have taken in this chapter on distributive justice is well borne out by the fact that the great majority of the world's non-Communist states do support financially the initiative shown by the primary educators.

CHAPTER IX

CONTROL OF THE STATE OVER
PRIVATE EDUCATION

IN CHAPTER VII we showed that the state has no authority over the establishment of schools founded by the Catholic Church, since she (the latter) has a directly divine commission to teach, a commission that supersedes any merely human authority. We wish to consider here the quite different question as to whether the state has authority to control the *establishment* of non-Catholic private schools.

ESTABLISHMENT OF PRIVATE SCHOOLS

That the state does have a right to control the founding of a private school seems to be a common opinion among American writers. The following view is illustrative of what we mean: "That the State could require all private and denominational schools, and particularly those of elementary and secondary grade, to secure a state permit as a condition to opening for instruction . . . probably could not be seriously questioned in the courts."[128]

As we have demonstrated in Part I, any of the state's rights and functions are to be drawn from its end or purpose, the preservation and promotion of the common good of the community. If the state, therefore, has any control over the establishment of private schools, that control must be required for the maintenance of the general welfare of society. For this reason we hold that if the establishment of a private school will hurt society at large, the state has a right and a duty to prevent the foundation of that school. It is for this reason that the state is bound to deny the faculty to open a school, however informal

---

[128] Cubberley, *op. cit.*, p. 714.

it may be, to organized crime or to the international conspiracy of Communism. That a given school or system of schools will harm the common welfare may not be antecedently presumed by the state without evidence, but on the contrary the danger must be clearly demonstrated.[129]

Outside of these exceptional circumstances the state does not have a right to require its permission or authorization as a condition for the establishment of a private school. Our reason is simply that if the state has such a right, it also has the right to deny authorization for a private school even when there is no demonstrable danger to the common good. Such would be an intolerable infringement of the natural right one man has to communicate with another.[130] Its logical conclusion would be the granting to the state of the power to abolish private schools if it so chose.

It may be objected that the position we have taken opens the door to an undue multiplication of schools and to uncontrolled and consequently inferior teaching. These two difficulties are theoretically possible but hardly likely to be realized to any appreciable extent. In much the same way one might argue that a failure to require permission for the opening of department stores will result in more stores than can be supported and in inferior merchandizing. In both cases excessive multiplication is forestalled by the law of supply and demand, while inferiority is precluded by competition and, if necessary, state inspection.

Since we have examined in the preceding chapter international prac-

---

[129] This principle is true also of the state's licensing function in general. When there is a genuine danger to the public, government may require a license as a condition to the operation of an enterprise, but it may not presume that danger without proof. Otherwise the state becomes potentially a universal overlord.

[130] Cronin seems to touch upon our problem. "If by means of combination amongst many families it is possible to maintain a private school, conducted according to a programme either drawn up or at least approved by themselves (the parents), then it is their right to maintain such a school and without interference from the State. In two cases only would interference be possible, vis. where it is evident that the child is not really being educated, for then an injustice is being done to the child, and the State could interfere on its behalf just as it can interfere if a child is not being properly fed. But such interference is, in general, invidious, and so far as education is concerned could be justified only on very rare occasions." *Op. cit.,* II, 487. His other case refers to the level of education required by the state for the common good. Cavagnis discusses our problem at great length and finally seems to conclude that the state has a right to certify the capability of the teachers in private schools but has no other right of authorization outside of the extreme cases we have mentioned. *Op. cit.,* II, 188–202.

tices regarding the state's relationship to the establishment of private schools, there is no need to review those practices here.

INSPECTION OF PRIVATE SCHOOLS[131]

The purposes of governmentally authorized inspection of an educational institution can be both scholastic and nonscholastic. In the present discussion we are not concerned with the latter, and hence are not asking whether the state may examine a school building for construction or fire safety or the pupils for the sake of public health. These we assume any reasonable man will grant, since there is no doubt that they fall within the competency of the state. We are asking, rather, whether the state in view of the fact that it is only a supplementary educator has the right and/or duty to investigate the condition of educational matters in the private school, which latter, of course, lies immediately in the hands of the primary educators. The answer to this question is not so clear as might first appear.

Writers, both Catholic and non-Catholic, are divided in their solutions to the problem. One denies to the state any right to inspect private schools. He reasons that since the private school is private, the state may not assume any deficiency in it without any reason for that assumption. Just as government officers may not enter the privacy of a home for the sake of investigation without some well-established basis for supposing something to be wrong, so also they may not enter a private school for the sake of inspection without some proof that there is a notable deficiency in that school.[132] "We hold, therefore, as a matter of principle, that the government has no right to inspect or control private schools, or to examine its teachers, or to prescribe the order and method of teaching, *as long as it has no evidence* that the children in these schools do not acquire sufficient elementary knowledge to secure their social well being or that of their future fellow citizens."[133] He adds that the burden of proof that there is a deficiency lies with the state. Holaind agrees with Messmer's presentation of the case.[134]

---

[131] We are here considering all private schools, Catholic and non-Catholic alike.

[132] S. G. Messmer, "The Right of Instruction," *American Ecclesiastical Review*, VI (Feb., 1892), 113.

[133] *Ibid.*, p. 114. Italics are Messmer's.

[134] *Op. cit.*, p. 12. Edmund F. Dunne, arguing in the well-known Ohio compulsory education case, likewise held that the state has no right to inspect or regulate private

In debating the question of state inspection of private schools before the Massachusetts legislature in 1888, Thomas Dwight of Harvard's medical school opposed inspection by public authorities because he did not believe that school boards could know with certainty just what is a good education and how much each child should have of it.[135] Another participant in this same dispute, Augustus D. Small, argued that there is no need to inspect private schools because parents are surely not going to spend their money in order that their children may avoid an education.[136] He also remarked that the genuine character and real worth of a school can be ascertained only by a thorough series of inspections and not by the mere isolated visit.[137] Furthermore, competition with the public school and a healthy self-interest were in themselves sufficient guarantees of educational excellence for the private institution.[138]

On the other hand, the editor of *America* asserted in 1925 that Catholic writers have again and again admitted both the right and the duty of the state to supervise education, to examine teachers and to inspect schools. His reasons were the protection of the parents and children and the common good of society. On this latter point he observed that the common welfare of society would obviously suffer harm if any group of men or women were permitted to organize schools and operate them as they chose and at their own good pleasure.[139] González grants to the state the right to watch over teaching in all schools, both public and private,[140] but it must be noted that watching over is not precisely the point at issue here, for the state is watching over when it merely corrects abuses that are brought to its attention or that cannot be missed by its own observation. Whatever he intends by this watching over, González favors us with some ex-

schools. Patrick F. Quigley, *Compulsory Education* (New York: Robert Drummond, 1894), p. 319.

[135] Massachusetts General Court, Committee on Education, a digest of the remarks of the Remonstrants at the hearings of the Legislative Committee on Education in March, 1888, n. pub., n. date, p. 13.

[136] *Ibid.*, p. 16.

[137] *Ibid.*

[138] *Ibid.*, p. 17.

[139] "The State's Power to Regulate," *America*, XXXII (Mar. 28, 1925), 567.

[140] "Status habet ius invigilandi ne pravae doctrinae tradantur in omnibus scholis, tam privatis, quam officialibus . . ." Joseph Hellin and Irenaeus González, *Philosophiae Scholasticae Summa* (Matriti: Biblioteca de Autores Christianos, 1952), III, 818–819.

amples of matters that the state may, in his opinion, watch over: (1) that nothing contrary to public peace and order be taught; (2) that public morality be not neglected; (3) that the elementary rules of health be observed; and (4) that all children be given a fit education.[141] Cavagnis likewise speaks of this vigilance of the state.[142]

Pope Pius XI states that the state "can exact, and take measures to secure that all its citizens have the necessary knowledge of their civic and political duties, and a certain degree of physical, intellectual and moral culture, which, considering the conditions of our times, is really necessary for the common good."[143] This statement of the Holy Father seems to be the best argument the supporters of this second opinion have to offer. From it they can conclude that if the state can take measures to see that all citizens have necessary knowledge, it can also examine all institutions in which that knowledge is being given. This argumentation, however, is not apodictic, for the Holy Father may have been thinking merely of the general right of the state to correct flagrant and obvious educational abuses that result in inadequate instruction. In other words, he may not have been considering at all the question of inspection of schools.

A final word regarding the state's relationship to Catholic seminaries. It seems manifest to me that the state has the same right of inspection over seminaries in matters of health and safety as it has over other private institutions. Seminarians and seminary faculties although functioning in institutions devoted (at least on the major level) exclusively to religious matters, yet remain citizens of the state and therefore subject to the state in temporal affairs.

In regard to religious instruction, however, the government has no competency. Bouquillon is clear on the question: "I have said that the State has no authority and right of inspection over the Church's schools for the training of the clergy, seminaries theological and classical, not even so far as the profane sciences are concerned."[144] Since the seminary is geared to the supernatural salvation of men and the state looks directly to the natural and temporal order, the instructional activity of

---

[141] *Ibid.*, pp. 810, 811.

[142] *Op. cit.*, p. 202.

[143] *Christian Education of Youth*, p. 17.

[144] *Education: to Whom Does It Belong? — A Rejoinder to Critics*, p. 31. Father Bouquillon points out that in this matter "the Church is at times tolerant and makes concessions to the State according to circumstances."

the former is entirely removed from the competency of the latter.[145]

As might be expected, nations of the world vary considerably in their attitudes and practices regarding the inspection of private schools. Under the Education Act of 1944 all schools in England, including independent ones, are subject to governmental inspection.[146] Cuba provides for inspection but explicitly exempts religious instruction from it: "Centers of private instruction shall be subject to regulation and inspection by the Nation; but in every case shall retain the right to give, separately from the technical instruction, the religious instruction which they desire."[147] Netherlands likewise inspects state-financed private schools but stipulates that the religious tendencies of the curriculum be not submitted to the inspection.[148] The Bombay Primary Education Act of 1947 provides for inspection of instruction, compliance with compulsory education, health of pupils, and records.[149]

Uruguay intervenes in private education in order to maintain hygiene, morality, safety, and public order.[150] Although Libya provides in article 28 of its constitution for governmental supervision of private schools, yet in article 29 it suggests that the state will not interfere unless some notable harm is being done.[151] The Union of South Africa tends to keep regulation of private schools to a bare minimum. The Transvaal and the Orange Free State practice a limited inspection policy, while in Natal and the Cape province unaided private schools are inspected at the request of the schools themselves. In the Cape Province, however, an inspector may visit any private school in order

---

[145] For this same reason the state has no right of inspection over the teaching of religion in Catholic schools.

[146] *Education in Great Britain,* p. 7.

[147] *Constitution of the Republic of Cuba,* July 5, 1940, article 55. Peaslee, I, p. 536.

[148] *Education in the Netherlands,* pp. 25–26.

[149] "Every approved school shall be open during the school hours to inspection by the inspecting officers of the (State) Government for the purpose, in particular of ascertaining — (a) whether instruction is given in accordance with the provisions of section 38; (b) whether the provisions of this Act for the compulsory attendance of children are being carried out; (c) whether the health of the school children is satisfactory; (d) whether the instruction given is not of a pernicious nature; (e) whether the registers and records are being maintained as required by the Director." *Bombay Primary Education Act, 1947,* section 40, from a printed excerpt furnished by the Embassy of India, Washington, D. C., Feb. 24, 1955.

[150] *Constitution of the Oriental Republic of Uruguay,* Oct. 26, 1951, article 68, U.N.Y. for 1951, p. 386.

[151] "Teaching shall be unrestricted so long as it does not constitute a breach of public order and is not contrary to morality." *Constitution of the United Kingdom of Libya,* Oct. 7, 1951, article 29, U.N.Y. for 1951, p. 227.

to ascertain its condition.[152] Afghanistan suggests that private schools are not inspected: "The public schools of Afghanistan are under the supervision of the Government. . . ."[153]

The practices among the states of the United States vary considerably. In its summary of inspectional activities among the states the appellee in the Oregon Case mentioned only twenty-three of the forty-eight as having regulations on this point. Nebraska and Washington require visitation of private schools twice a year. New Hampshire, Rhode Island, and North Dakota specify approval for "compulsory education purposes." New York examines courses in patriotism and citizenship, while Kansas looks into the use of English and the teaching of civil government. Courses of instruction must be approved by the civil government in New Mexico, Michigan, Maine, and Kentucky. Maine examines methods of instruction also. Connecticut and Wisconsin inspect "registers" and "attendance records" respectively.[154]

SUBMISSION OF RECORDS TO THE STATE

Since the submission of private school records to the civil government is so closely related to the problem of the inspection of these schools, there is little to be added here. It seems safe to infer that opinions on this question would parallel those we have discussed in the preceding section.

We might note, however, that once the state is granted the right to enforce compulsory education,[155] it follows necessarily that it has the right to whatever records are required for the execution of compulsory education laws.

STATE REGULATION OF PRIVATE SCHOOL CURRICULUM

We do not aim to discuss in this present section whether or not the state may determine to the last detail what the curriculum of the private school is to be. Such would be on the part of the state to as-

---

[152] Union of South Africa, *Education,* a preprint from the *Official Yearbook of the Union of South Africa* (Pretoria: Government Printer, 1947), p. 53.

[153] *Fundamental Principles of the Government of Afghanistan,* Oct. 31, 1931, article 22. Peaslee, I, p. 27.

[154] *Op. cit.,* "Appendix II to Brief in Behalf of Appellee — State Laws Relative to Private Schools and Classified Summary Thereof," pp. 925–926.

[155] This question we take up in Chapter XII.

sume the role of a primary educator, a role it does not enjoy. We do ask, however, whether or not the state may determine some minimum requirements in the curricula of private institutions.

It seems to me that an affirmative answer must be given to this last question. If the state has the power to enforce compulsory education, it is difficult to see how it would not also have the power to determine what the minimum of education shall be. As Bouquillon indicates, the former would be pointless without the latter.[156] We shall see in the next chapter that the state does have the power to enforce compulsory education.

Holaind did not allow this line of argumentation. He reasoned that the state may intervene in the parents' exercise of their right to educate only in cases of neglect and when there is a public wrong committed. In the same way the state may punish parents who starve their children, but it would make itself ridiculous by establishing a minimum food scale. Minimum education like minimum food is *a priori* undefinable. The existence of a public crime must be determined by the judge in each case. No other course of action is possible.[157]

We might answer that minimum food and minimum education are undefinable in precise and minute terms, but no one expects that the state define them in such terms. Dietitians do know approximately (the theologian's *moraliter*) what kind and how much food is necessary for health, and prudent officials can decide approximately what kind and how much education is needed at any given time for the preservation of the common welfare of society. We would allow, however, some probability to the position that the state may not question whether a private school is giving the minimum without some prior basis for its suspicion. This returns us to the problem of the state's inspection of private institutions.

It must be noted again in this connection that the state has no competency in fixing or modifying the curriculum in matters of religious

---

[156] *Education: To Whom Does It Belong?* p. 26. Pope Benedict XV taught the right of the state to prescribe at least the vernacular as part of the curriculum: "Nobody can deny that the civil government of Ontario has the right to exact that children should learn English in the schools. . . . Nor on the other hand is there any reason to contest the right of French Canadians, living in the province, to claim in a suitable way, however, that French should be taught in schools attended by a certain number of their children." The context indicates that the Holy Father was speaking of both Catholic and public schools. On the Canadian Language Controversy, *Catholic Mind,* XV (Jan. 22, 1917), 31.

[157] *Op. cit.,* p. 20.

instruction. This observation applies, of course, to primary and secondary education and, *a fortiori*, to seminary training.

Among the nations of the world Bolivia stands for strong state control over the curricula of private education: "Private schools shall be subject to the same authorities and the same official plans, programs, and regulations (as public schools)."[158] It specifically exempts religion, however, from this control. Cuba provides that the literature, history, and geography of Cuba in addition to civics and its constitution must be taught in all schools of the nation.[159] Lebanon requires that private schools follow the official curricula, but allows additional subjects to be added.[160] Syria has the same provision as Lebanon but restricts the additional subjects to such "material as may be defined by law."[161] Jordan merely stipulates that private schools must submit to "government supervision with regard to their curricula and educational policy."[162] The constitution of Panama requires that national history and civic education be taught by national professors and it forbids private schools to use a foreign language in instruction without the permission of the ministry of education. On the primary level private institutions must offer the same programs as the public schools, but they may obtain permission for additional courses in any language. On the secondary level they must include courses in national history, geography, and civic education.[163] In private schools supported by public funds the Netherlands determines not only the subjects that must be taught, but it also specifies the number of weeks per year and hours per week for which they are to be taught.[164] To the standard subjects others may be added.[165]

The English Education Act of 1944 spells out in considerable detail the extent of control the civil government exercises over the various categories of schools, public and private, to be found in England.[166]

---

[158] *Political Constitution of the Bolivian State*, Nov. 23, 1945. Peaslee, I, p. 173.

[159] *Constitution of the Republic of Cuba*, July 5, 1940, article 55. Peaslee, I, p. 536.

[160] *Decree of May 23, 1950*, U.N.Y. for 1950, p. 187.

[161] *Constitution of Syria*, Sept. 5, 1950, article 28, U.N.Y. for 1950, p. 282.

[162] *Constitution of the Hashemite Kingdom of the Jordan*, Dec., 1951, article 19, U.N.Y. for 1951, p. 213.

[163] *Constitution of the Republic of Panama*, Mar. 1, 1946, article 81. Peaslee, II, p. 711.

[164] Idenburg, *Education in the Netherlands*, p. 26.

[165] *Ibid.*, p. 20.

[166] Terminology used in this act is quite different from American usage. A county school is one established and maintained by a Local Education Authority (L.E.A.). It is equivalent to our public school. Private schools are called voluntary schools and are

The Local Education Authority has control over the secular instruction imparted in every county school and in every voluntary school. The governors of aided secondary schools, however, control the secular instruction given in their institutions. Both of these regulations are subject to other provisions for religious instruction and to other special articles of government that may provide for a school's operation. The authority to control the secular instruction in the county and voluntary schools includes also the power to determine the hours of the school day, the length of the school year, and the number of school holidays.[167]

The practices of the states in the United States show a considerable degree of uniformity. In its summary of American laws on this point the appellee in the Oregon Case listed twenty-nine states as having regulations controlling the curricula of private schools. Alabama, California, Delaware, Illinois, Maryland, Nebraska, New Hampshire, North Dakota, Oregon, Rhode Island, South Carolina, and Vermont are indicated as requiring at least the equivalent of a public school education. Many of the other states enumerate the required branches of study.[168] As an example of this latter group we might mention Connecticut which requires in all schools, both public and private, two courses in the duties of United States citizenship, one on the grade school level and the other on the high school level. Officials of both types of schools must file a copy of these courses with the secretary of the state board of education.[169]

Several nations of the world legislate on the teaching of religion in private schools. Portugal simply stipulates that no authorization is needed for the teaching of religion in private schools.[170] Egypt makes instruction in religion and ethics compulsory in private institutions but

---

themselves subdivided into four broad categories: (*a*) controlled schools — those for which the L.E.A. pays all improvement costs and over which it has much control; (*b*) aided schools — those for which the educational ministry pays one half of improvement costs and in which the L.E.A. appoints only one third of the school managers; (*c*) special agreement schools — those for which 50–75 per cent of the cost of new buildings is paid by the L.E.A.; (*d*) independent schools — those which receive no grant of public money. This line-up is a simplification. For a more complete treatment see British Information Services, *Education in Great Britain*, pp. 8–18.

[167] *Education Act, 1944*, section 23.

[168] *Op. cit.*, pp. 926–927.

[169] School laws, Chapter 67, sections 1352, 1353, Huston, *op. cit.*, under "Connecticut," I, p. 18.

[170] *Political Constitution of the Portuguese Republic*, Mar. 19, 1933, article 43, U.N.Y. for 1951, p. 299.

forbids these institutions to teach a child any religion other than his own.[171] As far as I know this regulation is unique among the family of nations, although it may actually be similar to that described in footnote number 174 below.

Syria excludes religion from the curriculum of at least some private schools by its refusal to permit the establishment of private schools for missionary purposes.[172] Spain provides that the curriculum in religion for both state and private schools shall be drawn up by agreement with competent ecclesiastical authority.[173] Madras in India permits religious instruction in private schools provided no proselytization is carried on.[174]

DETERMINATION OF PUPILS IN PRIVATE SCHOOLS

The problem here envisioned is that of the right of the state to prescribe who may or must attend a private school. I have not seen the ethics of this question discussed anywhere. I am of the opinion, however, that the state at least in ordinary circumstances does not have the right to force a private institution to accept persons it does not reasonably wish to accept. The reason for this position is that one group of parents is not obliged to provide education for the children of some other group. If the latter does not have the capability to care for its educational needs, the obligation to provide for them devolves on the state, not on some private group within the state.

In unusual circumstances, however, it could happen that the state could force a private group to admit a certain class of students into its institution. Such would be an extremely small number of students in a given locale, a number so small that there would be no justification for the erection of a public school, since a private school would presumably be in operation. It goes without saying that if the state

---

[171] Denver *Register,* Jan. 8, 1956, p. 5.

[172] Decree No. 175 of Mar., 1952, articles 2 and 8, U.N.Y. for 1952, p. 266.

[173] *Concordat between Spain and the Holy See,* article 27, No. 8.

[174] "(1) Where the religious instruction given in an institution is a faith other than that to which a pupil belongs, the pupil shall not be permitted to attend the religious instruction class unless his parent or guardian specifically demands in writing that he should be permitted to do so. (2) The religious instruction given shall not constitute an attack on other faiths. (3) The staff, pupils or buildings of any school or college shall not be utilized for proselytization purposes." "Extract of the rules 8 and 9 (A) of the Madras Educational Rules," sent to me by D. K. Hingorani, Education Department, Embassy of India, Washington, D. C., Nov. 4, 1955.

forces a private school to accept outside students, it is bound to pay for their education. If, on the other hand, the state is already fully supporting the private school financially, it would seem to me that it could much more easily require admission of students that would not disrupt the purpose and smooth functioning of that school. Most countries seem not to legislate on this problem in their primary educational documents. A few, however, do make mention of it. Panama provides that "no educational establishment may refuse to admit pupils because of the nature of the union of their parent or guardian or because of social, racial, or political differences."[175] The penalty for violation of this provision is the loss of state subsidy, recognition of degrees, and finally, if the violation is persistent, loss of permission to give instruction. India requires any educational institution that receives financial aid and recognition from the government to admit applicants from any class or group in the community.[176] Syria likewise stipulates that private schools must admit all applicants without discrimination.[177] The United States makes no regulation binding private education to admit or to reject any particular group.

FORCING PRIVATE PERSONS TO ESTABLISH AND MAINTAIN SCHOOLS

This is a difficult question and one that does not arise often. It is obvious that the state can compel parents to fulfill their natural law duty to care for and educate their children, but it is not quite so obvious that it can force them to discharge this duty by the maintenance of schools. This much at least seems demonstrable, however, that if parents *should* establish and maintain a school for the proper education of their children and if they neglect to do so, the state may interfere on the basis either of protecting the children in their rights or of obtaining the common good. Bouquillon ascribes to Taparelli the opinion that "the State can force the denominations to provide schools for their members."[178] I would agree with that opinion on condition

---

[175] *Constitution of the Republic of Panama,* Mar. 1, 1946, article 80. Peaslee, II, p. 711.

[176] Typed memorandum from the Embassy of India, Washington, D. C., to the writer, n.d.

[177] Decree No. 175 of Mar., 1952, U.N.Y. for 1952, p. 266.

[178] *Education: To Whom Does It Belong?* — A Rejoinder to the Civilta Cattolica, p. 14, footnote 1.

that the children's right to proper instruction would otherwise suffer. Few nations of the world provide in their primary educational documents for the compulsion of private persons in this matter, and the nations that do seem concentrated in South America. A decree of Ecuador's Congress in 1821 directed that "all convents should maintain schools for children."[179] Guatemala provides that "owners of plantations, factories and other major enterprises are obliged to provide and sustain schools for the rural or working school population of their properties, with the organization, appointment of personnel, and inspection of the same a duty of the State."[180] Peru has a similar stipulation.[181] Brazil requires industrial, commercial, and agricultural establishments employing more than one hundred persons to maintain free primary instruction both for employees and for their children.[182]

Spain was the only European country found to illustrate the present problem. In 1940 the Ministry of Industry and Commerce imposed the obligation on all companies employing over one hundred skilled workers to maintain at their own expense schools for apprentices. Approximately 800 of these centers can now be found in Spain.[183]

RECOGNITION OF PRIVATE SCHOOLS AND THE GRANTING OF DEGREES

The recognition of private schools by the state is reducible actually to the recognition of the fitness of the products they produce. Our problem here, therefore, is a problem of degrees and diplomas. We shall attempt to determine precisely what authority the state has over the certificates issued by private education.

A distinction must be made, first of all, between a diploma certifying that a student has successfully passed a given course of studies and a certificate which guarantees that he is suitable for some public office or profession. The first is usually granted upon examination by the educational institution, whereas the second is issued by the state upon

---

[179] Emilio Uzcategui, *Compulsory Education in Ecuador* (Paris: UNESCO, 1951), p. 13.

[180] *Constitution of the Republic of Guatemala*, Mar. 11, 1945, article 82. Peaslee, II, p. 85.

[181] *Constitution of the Republic of Peru*, Apr. 9, 1933, article 74. Peaslee, II, p. 770.

[182] *Constitution of the United States of Brazil*, Sept. 24, 1946, article 168. Peaslee, I, p. 212.

[183] Diplomatic Information Office, *Fifteen Years of Spanish Culture*, p. 126.

examination or some other assurance of fitness. In this second case González points out that the state, if it demands a professional title for a determined profession, ought to grant that title through the agency of some independent and impartial tribunal, one, that is, that would treat alike the graduates of both public and private institutions.[184]

The state not only may but must certify to the fitness of candidates for public office. Since these functions are civil, it is the state's duty to protect the common good by seeing to their proper discharge. The fitness of candidates may be ascertained by examination, by degrees from trustworthy institutions, public or private, or by any other adequate means. Catholic philosophers and theologians commonly teach this doctrine.[185]

Regarding the function of the civil government in the granting of degrees certifying to the successful completion of scholastic work, a distinction must again be made. There can be no doubt that the state may grant degrees in the institutions it operates.[186] Even though it is only a secondary educator, the state does have a right to maintain schools. Certifying to a student's successful completion of the course of studies is a mere corollary of that right.

The state may not, however, reserve to itself the sole authority to grant degrees. Both Ottaviani and González point out that the one capable of judging scholastic fitness at the completion of a course is the one who taught the course. And that of course means the institution itself, private or public. A second reason for this position is that the reservation of degree-granting power to the state alone is equivalent to a state monopoly in education, for it could force students to frequent government schools alone.[187]

Discoverable international regulations on the issuance of academic degrees tend for the most part to a statistic extreme. Bolivia provides that "public universities are the only ones authorized to issue academic diplomas. Degrees shall be granted by the government in the name of the State."[188] All essential certificates for all levels of education are

---

184 *Op. cit.,* p. 816, footnote 20.

185 Ottaviani, *op. cit.,* p. 244; Cavagnis, *op. cit.,* p. 214; Ciarlantini, *op. cit.,* p. 121.

186 We are not thinking here of state schools aimed at furnishing candidates for civil service (the right to grant degrees from these is patent), but of the ordinary public institution.

187 Ottaviani, *op. cit.,* p. 243; Hellin and González, *op. cit.,* p. 815.

188 *Constitution of the Bolivian State,* Nov. 23, 1945, article 160. Peaslee, I, p. 174.

conferred by the government alone in France.[189] In Panama "only the academic and professional degrees issued by the State or authorized by it in accordance with legal provisions are recognized."[190] Portugal stipulates that private schools may be authorized to grant diplomas provided their standards are not inferior to those of state schools.[191] In Syria only the state may grant diplomas, although private schools may issue certificates indicating classes attended by the pupils.[192]

CERTIFICATION OF TEACHERS IN PRIVATE SCHOOLS

We propose to examine here whether or not the state has a right to examine candidates for the position of teaching in private schools together with the right of certifying or not certifying them for that work. As might be expected (because the problems are so similar), there is on this question the same sort of disagreement of opinion that we noted above when discussing the inspection of private institutions.

Messmer denies that the state has a right to examine teacher-candidates for private schools.[193] Interesting support for Messmer's view can be seen in A. P. Marble, a stanch nineteenth-century patron of public education.[194] When he was asked "how the competence of private school teachers to impart the required schooling shall be known without an examination, Mr. Marble said that the parents who patronize the school can be trusted to look out for that."[195] An unsigned article (probably by the editor, the name of whom is not indicated in the volume) in the *American Ecclesiastical Review* for April, 1892, denied to the state a right to select and appoint teachers for private schools. The reason given was that the private school teacher represents not the state but the family. The writer granted, however, that the

---

[189] Henri Laugier, "France," *Educational Yearbook*, 1944, ed. I. L. Kandel, p. 139.

[190] *Constitution of the Republic of Panama*, Mar. 1, 1946, article 85. Peaslee, II, p. 711.

[191] *Political Constitution of the Portuguese Republic*, Mar. 19, 1933, article 44, U.N.Y. for 1951, p. 299.

[192] Decree No. 175 of Mar., 1952, article 9, U.N.Y. for 1952, p. 266.

[193] S. G. Messmer, "The Right of Instruction," *American Ecclesiastical Review*, VI (Feb., 1892), 109.

[194] Marble's position on Catholic education seems to have been a strange one. In a hearing held on March 13, 1888, before the Massachusetts legislature we read: "Getting to the question of Catholic parochial schools, Mr. Marble, while deprecating their establishment, could not say that he would do differently if he were a Catholic." Massachusetts General Court, Committee on Education, *op. cit.*, p. 6.

[195] *Ibid.*

state has a right to assure itself of the teaching competency of all teachers, but "if this assurance is obtainable without examination, as *per se* it is, the right of the State to examine is precluded."[196] In conformity with the trend of thought of this school as expressed elsewhere, we might observe that these writers in all likelihood would argue that the state may not enter the private sphere of activity unless some notable harm is being done. This harm likewise must not be presumed but proved. Hence, the state may not examine and certify private school teachers unless it has some well-founded reason for supposing that they are deficient and consequently hurting society.

On the other hand we have the editor of *America* in 1925 readily admitting the right and the duty of the state to examine teachers.[197] Although González is of the opinion that parents will see to the fitness of teachers in private institutions, he allows the state a right to examine the aptitude of teachers in those schools.[198] Cavagnis makes the distinction that the state may examine teachers but that it ought not always to exercise its prerogative. The right to examine he derives from the good that accrues to society and from the fact that such examination is no great burden to private education when it is not carried to extremes. When, however, the cultural level of a society is such that the danger of inferior teaching is decidedly remote, the state ought not to burden its subjects by useless cautions.[199]

Laws requiring the certification of teachers are common in the world today. The Japanese system of certification applies to all types of educational workers: ordinary teachers, assistant teachers, school nurses, teachers of the handicapped, principals, and the superintendent of the board of education.[200] Ceylon, along with many countries, differentiates its teaching certificates according to the educational level for which each is meant. For the primary grades a "vernacular" certificate is required; for the English schools (which are mostly secondary) an "English School Certificate" is needed; on the upper levels a "Higher School Certificate" or a degree is necessary.[201] Being a highly segregated country, South Africa further distinguishes its certificates into Euro-

---

[196] VI, 301.
[197] "The State's Power to Regulate," *America*, XXXII (Mar. 28, 1925), 567.
[198] *Op. cit.*, p. 820.
[199] *Op. cit.*, pp. 199–200.
[200] Hideo Nakahara and Genji Takahashi, "Japan," *The Year Book of Education, 1953*, ed. J. A. Lauwerys and N. Hans, p. 520.
[201] T. L. Green, "Ceylon," *ibid.*, p. 492.

pean (primary, etc.) and Coloured and Native. Among the last named are specialized and distinct certificates for music, housecraft, physical education, agriculture, woodwork, domestic science, and infant education.[202]

The United States has hundreds of differently named teaching certificates among its forty-eight states. Traditionally, however, this country has tended to require certificates for private schools only if these latter seek accreditation by the state department of education. Only Alabama, Iowa, Michigan, Nebraska, and South Dakota have compulsory legal certification requirements for private institutions.[203] The law of the last named state declares that "no person shall be permitted to teach in any private school any of the branches prescribed to be taught in the public schools unless such a person shall hold a certificate entitling him to teach the same branches in the public schools of this state."[204]

---

[202] Union of South Africa, *Education*, pp. 26–27. It will be noted, however, that none of the above examples (Japan, Ceylon, South Africa) explicitly includes or excludes private education from national requirements.

[203] William F. Jenks, "Exceptional Job Done for Normal Children — Normal Job Planned for Exceptional Children," National Catholic Educational Association *Bulletin*, LII (Nov., 1955), 23.

[204] *1933 School Laws of South Dakota*, Sec. 15.1005, in Huston, *op. cit.*, under "South Dakota," p. 7.

CHAPTER X

PROVISION OF PUBLIC SCHOOLS CORRESPONDING TO THE NEEDS AND REASONABLE DEMANDS OF PRIMARY EDUCATORS

THUS far we have investigated the relationship of the state to the primary educators under the particular aspect of the schools operated by those primary educators. We now turn to the rights and duties of the state toward these same educators under the aspect of the schools the *state* operates in order to supplement their efforts. We have already demonstrated the obligation that lies on the state to provide schools wherever private enterprise fails or neglects to provide them. There remains for us here, therefore, merely the need to show the relationships that ought to exist among the primary educators, these public schools, and the sponsoring state.

INFLUENCE OF THE CHURCH AND FAMILY IN THE PUBLIC SCHOOL

Since the state's function in education is essentially subsidiary and supplementary, and since the public school represents the parents, it immediately follows that the state-operated school must remain in intimate contact with the agencies it is supplementing, the Church and the family. This means practically that the state is morally bound to operate its schools in a manner that recognizes the rights of the Church and corresponds to the reasonable demands of the parents who patronize its schools.[205]

---

[205] This position seems to have been included in the thought of Pope Pius IX when he taught that the Christian state does not have entire authority over the public school,

It is of course impossible for the state to satisfy every demand of every parent, and that is why we specify *reasonable* demands. If a sufficient number of parents object to subject matter or methodology and at the same time have a rational basis for their objection, the civil government is bound to conform to their will provided the rights of other parents are not thereby compromised. Cronin rightly points out that the fact that the state "does provide money for education, and that, consequently it is in the advantageous position of being necessary to parents, no more gives it a right to take the children out of their parents' hands and educate them according to its own ideas exclusively, than its necessity in the interests of public order bestows on the State a right of forcing a particular kind of dress or food or habitation on all those who are in the unhappy position of having to appeal to it for aid against thieves and robbers."[206]

The element of reasonableness in the parents' demands suggests, second, that they not interfere in the public school regarding matters in which they have no competence. Cronin feels that the state need not consult parents in matters in which it is supposed that they cannot judge rightly, and he cites as an example the teaching of mathematics, the extent of that teaching and its methods.[207] But, on the other hand, he feels that there are other matters in which the parents are quite competent judges and of these he mentions the matter of religion as an example. Because the state enjoys no competency in this latter, it may not use its (the state's) necessity to the parents to force a system of education on the children of which the parents do not approve.[208]

A person may object to the position we have taken on the grounds that a home-school co-operation, while fine in theory, is unrealizable in practice. This we question. The feasibility of parental influence in

---

an authority that would rule out the influence of any other agency. Condemned was the proposition that "Totum scholarum publicarum regimen, in quibus iuventus christianae alicuius reipublicae instituitur, episcopalibus dumtaxat seminariis aliqua ratione exceptis, potest ac debet attribui auctoritati civili, et ita quidem attribui, ut nullum alii cuicunque auctoritati recognoscatur ius immiscendi se in disciplina scholarum, in regimine studiorum, in graduum collatione, in delectu aut approbatione magistrorum." Syllabus, prop. 45, Henricus Denziger, *Enchiridion Symbolorum,* 29 ed. (Friburgi: Herder, 1953), No. 1745.

[206] *Op. cit.,* II, 489.

[207] We do not agree entirely with Cronin's example. Parents' judgments on the extremes of progressivism are far more accurate than those of many professional educationists.

[208] *Ibid.,* p. 488.

the school as we here envision it may be illustrated by the activities of over 10,000 citizens' educational committees operating in the United States at the present time. These work in conjunction with the school boards for the improvement of public education. In Cleveland Heights, Ohio, for example, the committees offered in the course of one year fifty-one recommendations to the board and of these twenty-six were accepted.[209]

In the concrete circumstances of human life the more crucial influence of parents in the public schools would most usually find expression in questions of morality, religion, and auxiliary services. A well-based and therefore reasonable judgment of a sizable group of parents on any of these points demands recognition on the part of the government. Sex education or instruction in the evils of narcotics, for example, are matters of parental concern and do not depend on the mere judgment of school officials. Parents, likewise, are usually at least somewhat competent judges regarding the kind of medical attention given their offspring and of the type of food served to them. Those parents, therefore, have a right to be heard in these and like matters.

Religious education, however, is the one question that touches most acutely the right of parents to influence the public school. There can be no doubt that parents are reasonable in demanding that the education of their children be informed by religious motivation and religious truth. There is likewise no doubt that extremely large segments of any population desire the religious formation of their children in the school. The truth of this last statement is amply borne out by the high percentages of parents who take advantage of religious instruction in the public schools of those countries which provide it.[210] That parents are reasonable in desiring religious training in the public school curriculum can quite readily be shown.

Experience is an apt teacher in showing that home and "Sunday-school" religious instruction is wholly inadequate in the modern day world. Only the starry-eyed optimist can seriously entertain the thought that today's typical parent is willing and equipped to give solid, thor-

---

[209] *New York Times,* Sept. 30, 1956, p. L 47.

[210] In Australia, for example, "New South Wales estimates the attendance (at religious instruction classes in the public schools) at about 90 per cent of the possible number, Victoria 90 per cent, Queensland 90 per cent, Western Australia and Tasmania an unspecified figure but much greater than 50 per cent." George S. Browne, "Australia," *Education Yearbook, 1932,* ed. I. L. Kandel, pp. 7–20.

ough, and intellectually based instruction in the truths of religion. And we need say nothing of the pervading anxiety and movement of modern family life as a deterrent to serious teaching and learning in the home even supposing parents are willing and capable.

Nor is Sunday church instruction adequate. On the one hand attendance at services and religion classes is irregular and sparse, and on the other one half hour per week is, of course, by no means sufficient for the amount of work to be done. Missing, too, is the indispensable weeklong religious atmosphere required for the genuine formation of the whole child. Archbishop Ireland was entirely correct when he referred to the opinion that children can be educated religiously at home or in Sunday school as an "airy dream."[211] In our own day the same conviction was expressed by Archbishop Muench when he said that "the religious formation given in the home or in a Sunday school is no longer adequate in the world in which we live."[212] The most authoritative statement, however, comes from the pen of Pope Pius IX who condemned the proposition that Catholics may approve of a kind of education that attends solely or primarily to natural truth and fails to concern itself with the teaching of Catholic truth.[213]

Perhaps the most telling reason why the public school may not be neutral in the matter of religion is that it cannot be neutral. There is, in other words, a question of impossibility. By omitting reference to matters of religion the school is teaching by silence that it considers secular affairs of greater importance than religious ones. Secularists are bankrupt in their efforts to meet this charge straight on. Thayer, for example, cites Father John E. Wise as alleging that *religious* indifferentism is represented in the American state school but that the teachings of the various faiths are not. In his answer, instead of discussing the religious assault on his position, Thayer swings off into morality and character. He utterly fails to touch the real issue of *religious* indifferentism. The kernel of his reply is the irrelevant, "Would that all departments of the state were staffed by men and women of an

---

211 Reilly, *op. cit.*, p. 96.

212 Aloisius J. Muench, "Religion in Education," *Social Justice Review*, XLVIII (Sept., 1955), 212.

213 "Catholicis viris probari potest ea juventutis instituendae ratio, quae sit a catholica fide et ab Ecclesiae potestate seiuncta, quaeque rerum dumtaxat naturalium scientiam ac terrenae socialis vitae fines tantummodo vel saltem primario spectet." Syllabus, prop. 48, Denzinger, *op. cit.*, No. 1748.

integrity, an earnestness, and high ideals equal, by and large, to those of the teachers of our public schools!"[214]

For the same reason, a "nonsectarian" instruction in public schools would decidedly be sectarian, namely, that sectarianism which holds doctrinal differences to be of little moment. The position of Horace Mann on this problem seems to bring out the impossibility of the secularist position, for he was really on both sides of the fence at the same time. On the one hand he unflinchingly opposed the introduction of sectarian teaching into the public school and yet on the other he firmly opposed a secularist education. He saw a place in the common school for the teaching of morality and scriptural theology.[215] But Mann probably did not see how sectarian his position really was. The mere reading of the Bible even without note or comment is, of course, decidedly sectarian, for behind the practice lies the Protestant doctrine of private interpretation and the implicit denial of a needed explanation by a divinely authorized Church.[216]

Likewise undeniable is the fact that any teacher, no matter how diligently he may strive to the contrary, is bound by nuance, stresses, and side observations to reveal some sort of attitude toward God, religion, and the Church. This is an accidental yet telling way of teaching religion. A student of American public education has acknowledged the fact that public school discipline has "all too often degenerated from a non-religious to an anti-religious discipline."[217] A German Bishop insisted on the fact that the nonreligious school not only fails to provide religious formation but that it positively misinstructs. "The secular public school, however, denies this truth (that religion must form the basis of all human concerns), because it knows nothing of the true destiny of man, and aims at nothing higher for the child beyond this life." He concludes that the secular school is

---

[214] *Religion in Public Education,* p. 152.

[215] Sister Aimee, F.C.S.P., "Religious Convictions of Horace Mann," Catholic Educational Review, XXV (Mar., 1937), 149–151. See also E. I. F. Williams, *Horace Mann* (New York: Macmillan, 1937), pp. 266–274.

[216] Even the seemingly nonsectarian subject, history of religion, is often not taught without large doses of bias. Father James J. Maguire has successfully exposed the extreme prejudice found in the required textbook for Wayne University's (a public institution) history course 571, "History of Religion." One may wonder how the secularistic brand of religion may be supported by public funds and no other be granted that privilege. See "Cocktail Lounge Theology," *Newman Review,* VI (3rd Quarter, 1955), 4–9.

[217] Isaac Doughton, *Modern Public Education, Its Philosophy and Background* (New York: Appleton-Century-Crofts, 1935), p. 274.

therefore "essentially based on infidelity."[218] Because the public school in some countries may not discuss God, Christ, and His Church, the child is formed in the habit of viewing all earthly things as though they had no relationship to God, Christ, and His Church. And this is positively misinforming.[219]

Holaind writes in the same vein when he remarks that "one who sets aside revelation makes himself unfit to teach Christian morals. Nothing is left but to teach *la morale civique* — a doubtful sort of education."[220] Anyone who has attended a typical American public school knows from experience that Holaind's last remark is perfectly true. I well remember from my grade school years that the clear impression produced on us in the public school was *la morale civique:* virtue was merely natural and the "saints" were the national heroes.

The right of parents to religion in the curriculum of the public school is further based on the fact that morality and the teaching of morality cannot be soundly based without religion. The man in the street readily sees the intimate and necessary connection between the two, but the secularist does not.[221] Thayer attempts to show that morality can be taught effectively without religion by citing the overworked prison argument. He tells us that "from a study conducted by Franklin Steiner on the religious preferences of prison inmates, it was found that of 85,000 individuals 80 per cent expressed a preference for Christianity; only 8000 indicated no preference at all, and a mere 150 identified themselves as either atheists or agnostics!"[222]

It is interesting to note, first of all, the fact that Thayer does not document his source for this "study." Then, too, the very roundness of the figures alleged suggests slipshoddiness of procedure or lack of exact memory.[223] But even granting for the sake of discussion the truthworthiness of the alleged data, it seems perfectly obvious that the figures prove nothing at all. That eighty per cent *prefer* Christianity proves only that prisoners tend to say that they prefer Christianity. It

---

[218] Wilhelm E. von Ketteler, *Public Schools or Denominational Schools* (New York: Benziger, 1892), p. 13.

[219] *Ibid.*, p. 15.

[220] *Op. cit.*, p. 15.

[221] Early America did not seem to question the connection. In the famous Northwest Ordinance we read that "religion, morality, and knowledge, being necessary to good government, and the happiness of mankind, schools and the means of education shall forever be encouraged . . ." July 13, 1787, Article III.

[222] *Op. cit.*, p. 110.

[223] See *ibid.*, pp. 110–111 for more of these undetailed studies.

does not prove that they know Christianity, that they are imbued with it, and, most of all, that they practice it.[224] That only 150 professed to be atheists or agnostics proves only that extremely few people in any walk of life see anything in atheism or agnosticism. Nor may we neglect to note that our institution of paroling may persuade prisoners that it is wise to "profess" Christianity and not to profess atheism.[225]

Perhaps our best answer, however, is a study we can document, a study that got down to details, details that mattter. As a service to the Knights of Columbus investigation the chaplain of the Illinois State Penitentiary made a study in order to furnish up-to-date and reliable information on the number of Catholics in the Joliet-Statesville branch. The results of this study are interesting for they show that the amount of previous religious influence and a later involvement in crime vary inversely.[226]

Since parents, therefore, have a right to influence reasonably the curriculum of the public school, their demand that religion form an essential part of that curriculum must be heeded by the state. The state is bound to provide for the religious instruction of those children whose parents request it. This provision can be cared for either by religious instruction classes for the various creeds in each school or by denominational public schools.

---

[224] In this connection the Knights of Columbus cite a report issued as a result of a twenty-year study of forty-six prisons: "In prison records, it suffices that the prisoner has at some time or another joined a Church or belonged to it, no matter whether this was five, twenty-five, or fifty years ago; no matter whether the prisoner has not put his foot inside a church nor performed a religious duty for an age. It even suffices that either the prisoner's father or mother or both have professed the religion assigned by him, though the prisoner himself never professed any religion. Yes, it suffices that the prisoner here and now state his preference or choice of the religion he might wish to profess if occasion were to arise. . . . Church affiliation among prisoners is very largely the merest label." The study from which this report is taken was conducted by two Catholic chaplains of Joliet Prison and is cited in Knights of Columbus, *Why the Catholic Church Says, "Investigate"* (St. Louis: Knights of Columbus, 1949), pp. 33–34.

[225] We are told that the "parole system increased church-attendance 260 per cent at Joliet." *Ibid.*, p. 34.

[226] "Out of 1031 men convicted from Cook County (which has a population 50% Catholic) only 369 were Catholics — a figure far below the 50% that would be expected proportionally. Furthermore, out of the 438 prisoners in the institution who are registered as Catholics, only about 100 had been actually practicing the Catholic religion before their commitment according to their own testimony. Of these 438, 56% had never received any Catholic education. Of the men who had received 'some' Catholic education, eighty had not gone beyond the fourth grade . . . eighteen had gone one or two years to a Catholic high school . . . only ten had graduated from a Catholic high school." *Ibid.*, p. 35.

The first solution is not ideal,[227] but in some cases it may be the only one possible. The second is the preferable, although in a religiously pluralistic country it presents problems of a practical nature (one of them being the number of different schools desired).[228] These practical difficulties are, however, by no means insuperable, as the practice of several nations well demonstrates. In any event the mere presence of difficulties does not do away with the religious rights of parents; it rather calls for the intelligent solution of those difficulties. How some of these difficulties have been solved may be noted in the examples we shall discuss below.

Because the present problem is one of the most crucial facing parents and nations today and because practice in the other countries of the world is often so different from that found in the United States, we will devote more attention here to illustration than we have been wont to do.

The public schools of the Union of South Africa begin each day's work with prayer and the reading of the Bible. The teaching of Bible history is compulsory (with a conscience clause), but no "sectarian" interpretation may be given except in Cape Province where catechism may be taught within prescribed limits.[229]

Scotland provides religious instruction in its public schools according to syllabuses issued by a committee representing Scottish churches, the Educational Institute of Scotland, and the Association of Directors of Education. This religious instruction is free from the inspection, control, and regulation of the Secretary of State.[230] In the free public schools of England there must be two periods of religious instruction each week and that according to an agreed syllabus.[231]

Various reports have come to me concerning current practice in India. While there is in all probability some variation from state to state, the general trend seems to be that religion may not be taught

---

[227] See canon 1374.

[228] The moral problem involved in the state's positively aiding the propagation of heresy by maintaining schools for the sects has already been solved by moralists. This they allow for grave reasons. Zalba permits Catholic civil officials to vote for financial aid to build Protestant schools provided the schools are not used to proselytize Catholics and provided the officials' vote is not considered as favoring heresy as such. Regatillo and Zalba, *op. cit.*, I, No. 987. See also Heribert Jone and Urban Adelman, *Moral Theology* (Westminster, Md.: Newman Press, 1953), No. 148–149.

[229] Union of South Africa, *Education*, p. 40.

[230] British Information Services, *Education in Great Britain*, p. 26.

[231] A.C.F. Beales, *op. cit.*, p. 1.

during school hours in institutions wholly supported from governmental funds. It may, however, be taught outside of school hours in public school buildings but not at state expense. In Madras, for example, the following regulations govern the teaching of religion in public institutions:

(i) Institutions under public management should not be used as a means of fostering any one religion at the expense of others and the principle of strict religious neutrality should be maintained.

(ii) Public funds should not be utilized for imparting religious instruction.

(iii) If, without infringing the above conditions, it is proposed to introduce religious instruction in a school under the management of a local body, a resolution approving the same should be passed by a majority of the members of the local body.

(iv) Religious instruction may be imparted both in boys' and girls' schools.

(v) The school premises may be utilized for religious teaching or simple prayers. There is, however, no need to reserve one or two room [sic] specially for the purpose.

(vii) The instruction will always take place either at the beginning or at the end of a school session, that is to say, immediately before the afternoon session or immediately after the morning session or immediately before the afternoon session or immediately after the afternoon session. [sic]

(viii) The services of the teachers in an institution, where they voluntarily undertake the work of religious instruction, shall preferably be utilized. The services of voluntary teachers from outside may be utilized if competent teachers are not available in the institution itself. The selection of such outsiders should be approved by the chairman or president of the local body maintaining the institution.

(ix) No pupil shall be permitted to attend any form of religious instruction or observance without the written request of the parent or guardian which request should be made in writing and will be in force until revoked.[232]

The Fundamental Law of Education in Japan provides that religious tolerance and the importance of religion shall be taught in the public schools, but that no specific religion will be promoted.[233] This pro-

---

[232] "Extract of the Rules 8 and 9 (A) of the Madras Educational Rules," typed memorandum furnished by the Embassy of India, Washington, D. C., Nov. 4, 1955.

[233] Ministry of Foreign Affairs, *Japan's Problems*, p. 30.

vision is in accord with the new constitution which stipulates that the government refrain from any religious activity.[234]

Among the comparatively few nations which do not provide for religious instruction in their public schools the Communist-dominated ones of course predominate. Because their philosophy and practice on this point are well known, it would seem superfluous to detail them here.

Sweden, through its Elementary Schools Act of 1921, made religion a compulsory subject in the primary schools.[235] The government also required that when parents requested exemption from religion classes for their children the local school board had to see to it that the parents themselves provided for the missed instruction. If the latter failed to furnish that instruction, the children were forced to attend religious instruction in the school.[236] The Principality of Liechtenstein provides for instruction in religion and requires that it be given by ecclesiastical authorities.[237]

The constitution of Burma states that religious instruction shall not be imposed in the schools on any minority.[238] Buddhism was being taught in the public schools when in 1950 the government decided that instruction in the other religions was to be given in those schools just as Buddhism was.[239] However, because influential Buddhist leaders objected strenuously to the teaching of Islam in state schools, the government decided to discontinue all religious instruction in order to avoid discrimination.[240]

In its concordat with the Holy See Spain made the teaching of the Catholic religion a compulsory subject in its public schools, although children of non-Catholic parents may be excused at the request of those parents. The civil and ecclesiastical authorities work closely in

[234] "The State and its organs shall refrain from religious education or any other religious activity." The strong American influence operating in the reconstruction of Japan is obvious here. *Constitution of Japan*, May 3, 1947, article 20, mimeographed copy furnished by the Embassy of Japan, Washington, D. C., n.d.

[235] Ingemar During, *The Swedish School-Reform*, p. 35.

[236] B. J:son Bergqvist, "Sweden," I. L. Kandel, *Educational Yearbook, 1932*, pp. 400–401.

[237] *Constitution of the Principality of Liechtenstein*, Oct. 5, 1921, article 16. Peaslee, II, p. 378.

[238] *Constitution of the Union of Burma*, Sept. 24, 1947, article 22. Peaslee, I, p. 252.

[239] U Nu, "Fair Treatment To All Faiths, Says Premier," *Burma Weekly Bulletin*, Sept. 15, 1954, p. 178.

[240] *Ibid.*, Buddhism is the predominant religion in Burma.

the appointment of religion instructors, the adoption of religion text-books and the determination of the religion curriculum.[241] Norway presents a religious educational picture quite similar to that of Spain. The chief difference from the point of view of religion in the public schools lies in the fact that in Spain the predominant religion is Ca-tholicism, whereas in Norway it is Lutheranism. In the public schools of Norway the Evangelical-Lutheran religion is taught, but pupils of other faiths may be exempted from such instruction.[242]

The states of the United States present on the whole a fairly uni-form attitude toward the teaching of religion in public schools. For the most part sectarian teachings are not tolerated. Often, however, Bible reading without commentary and some sort of prayer are per-mitted. Typical illustrations follow.

In its constitution the state of Pennsylvania stipulates that no money raised for public education may be used for sectarian schools.[243] This regulation has given rise to a number of court decisions. One declared that it prohibits sectarian religious exercises.[244] Another stated that public school buildings may not be used for religious meetings.[245] A third ruled that the constitution does not forbid Bible reading or the

---

[241] "1. The Spanish State guarantees the teaching of the Catholic religion as an ordinary and compulsory subject in all teaching establishments, whether or not belonging to the State, and of whatever kind or grade. The children of non-Catholic parents shall be dispensed from such lessons at the request of their parents or guardians. 2. In State primary schools, the religion lessons shall be given by the school teacher, except in the event of an objection to any of them being raised by the Ordinary for the reasons stated in canon 1381, paragraph three, of the Code of Canon Law. Such teaching shall also be given, periodically, by the parish priest or his deputy, by means of catechism lessons. 3. In State Secondary Schools, the religious teaching shall be given by masters, priests or religious, and, subsidiarily, by lay masters appointed by the competent civil authority, at the proposal of the diocesan Ordinary. . . . 8. Religion curricula for both State schools and others shall be drawn up by agreement with the competent ecclesiastical authority. No other textbooks for the teaching of religion shall be adopted than those approved by the ecclesiastical authority." *The Concordat between Spain and the Holy See*, article XXVII. These provisions are of particular interest to us for they indicate the mind of the Church regarding concrete educational problems as they exist in a predominantly Catholic country.

[242] Olaf Devik, "Norway," *Educational Yearbook, 1944*, ed. I. L. Kandel, p. 254.

[243] "No money raised for the support of the public schools of the Commonwealth shall be appropriated or used for the support of any sectarian school." Constitutional provisions, article 10, sec. 2, in Huston, *op. cit.*, under "Pennsylvania," II, p. 1.

[244] *Stevenson* v. *Hunyon*, 16 C.C. 186, 4 Dist. 395. 42 Pitts. 381. (1895), in Huston, *ibid.*

[245] *Hysong* v. *Gallitzin Borough Sch. Dist.*, 164 Pa. 629 in Huston, *ibid.*

singing of Protestant hymns.[246] This last stipulation is not typical of American practice. A final decision states that "there must be proof that sectarian instruction was imparted during school hours; such instruction out of school hours, though by teachers at the school house, is not within the prohibition by this section."[247]

Provisions in the state of Maine are both interesting and detailed. We will reproduce them just as they appear in Huston.

Sec. 27 [sic]. READINGS FROM THE SCRIPTURES IN PUBLIC SCHOOLS. To insure greater security in the faith of our fathers, to inculcate into the lives of the rising generation the spiritual values necessary to the well-being of our and future civilizations, to develop those high moral and religious principles essential to human happiness, to make available to the youth of our land the book which has been the inspiration of the greatest masterpieces of literature, art, and music, and which has been the strength of the great men and women of the Christian era, there shall be, in all the public schools of the state, daily or at suitable intervals, readings from the scriptures with special emphasis on the Ten Commandments, the Psalms of David, the Proverbs of Solomon, the Sermon on the Mount, and the Lord's Prayer. It is provided further, that there shall be no denominational or sectarian comment or teaching,[248] and each student shall give respectful attention but shall be free in his own forms of worship.

Sec. 128. SCHOOL COMMITTEE MAY PROVIDE FOR MORAL INSTRUCTION. The school committee of each city or town is authorized and empowered to provide for the moral instruction of pupils subject to the jurisdiction of such committee in the manner provided for in sections 128 to 134, inclusive.

Sec. 129. SURVEY OF RELIGIOUS AFFILIATIONS MAY BE MADE. The school committee of each city or town may authorize and complete a survey of the religious affiliations of all pupils attending the public schools within such city or town, and ascertain those pupils who desire and have the consent of parent or guardian for moral instruction. On a day in each week, to be fixed by the board, it may excuse such pupils for at least one hour for the purpose of attending their respective places of worship, or some other suitable

---

[246] *Hart* v. *Sharpsville Borough Sch. Dist.*, 2 Lane 346, in Huston, *ibid*. The permission of sectarian hymns seems inconsistent with the other decisions.

[247] *Hysong* v. *Gallitzin Borough Sch. Dist.*, 164 Pa. 629, in Huston, *ibid*.

[248] We have shown above how this type of provision is already denominational and sectarian.

place, there to receive moral instruction in accordance with the religious faith of said pupils.

Sec. 130. RULES AND REGULATIONS. Each school committee is authorized to adopt rules and regulations for carrying into effect the provisions of sections 128 to 134, inclusive, and to make such arrangement with the respective persons in charge of the several denominations for the giving of the aforesaid moral instruction.

Sec. 131. CREDIT FOR TIME SPENT AT PLACES OF WORSHIP. Pupils attending their several places of worship for moral instruction therein at the time specified and for the period fixed shall be credited with the time so spent as if such pupils had been in actual attendance at school.

Sec. 132. CHILDREN TO REMAIN IN SCHOOL OR BE PRESENT AT PLACE OF WORSHIP. Any child which, for any reason fails to receive the aforesaid moral instruction, shall remain in school during the period when such instruction is being given as herein provided, but such child shall not receive any educational advantage over children receiving such instruction.

Sec. 133. EXPENSE. The aforesaid moral instruction shall be given without expense to any city or town, the pupils of which receive such instruction, and no city or town, or the school committee thereof shall incur any expense for such instruction beyond the cost of the original survey, hereinbefore mentioned.

Sec. 134. INTENT. It is declared to be the intent of the legislature that the provisions of sections 128 to 134 inclusive, shall be permissive and not mandatory.[249]

After declaring that no student or teacher in the public schools shall ever be required to attend any religious service, Colorado adds that "no sectarian tenets or doctrines shall ever be taught in the public schools, nor shall any distinction or classification of pupils be made on account of race or color."[250]

The state of Kentucky has provisions for moral instruction quite similar to those of Maine. It likewise provides for the reading of the Bible, and in a court decision has declared that "the Bible is not a sectarian book and the reading thereof does not constitute sectarian instruction."[251] Kentucky stipulates also that "no book or other publication of a sectarian, infidel or immoral character, or that reflects on

---

[249] School Laws of Maine, *op. cit.*, under "Maine," I, p. 16.

[250] Constitutional provisions, article 9, sec. 8, in Huston, under "Colorado," I, p. 9.

[251] *Hacket* v. *Brooksville*, 120 Ky. 608, in Huston, under "Kentucky," I, p. 18.

any religious denomination, shall be used or distributed in any common school."[252]

Arab countries commonly provide religious instruction in their public institutions of education. That this instruction is for the most part quite extensive may be seen from the following table.[253] The numbers indicate the hours per week during which religion is taught for the first nine years of a child's education.

	First	Second	Third	Fourth	Fifth	Sixth	Seventh	Eighth	Ninth
Egypt	2	2	4	4	3	3	2	2	1
Iraq	4	4	3	3	2	2	1	1	1
Syria	4	4	4	3	3	1	1	1	1
Jordan	4	5	5	4	4	4	3	0	0
Lebanon	1	1	1	1	1	1	1	1	1

The religion taught in these courses is that of the majority of the pupils in the school.[254] Those not belonging to that religion are exempted from the instruction.

Iraq provides free religious schools on the elementary and secondary levels. Students likewise receive books and school supplies without charge and are given a monthly allowance.[255] On the elementary level Egypt provides classes in the Koran for the first and last hours of the school day.[256] Syria stipulates that "religious instruction for each religion in accordance with its faith shall be compulsory in primary and secondary stages." No distinction is made between the public and private schools in this matter.[257]

The religious instruction in the public schools of New South Wales, Australia, is put on the same footing as other subjects, "and when the school is inspected each year, the nature of the instruction in Scripture

[252] Sec. 158–190, *ibid*.

[253] This table is taken from Sati el Hussri, "Arab Countries," *The Yearbook of Education, 1951*, ed. J. A. Lauwerys and N. Hans, p. 599.

[254] The reader will note the frequency with which this arrangement occurs both in predominantly Christian and predominantly non-Christian countries.

[255] Regulation No. 45 of 1942, U.N.Y. for 1952, p. 137.

[256] *Elementary Education Act of 1951*, U.N.Y. for 1951, p. 81.

[257] *Constitution of Syria*, Sept. 5, 1950, article 28, U.N.Y. for 1950, p. 282.

is carefully tested by the inspectors."[258] All teachers of whatsoever creed are required to teach these Scripture lessons but they may not enter into questions of dispute. Parents may withdraw their children from this instruction if they so choose. Queensland has similar provisions, while the other states (with one exception) allow Bible reading and/or the telling of Bible stories. The state of Victoria forbids any but secular instruction in its public schools. This last state, however, along with most of the other states has in its schools a well-organized system of instruction given by clergymen and visiting teachers.

It may be seen, therefore, that most of Australia provides a twofold program of religious instruction in its schools, a general one conducted by teachers, and a special one offered by visiting instructors.[259]

The Province of Quebec in Canada affords an interesting and seemingly successful picture of denominational public schools.[260] This province, which is ninety per cent Catholic and eighty-five per cent French speaking, provides two systems of public schools, one for the Catholic majority and one for the Protestant minority. Each system is governed by a committee representing both the civil government and the religious group. Supervising the whole educational effort of the province is a civil department of education. The schools are financed by public tax money and the religion of each group is taught in its schools. We are told that "such public financing of denominational education gives satisfaction to all and has brought a century of peace between the two groups."[261]

Ceylon stipulates that "instruction in the religion of the parent of each pupil in a Government school shall be given to that pupil, as a part of his course of studies in the school, by a person who is an adherent of that religion and who has been approved by the Director."[262] Indonesia likewise makes provision for religious instruction during school hours and in accordance with parents' wishes.[263] In

---

[258] George S. Browne, "Australia," *Educational Yearbook, 1932,* ed. I. L. Kandel, p. 9.

[259] We have already mentioned the favor with which this plan has been received by Australian parents. See above, p. 146, footnote 210.

[260] We have previously cited Quebec during our discussion of distributive justice in education, since this present plan bears on that question also.

[261] Bilodeau, "Canada," *The Yearbook of Education, 1951,* p. 397.

[262] Education Ordinance of 1947 found in K. Nesiah, "Ceylon," *The Yearbook of Education, 1951,* p. 588.

[263] *Provisional Constitution of the Republic of Indonesia,* Aug. 15, 1950, article 41, U.N.Y. for 1950, p. 155.

Belgium's secondary schools religion classes are held twice a week. Pupils excused from these classes take instead a course in morality.[264]

Brazil requires religion as a part of its public school program and stipulates that it shall be given according to the convictions of the student: "Religious instruction shall be a part of the teaching schedule of official schools, matriculation therein shall be optional, and shall be administered in accordance with the religious confession of the pupil, manifested by him, if he is capable, or by his legal representative or person responsible for him."[265] The state of Rio de Janeiro in Brazil images the country's policy by providing that optional religious instruction shall be included in the public school curriculum and that it shall be in accordance with the religion of the pupil.[266]

Panama has the simple stipulation that since the Catholic religion is that of the majority of its citizens, that religion "will be taught in the public schools, but learning it and attendance at acts of religious worship will not be obligatory for the pupils, when their parents or guardians so request."[267]

The public system of education provided by the Federal Republic of Germany is unique in its attempt to meet the preferences of all parents within its boundaries. The school system is set up in the constitution:

Article 12.   1. The elementary schools comprise denominational schools (Bekenntnisschulen), interdenominational schools (Gemeinschaftsschulen) and schools teaching certain systems of philosophy (Weltanschauungsschulen).

2. In the denominational schools, children of the Catholic or Protestant faith will be educated and instructed in the spirit of their creed.

In the interdenominational schools, children of different denominations will be educated and instructed on the basis of Christian educational and cultural values.

In the schools teaching certain systems of philosophy, which expression includes undenominational (bekenntnisfrei) schools, children will be educated and instructed in the spirit of the particular system of philosophy.

3. The parents or guardians of the children are entitled to choose

---

[264] Julius Hoste, "Belgium," *Educational Yearbook, 1944,* ed. I. L. Kandel, p. 27.

[265] *Constitution of the United States of Brazil,* Sept. 24, 1946, article 168. Peaslee, I, p. 212.

[266] *Constitution of the State of Rio de Janeiro,* June 20, 1947, article 149, U.N.Y. for 1948, p. 22.

[267] *Constitution of the Republic of Panama,* Mar. 1, 1946, article 36. Peaslee, II, p. 706.

the type of school to be attended by the children. Schools shall be established, in the manner to be prescribed by statute, in conformity with the provisions of paragraph 2 hereof at the request of the children's parents or guardians wherever the possibility of an ordered school organization exists. Even schools which do not provide a great variety of courses and which are not divided into classes shall, as a rule, be regarded as providing an ordered school organization.

4. Teachers must possess the personal and academic qualifications required by the nature of the school organization concerned.

Article 14.   1. Religious instruction shall be a regular part of the curriculum in all schools with the exception of schools teaching certain systems of philosophy (undenominational schools). Teachers imparting religious instruction must be authorized to do so by either the church or the religious society concerned. No teacher may be compelled to impart religious instruction.

2. Syllabuses and textbooks for religious instruction shall be determined by agreement with the church or religious society concerned.

3. Without prejudice to the State's right of supervision, the churches or religious societies shall be entitled, in a manner to be agreed upon with the education authorities, to inspect schools for the purpose of ensuring that religious instruction is being imparted in accordance with their teachings and requirements.

4. Exemption from religious instruction may be granted only if the parent or guardian or, when he has reached the age prescribed by law, the pupil himself, makes an application in writing for exemption from religious instruction.[268]

Summary observations: From our above survey of international practices dealing with the teaching of religion in public schools some rather noteworthy conclusions emerge. 1. The teaching of religion (not merely about religion) in publicly supported schools is a common practice among the nations of the world. These countries thus recognize the right of parents to be heard in the formation of the public school curriculum. 2. The teaching of religion in the public school is a common practice even in religiously pluralistic societies. 3. Among the free, democratic nations of the world the United States of America seems to be one of the few exceptions to the rule. 4. The various systems adopted for the teaching of religion in public institutions seem on the whole to work out well. Available evidence points to the fact that the great majority of parents favor the teaching of religion in their state

---

[268] *Constitution of North-Rhine-Westphalia,* June 28, 1950, U.N.Y. for 1950, pp. 101–102.

schools and enthusiastically avail themselves of the program when it is available. 5. The fears and obstacles to religious instruction in the public schools of the United States so often alleged by American secularists are shown to be vain and for the most part baseless. One may not raise up phantoms to counteract fact.

Religious Garb

Somewhat related to our present discussion is the further question of whether or not a government may exclude from its schools a teacher wearing a religious garb when that teacher belongs to a church different from that of some of the pupils. It seems to me that while a religious garb does not teach a particular religion, it is likely to create an atmosphere favorable to that religion. The two possibilities are quite different. Yet even in the latter case whether or not a nun causes a favorable reaction to her Church depends not on her habit but on the nun herself. If she were of unpleasant disposition an unfavorable reaction would likely follow.

In this connection Kentucky's Court of Appeals upheld in a 6–1 decision the right of sisters wearing their habits to teach in the public schools of the state. The opinion of the court, written by Judge Porter Sims, stated that Kentucky law had "not yet prescribed what dress a woman teaching in the public schools should wear, or whether she may adorn herself with a ring, button or other emblem signifying she is a member of a sorority." The court further said that the garb does not teach, but rather the woman within. "The dress of the Sisters denotes modesty, unworldliness and an unselfish life."[269]

CENTRALIZATION OF THE STATE EDUCATIONAL EFFORT

Closely related to our preceding discussion of the parents' influence in the public school is our present problem of centralization. We have already shown that the state does have a role to play in education, albeit a subsidiary and supplementary one. We now propose to discover on precisely what level of government ought that role to be played, national, regional, or local. Or, to put the question in other words, we might ask who among the vast army of civil servants ought to run the public schools. Should these schools be directed ultimately from one office or should there be many ultimate offices? Should the educational

---

[269] Brooklyn *Tablet*, Feb. 18, 1956, p. 3.

system of a nation be subjected to a single, centralized authority or should it be fanned out and subjected to many, decentralized authorities?

This problem can be settled (if it can be settled at all) on the basis of reason alone. Neither revelation nor the Church has said anything about the matter. The political philosopher must, therefore, judge the problem on the merit of the reasons alleged pro and con. As we might expect, there are two schools of thought, the one favoring centralization, the other favoring decentralization.

We will consider the former first. The reasons supporting the opinion that the work of public education be lodged ultimately in one, centralized, national authority are the following: (1) A centralized system of education enables the government to aid the financial disabilities of poorer areas more effectively. When education is financed and controlled by an impoverished local administration, it cannot pull itself up by its own boot straps and so remains inferior. (2) A unified educational system likewise aids the backward districts to progress in administrative techniques, instructional procedure, and teaching methodology. The local unit learns more easily from the larger. (3) Centralization makes it possible to keep standards uniformly high in all areas of a country. Salary schedules, working conditions for teachers, and building equipment may serve as examples of what we mean. (4) There is a reduction of administrative waste since there is less administration on the top level. (5) When a population tends to be mobile, a centralized system makes the transfer of pupils from one district to another easier.[270] This is so because administration is unified and standards tend to be more constant.

Before we delve into the reasons favoring decentralization, we might indicate the possibility of a middle ground, namely, a system that combines centralized and decentralized elements. Bestor, a professor of history at the University of Illinois, seems to favor some sort of regional centralization tempered by a local role. He feels that a local authority is, for example, a much more competent judge of a prospective teacher's personal teaching qualifications than is the distant official since the local authority enjoys a personal contact with the candidate. On the other hand, the regional office is a better judge of the teacher's subject competence since it can administer standardized tests and compare the

---

270 Counts mentions this as one of the reasons favoring centralization. *Op. cit.,* p. 56.

candidate's subject fitness with that of candidate's over a much wider area.[271]

Reasons militating against the centralization of the state's control over public education are the following: 1. The principle of subsidiarity to which we have referred so often is again applicable here. This guiding norm in the field of political science states that in the conduct of human affairs the private, the small, the local are not to be superseded by the public, the large, and the national unless necessity demands it. Applied to the state's educational function, subsidiarity means that a centralized arm of government ought not to undertake the work of education if that work can be done effectively by a local unit. Findlay referred to this point when he insisted on the right of the local community to conduct its own business until its inability to do so be proved.[272] 2. Cathrein observes that since the family has the natural law right to educate, when it cannot of itself build schools the duty does not devolve on the whole of society but on the local unit.[273] This is so because the local unit of government is closer to the family than is the national. He remarks further that if local units cannot or neglect to carry out their educational duty, the higher must discharge it.[274]

3. A governmental agency on the local level is better fitted to respond to parents' wishes and to safeguard their rights in the education of their children. This flows from the very nature of government. The more centralized it is, the less direct is the influence exercised by the individual citizen. The advantage of a decentralized system is clearly seen in those municipal boards of education that are selected by the votes of the parents themselves. There is a tendency under such an arrangement for the board members to be extremely sensitive to the desires of the voters.

4. Findlay points out several reasons for the Anglo-Saxon tendency to conduct education on a local level and they are reasons based on the political philosophy of the matter. (a) Children are first citizens of

---

[271] Arthur Bestor, *The Restoration of Learning* (New York: Alfred A. Knopf, 1955), p. 261.

[272] *Op. cit.*, I, pp. 129–130.

[273] *Op. cit.*, No. 660.

[274] *Ibid.*, No. 661. President Eisenhower recently said that education "should be under the control of the family and the locality. It should not be controlled by a central authority." To the White House Conference on Education, 1955, reported from *Human Events*, Dec. 24, 1955, in the Catholic Digest, XX (Mar., 1956), p. 30.

the local group before they are citizens of the nation at large. (*b*) The whole time they spend and the environment in which they spend it embrace the local community and its activities. One can notice especially in rural areas how oblivious the inhabitants seem to be of anything that does not concern immediately the locale itself. (*c*) The nourishment of the child's emotional and intellectual life derives chiefly from the neighborhood. (*d*) The child's health, recreation, and employment are interests especially of the local community.[275]

5. When government and the financial support of it are far removed from the local scene, people tend to demand more and more from state agencies, oblivious of the fact that in the end they must pay the bill.[276] In this way the citizen may contribute to the growth of bureaucracy and its attendant extravagance.[277]

6. Counts has rightly observed that a decentralized educational system cannot be radically and suddenly changed, since there is no one center through which all can be reached in an authoritative manner.[278] His reasoning is, of course, based on the premise that a sudden and radical change is seldom if ever desirable.

7. Independent and therefore decentralized systems of education can easily aid one another by competition, experiment, and the free circulation of diverse ideas. The uniformity introduced by centralization tends to decrease the effectiveness of these advantages.

While we favor the decentralization of public education and judge the reasons advanced in its behalf more firm, we do not think that those reasons demonstrate that every state system must be decentralized or that centralization is necessarily and always inferior to decentralization. One can easily imagine the conditions of a culture to be such that educational progress could be assured only by a strong unit of central authority. This would be true in a backward country that showed little interest in intellectual or moral improvement.

Instances both of centralization and decentralization can be found

---

[275] *Op. cit.,* pp. 130–131.

[276] This tendency has been noticeable in the United States during the long struggle to obtain federal aid for public education.

[277] Isaac Doughton, *op. cit.,* p. 433.

[278] *Op. cit.,* p. 54. While he has probably oversimplified the matter to some extent, the Jesuit sociologist, Joseph H. Fichter, points out some of the rigidity that can result from an overgoverned educational system. He supports the thesis that there is much less authoritarianism and uniformity in a typical parochial school than in a typical public school. See Joseph H. Fichter, "Parochial School Teacher," *Catholic World,* 185 (Apr., 1957), 51–55.

among the nations of the world. Among the former we can mention the systems of France, Indonesia, Turkey, and Hungary (Communist). Among the latter there are England, Canada, Netherlands, Japan, Finland, and the United States. The Union of South Africa and New Zealand occupy a middle position.

We are told that in France the administration of the school system is characterized by centralization. "All functionaries in the public school system are appointed by the minister and paid out of the general budget of the state."[279] The activities of the schools are controlled by delegates of the national minister of education.

According to a report I received from the Indonesian embassy in Washington, the centralization of public education in Indonesia is of the extreme variety. All institutions are administered directly by the Ministry of Education and there is no local control.[280] In Turkey teachers, administrators, and superintendents on all levels are appointed by the Ministry of Education.[281] In each province, however, there is a consultative committee which aims at exchanging information between schools and at standardizing local policies.[282] The Communist government of Hungary nationalized private schools in 1948.[283] Soviet Russia recently introduced a somewhat unusual centralized practice in its efforts to raise standards for the doctor's degree. In order to improve the quality of dissertation research, a Central Certification Commission consisting of seventy-seven members has been established to review all dissertations.[284]

The administration of South African education is both centralized and decentralized, for it is dual. On the one hand, there is the provincial system which administers primary, secondary, and teacher training education. On the other, there is the Union Government system which handles other educational activities, among which is higher education. We are told that

---

[279] No author, *France,* n.d., n.p., p. 144.

[280] "All public schools, including several universities, are administered directly by the Ministry of Education on a nation-wide basis, with no provision for local control." Letter from Alice E. Lovely, Educational and Cultural Assistant, Embassy of Indonesia, Washington, D. C., Nov. 5, 1954.

[281] Letter from Emin Hekimgil, Educational Attache, Turkish Embassy, New York City, Nov. 5, 1954.

[282] *Ibid.*

[283] Max Morris, *Hungary Builds a New Education,* 2nd ed. rev. (London: Hungarian News and Information Service, 1952), p. 3.

[284] *New York Times,* Oct. 14, 1956, p. L 9.

. . . there is an essential difference between the administrative system of South Africa and that of the other Dominions, like Canada and Australia, or that of the United States of America. In the first place, the powers of the four Provincial Councils in South Africa are distinctly limited. They are constituted parts of a union and *not of a federation,* and they are always subject to the "overriding power" of the Union Parliament. While certain definite powers and functions (the chief of these being primary and secondary education) were allocated to the provincial authorities by the Act of Union in 1910, they retain these powers at the pleasure of the Union Government, which may even abolish the Provincial Councils altogether if it finds such a measure expedient. Yet while there is nothing in the South African Constitution like, e.g., Section 93 of the Canadian Constitution, which stipulates that the provincial legislature "may *exclusively* make laws in relation to education in and for each province," the South African provincial authorities are in actual fact free from interference from the Union Government in dealing with those functions, e.g., primary and secondary education, etc., allocated to them by Article 85 of the Union Constitution.[285]

Since 1910 the Union Government has decided on a number of occasions that for the good of the nation it should step in and take over certain educational functions. "Thus, *industrial education, child welfare, agricultural education, vocational* and *technical education, special education,* etc., were by successive acts of legislation declared by the Minister to fall under 'higher education,' and so under the Union Government."[286]

While New Zealand like South Africa occupies a middle position in the centralization-decentralization issue, the trend in that country during the present century has been toward centralization. At the present time there are three levels of administration: the national Department of Education, the District Education Boards, and the School Committees. The Department of Education in Wellington has in recent years been given a greater control of the nation's educational system. At the present time we learn that the decentralized School Committee's

. . . primary function is the care of school buildings, grounds, and equipment, but, in addition to this, many interest themselves very

---

[285] Union of South Africa, *Education,* p. 1. Italics in the original.
[286] *Ibid.* Italics in the original.

keenly in the general activities of the school and provide in each district a focusing-point for local opinion on educational matters.[287]

At the same time, the next level of administration, the District Education Boards

. . . are still the initiating bodies on matters of buildings, sites, conveyance of pupils, consolidation, and provision of school facilities generally; and, although the final word often lies with the Minister of Education or the Department, the Boards have no small influence in the fixing of policy within their districts. The schools are legally their schools and the teachers their teachers, and, although in general the Board's choices of applicants are limited by the (national) grading system, they have much more discretion in the selection of applicants for special or key positions. The teachers' class-room activities are under the control of the Inspectors, but their general responsibility is to the Boards, and their professional life tends to centre on the Boards rather than on the Department. In spite of the apparent clumsiness of the administrative structure and of periods of strong feeling in the past, the system at present functions remarkably smoothly, and has achieved a balance, workable if not ideal, between the claims of local initiative and national efficiency.[288]

We may proceed now to state systems of education that are notable for their decentralization.

Even though its educational system is decentralized, England does have a national Ministry of Education with a political head, the Minister of Education. This minister has the authority to establish a national policy for education, but neither he nor his department owns, operates, or controls any kind of school. These latter functions are executed by the Local Education Authorities, local governing bodies to whom many services other than education are entrusted. Each L.E.A. (their popular term of reference) selects an education committee and to it commits the supervision of education.[289] However, when even these divisions are too large to care for local circumstances and problems, provision is made for them to delegate certain duties to divisional executives who are usually responsible for an area of at least 60,000 population.[290] As a result of this decentralization, the

[287] *Education in New Zealand*, no author, mimeographed. Sent to me by the New Zealand Embassy, Washington, D. C., under date of Nov. 8, 1954, p. 2.
[288] *Ibid.*
[289] British Information Services, *Education in Great Britain*, pp. 7–8.
[290] *Ibid.*, p. 8.

educational system of England enjoys a large measure of freedom for local initiative.[291]

Canada's control over its educational system closely resembles that of the United States. The Dominion Government provides directly for education only in the case of those persons not directly under the jurisdiction of any one of the provinces, such as those in the Yukon Territory. It also grants subsidies for special kinds of training.[292] Decentralization in the Netherlands is exemplified by the right of parents to control the spiritual and moral attitudes of teachers by recourse to local school boards. The teachers, however, are protected in case of controversy with the school board by another board of appeal, from which a final decision can be obtained.[293] Prewar Japan's educational endeavor was administered by the centralized Education Ministry, but since the war the power of this ministry has been transferred to local boards of education. The role of the Education Ministry at the present time is one of advice on specific questions.[294]

The educational philosophy of the United States has been one of decentralization from the very inception of its existence as an independent nation. The root of this philosophy is found in the constitution itself.[295] It is explicitly stated that any power not delegated to the Federal Government by the constitution nor prohibited by that constitution to the states is reserved to the states or to the people. Since education is given no notice in the constitution, it follows that care for this activity is withdrawn from one centralized source and committed to the individual states and/or the people.

As a consequence of this disposition the Federal Government has extremely little authority over American public education, while the prevailing philosophy looks upon the fifty states as the proper executors of the educational function. But the relationship between the state education office and the local school board varies widely

---

[291] "The central government does not own any school, employ any teacher, or prescribe the curriculum. The teachers are not civil servants; they are employed and paid by local authorities or by the governing bodies of their school. Head teachers are free within broad limits to organize their schools according to their own ideas, and the assistant teachers play a significant part in devising the syllabuses, choosing the textbooks and formulating the methods used in the school." *Ibid.,* p. 1.

[292] J. G. Althouse "Canada," *Educational Yearbook, 1944,* ed. I. L. Kandel, pp. 36–37.

[293] B. H. M. Vlekke, "Netherlands," *Educational Yearbook, 1944,* ed., I. L. Kandel, pp. 223–224.

[294] Ministry of Foreign Affairs, *Japan's Problems,* p. 35.

[295] Bill of Rights, article X.

throughout the country. In New York City the local school board is almost entirely subject to the local city government (e.g., the board is appointed by the mayor). In the larger cities of New Jersey, Massachusetts, Ohio, and Indiana the boards are independent of local government except for financial support. In other cities the school board is completely independent of local government and responsible directly to the state.[296]

The administration of the Finnish public school system is divided off into school districts, each of which is placed under a Folk School Committee. Within the district "the local administration of each school is managed by the Board of the Folk School, to which the Community Council has to elect six members, chiefly parents of the pupils."[297] In this last provision the influence of the parents in the school is obvious.

STATE PROVISION FOR EXCEPTIONAL CHILDREN

The legal meaning of the term, exceptional children, is often, if not exclusively, negative, that is, indicating some defect. The law of California, for example, understands by exceptional children those who are either mentally or physically handicapped.[298] Illinois includes also truant, incorrigible, or delinquent children under this same heading.[299] Here, however, we wish to be understood as including all children who differ from the average in a marked way, whether positively or negatively. We envision, therefore, the physically and mentally handicapped, the intellectually gifted, and those who are truant or delinquent.

About these children we wish to investigate whether or not the state has some kind of obligation to provide a special training, one that deviates from the training that is offered to the great mass of citizens. At first blush it might appear that the state has no extraordinary duty toward these children, that it suffices to offer them the usual, the common, the ordinary. We, however, take the position that the state may easily be obligated to take unusual, uncommon, and extraordinary

---

[296] Edgar L. Morphet, "Relationships of Education to Government," *Forty-fourth Yearbook of the National Society for the Study of Education*, Part II (Chicago: University of Chicago Press, 1945), p. 169.

[297] Niilo Kallio, *The School System of Finland*, p. 12.

[298] See *Education Code* of California, Sec. 7801, in Huston, *op. cit.*, under "California," *1953 State School Supplement*, I, p. 23.

[299] See Illinois law, Sec. 12–20, in Huston, under "Illinois," I, 23.

means to care for the needs of exceptional children.[300] Three reasons may be advanced in support of this thesis.

Every child has a right to the full development of whatever talents he possesses whether they be great or small. If that right is not honored by the family, the state as a subsidiary educator is bound to enter the picture and protect the child. In the case of physically or mentally deficient children the state must then provide the treatment and formation that will enable them to assume as useful a place in society as possible. For the unusually bright the state should offer an education that will challenge their abilities and bring them to full flower. On somewhat different grounds the state must protect the rights of the delinquent child by aiding him to learn to live a sound moral life. Those grounds are the obligation of fraternal correction.[301]

The common good of the community requires that all types of exceptional children receive adequate and therefore special attention. The state must, as a consequence, provide educational facilities for the deficient and the delinquent (when primary educators either do not or cannot provide them) lest they become unnecessary burdens to society. The gifted, on the other hand, are much more valuable to the community when their talents are explored to the full. When necessary, therefore, the state should provide these people with the complete means necessary for entire development when those means are otherwise lacking.

The prohibitive cost of the education for exceptional children — our third reason — is often unequal to the financial resources of the family including within its membership one such child. For this reason there is frequently even greater need for state supplementation here than in the usual case of the ordinary child.

The nations of the world recognize at least to some extent their obligation to provide for the peculiar needs of the unusual child.

The Union of South Africa reflects a common international practice in its provision of schools for the mentally retarded and the physically handicapped and of industrial institutions for the juvenile delinquent.[302] Romania runs special schools for the blind, the deaf

---

[300] In the philosophical discussion of this problem I cite no supporting (or opposing) authorities for I have met none in my investigations.

[301] The purpose of prisons is not merely to protect society, but also to rehabilitate the prisoner for his own good.

[302] W. F. Grant, "Union of South Africa," *Educational Yearbook, 1944*, ed. I. L. Kandel, pp. 301–302.

and the dumb.[303] England charges each Local Education Authority with the duty to provide for pupils suffering from any disability of mind or body. These children are to be cared for either in special schools or otherwise and they are to be treated by special methods appropriate for each disability.[304] The United States has an extensive program caring for over one-half million exceptional children, and yet over three times that number of children need special service and are not receiving it.[305]

For children on the upper levels of intelligence Luxembourg states that special funds for the education of gifted persons shall be established by law.[306] Brandenburg in Germany determines in its constitution that gifted pupils from all ranks of society shall be enabled to attend secondary and higher institutions of education.[307] Australia aids candidates for the higher reaches of schooling by awarding Commonwealth scholarships to successful applicants working at universities and other approved institutions.[308] The State of Piaui, Brazil, has established scholarships "for poor students of high intellectual ability and good character."[309] Italy provides that "capable and deserving students even if without means, have the right to attain the highest grades of education." Scholarships, grants, and other kinds of assistance are awarded through the results of competitive examinations.[310] Bolivia stipulates that it shall aid financially any capable student who, because of lack of means, cannot go on to higher educational levels.[311]

---

[303] *Education Reform Act*, Aug. 3, 1948, article 7, U.N.Y. for 1948, p. 180.

[304] *Education Act, 1944*, Part II, section 8.

[305] "There are about twenty-five thousand special teachers in the country today caring for over five hundred thousand exceptional children enrolled in local school systems." William F. Jenks, *op. cit.*, p. 21. Spain's provisions are described in *Fifteen Years of Spanish Culture*, Diplomatic Information Office, pp. 98–99.

[306] *Constitution of the Grand Duchy of Luxembourg*, Oct. 17, 1863, article 23 (as amended May 21, 1948), U.N.Y. for 1948, p. 142.

[307] *Constitution of the Mark Brandenburg*, Feb. 6, 1947, article 59, U.N.Y. for 1948, p. 75.

[308] *Education Act of 1945*, U.N.Y. for 1951, p. 6.

[309] *Constitution of the State of Piaui*, Aug. 22, 1947, article 141, U.N.Y. for 1948, p. 20.

[310] *Constitution of the Italian Republic*, Jan. 1, 1948, article 34. Peaslee, II, p. 283.

[311] *Political Constitution of the Bolivian State*, Nov. 23, 1945, article 154. Peaslee, I, p. 173. Governmentally sponsored scholarships are becoming increasingly more popular in the United States. See, for example, Theresa Birch Wilkins, "New State Scholarship Programs in California and New York," *Higher Education*, XIII (Oct., 1956), 25–26.

ACADEMIC FREEDOM FROM STATE-IMPOSED INSTRUCTION

Academic freedom as it is viewed in the many and often acrimonious debates that center upon it usually turns about two persons, the teacher and the student, the latter being frequently neglected in these debates in favor of the former. Educational freedom for the teacher involves his right to seek and speak truth wherever he may find it. For the student this same freedom insures his right to be given *reality:* certain truth as certain and probable opinion as probable. We do not propose to detail here the nature and limits of academic freedom,[312] but merely to indicate at what point the state must desist from enforcing a doctrine or policy on the teacher or the school, public or private.

As we have already seen, the state is a teacher, neither by definition nor by nature, but merely by way of supplementation. More obvious still, the state is not an inviolable source of truth. It lacks both omniscience and infallibility. Admittedly, therefore, the state possesses no right to impose a teaching on its own naked authority.

Whatever function the state does have in the realm of truth and error it has in virtue of its double purpose: to protect and foster the common good of society. On this ground the state is competent and here it may function. In outlining this function we will first indicate negatively what the state may not do: (1) The state may not impose any doctrine that conflicts with any certainly known truth, whether that truth be religious, historical, philosophical, or scientific. (2) It may not impose a teaching which, while true, is either dangerous or useless. Such would be, for example, a public exposition of the complete physiology of sex for the very young. (3) It may not teach revealed religion.[313] God has committed to His one Church the single authority to teach His revealed truth. The state is therefore incompetent in the matter. (4) It may not demand that mere opinions be taught as fact. Rudimentary honesty reprobates the practice in any person or institution, public or private. (5) The state, finally, may not

---

[312] For a general discussion of academic freedom the reader may consult Daniel C. Sullivan, "Freedom and Education," *Concept of Freedom,* ed. Carl W. Grindel (Chicago: Henry Regnery Co., 1955), pp. 363–389.

[313] We specify *revealed* of set purpose. There could conceivably exist a situation in which the community knew natural religion alone and for which situation the state would be the sole central authority capable of organizing instruction in that religion.

forbid the teaching of any truth, religious, historical, philosophical, or scientific unless that teaching be harmful to the common good. We may add that the fulfillment of this condition would be extremely rare. It goes without saying, of course, that the state may never substitute a lie for the truth, not even if the common good would seem to benefit by the substitution. A good end never justifies a bad means.

Positively, the state may promote the common good in the realm of truth and error in the following ways: (1) It may (and sometimes must) proscribe errors known with certitude to be errors. A government would not manifestly proscribe every error that sees the light of day, but only those that may work notable harm on society. (2) The state may proscribe any teaching that is genuinely and honestly dangerous to public order and sound morality. (3) In the schools of the nation the state may require that certain subjects necessary or beneficial to the general welfare be taught. Such may be, for example, civic duties, the rudiments of reading and writing, and the use and abuse of alcohol and narcotics. This point raises the question of compulsory education, a question we shall discuss in the next chapter.

Among the nations of the world it is common knowledge that Communist-dominated countries sin against almost every one of the above norms. We may even say that the torture of truth and the denial of academic freedom are among the most obvious characteristics of the whole Communist movement.

Most of the other nations, however, both profess and for the most part, demonstrate in fact a devotion to the principles of intellectual honesty and liberty. The constitution of Nicaragua declares that the government guarantees academic freedom as long as there is no violation of good morals and public order.[314] Japan, which before World War II exercised a state inspired thought control, now asserts in its new constitution that "academic freedom is guaranteed."[315] Panama provides that the "freedom of the lecture-room is recognized without limitations other than those established by the university statute for reasons of public order."[316] Costa Rica approaches the problem from the point of view of censorship: "Every one can communicate

---

[314] *Constitution of the Republic of Nicaragua,* Jan. 21, 1948, article 91. Peaslee, II, p. 644.

[315] *Constitution of Japan,* Nov. 3, 1946, article 23. Peaslee, II, p. 309.

[316] *Constitution of the Republic of Panama,* Mar. 1, 1946, article 88. Peaslee, II, p. 712.

his thoughts by word or writing and publish them by means of the press, without previous censorship, being responsible for abuses committed in the exercise of this right in the cases and manner which may be established by the law."[317]

Some nations offer specific restrictions. Lebanon allows in private schools no textbooks other than governmentally approved ones for the teaching of Lebanese history, geography, civics, and government.[318] The state of Alabama provides that no book may be used in the public schools of the state unless it carries a clear statement by the publisher or author that the latter is or is not a supporter of Communism or a member or ex-member of the Communist party or of a Communist front organization.[319] Iran stipulates that "all publications, except heretical works containing matter harmful to the religion of Islam, are free, and it is forbidden to make distinction between them." If anything at variance with the law is found in a book the publisher or author is punished.[320]

---

[317] *Political Constitution of Costa Rica,* Dec. 7, 1871, as amended, article 37. Peaslee, I, p. 506.

[318] Decree of May 23, 1950, U.N.Y. for 1950, p. 187.

[319] Act No. 888, sec. 1, "1954 State School Supplement," in Huston, under "Alabama," I, 1.

[320] *Iranian Constitutional Law,* Oct. 8, 1907, article 20. Peaslee, II, p. 207.

CHAPTER XI

THE STATE AND THE TEACHING OF MORALITY

THE problem we envision here is closely related to, but not identical with the problem of the state's relationship to the teaching of religion. While there are those who confuse the term, "moral values," with "religious values," we wish to be understood here as clearly differentiating the two. A religious truth is a proposition, naturally known or divinely revealed, enunciating a judgment about God, man, or a relationship between the two. A moral truth is likewise a proposition, but it deals with activity, the way man ought or ought not to act in order to fulfill the implications planted in his nature and in order to reach his supernatural end.

We have already discussed in detail the relationship of the state to the teaching of religion. We now wish to explore its relationship to the teaching of morality.

Since the state is not by definition a teacher, it is not by definition a teacher of morality. If the state has any function in the imparting of morality that function will have to flow from the nature and end of the state as a state, which is to say from its obligation to provide for the temporal common good of the community. The society which is by definition a teacher, and a teacher of morality, is the Catholic Church. She has been divinely authorized and commissioned to teach morality as well as religion: "Go, therefore, and make disciples of all nations . . . teaching them to observe all that I have commanded you. . . ."[321]

Pope Leo XIII was clear on this point. The Catholic Church, he

[321] Mt. 28:19-20.

said, "is the true and sole teacher of virtue and guardian of morals."[322] And further "it is the Church, and not the State, that is to be man's guide to heaven."[323] This does not mean, however, that the Catholic Church envisions herself as having a complete monopoly on moral truth. Pope Pius XI highly praised the words of Manzoni when he (the latter) explained that the Church in making statements such as those cited above by Leo XIII does not mean that she alone possesses morality but rather that she possesses it entirely. The Catholic Church has never maintained that those outside her fold cannot reach any moral truth, but rather that she alone possesses and can never lose the whole of moral truth committed to her by God Himself.[324] This, of course, flows from what we said in Chapter V about the Church's directly received commission to teach, a commission deriving from Christ Himself.

The state, nonetheless, does have a role in the teaching of morality, and it is a role that stems both from its end and from its subsidiary nature. From its duty to preserve the community from harm issues the state's obligation to prevent the teaching of immorality when that teaching tends to harm the common good. Van der Aa observes that since the state is not infallible, it may suppress a teaching only when that teaching is obviously false or when from experienced effects it is shown to be harmful.[325] Cathrein concurs with this opinion.[326]

The state's second function in the teaching of morality is the protection and supplementation of the primary educators in their efforts to impart sound morals. This protection and supplementation as applied

---

[322] *Immortale Dei,* Nov. 1, 1885, no ed., *The Great Encyclical Letters of Pope Leo XIII* (New York: Benziger Bros., 1903), p. 124.

[323] *Ibid.,* p. 113.

[324] *Christian Education of Youth,* pp. 8–9. In this connection Valton remarks that "il faut observer en outre que, dans les rapports juridiques de l'Etat avec la famille, il ne peut etre question que de l'education physique et intellectuelle des enfants; car, pour ce qui regarde l'education morale, et surtout l'education religieuse, la mission de suppleer la famille, et meme de la diriger dans l'accomplissement de ses devoirs, est devolue a une autre societe parfaite, en vertu d'une vocation special et d'un droit predominant: cette societe est l'Eglise." E. Valton, "Etat," *Dictionnaire de Theologie Catholique,* ed. A. Vacant and E. Mangenot, V (1913), 896.

[325] "Quum auctoritas civilis infallibilis non est eos solos errores prohibere potest, qui vel evidenter omnibus ex ipsa ratione appareant esse falsa doctrina, ac proinde nociva intellectibus, vel ex effectibus practicis clara experientia deprehendantur exitiales esse." Quoted in "State Control and Relative Rights in the School," no author, *American Ecclesiastical Review,* VI (Apr., 1892), 301.

[326] "In ordine *naturali* auctoritas civilis habet ius et officium impediendi, ne doctrinae legi naturali aperte contrariae et perniciosae publice doceantur." *Op. cit.,* No. 678.

to private education occasions no problem, for the same principles we discussed above in connection with religion in private institutions are pertinent here. The teaching of morality in state schools, however, is a more complex question.

It would seem that the state has a free hand in the teaching of morality, since much of morality is based on mere natural law and on the natural plane the state is competent. This same conclusion seems to issue from the fact that since the state may do whatever is necessary for the common good of society, it may teach morality, for a knowledge of right and wrong is essential to the common good. We may note, finally, that the state may instruct in civil duties, and yet civil duties are nothing but a part of the moral code. From these three considerations it would seem to follow that the state is in its own right a teacher of morality.

Such, however, is not the case. From these observations we may conclude that the state is on occasion *a* teacher of morality, not that it is the ultimate teacher. We may conclude that the state may teach morality in some instances, not that it may teach in all. We have already noted that the state is not by definition a teacher of morality and that it is certainly not an infallible teacher. When the state, therefore, teaches in the field of right and wrong it teaches dependently, namely, on one who *is* a teacher by definition and mission, an infallible teacher, the Church.

In its own public schools the state not only may but must provide for instruction in morality. As we have already pointed out, this obligation flows from the necessity of moral formation in the citizen for the preservation of peace and prosperity in society.[327]

It seems obvious that this instruction in right and wrong cannot be separated from religion if any appreciable result is to be expected.[328] In June of 1954 Senator Robert C. Hendrickson reported to the Congress of the United States on the results of a survey questionnaire sent out to approximately 2500 high school students and 1000 college students. The futility of our present religionless morality in the public

---

[327] See Gredt, *op. cit.,* II, No. 1044. Bishop Buddy of San Diego has issued a strong plea for the introduction of courses in natural law morality into the public schools. These courses he would have based on the natural philosophy of God and taught by specially trained public school teachers. Nowhere does he make mention of clergymen entering the schools. See Charles F. Buddy, "Bring the Ten Commandments Back into the Schools," *America,* XCIII (Sept. 24, 1955), 613–615.

[328] We touched upon this point above, pp. 149–150.

school is suggested by some of the evidence adduced. "Three-fourths of the 3,500 students polled did not think it wrong to lie or cheat; twelve per cent saw nothing wrong in stealing, nine per cent in committing robbery, fifteen per cent in destroying property, and seventeen per cent in indulging in sex relations."[329]

The necessity of religion as the base and end of instruction in morality is further illustrated by the fact that the very obligations bound up in the practice of religion are the most important part of morality itself. A man is not a moral man by the mere observance of the golden rule. Each attempt to instruct in right and wrong without reference to religion will at best issue in a truncated morality.[330]

The final competency of the state in the field of instruction in morality is its obligation to teach civic duty to the citizenry. Pope Pius XI has pointed this out and at the same time indicated that the state can require a minimum knowledge both of civic duty and of morality.[331]

Because legal citations here would be so similar to, and sometimes identical with those we have already reviewed in connection with religious instruction, we see no usefulness served by introducing contemporary international practices illustrating the teaching of morality in private and public education.

---

[329] Aloisius J. Muench, "Religion in Education," *Social Justice Review*, XLVIII (July–Aug., 1955), 141.

[330] Cavagnis, *op. cit.*, p. 157. The obligation, for example, to worship God according to the manner which He has stipulated is at one and the same time an affair of religion and of morality.

[331] "The state can exact, and take measures to secure that all its citizens have the necessary knowledge of their civic and political duties, and a certain degree of physical, intellectual and moral culture, which, considering the conditions of our times, is really necessary for the common good." *Christian Education of Youth*, p. 17.

EDUCATIONAL DUTIES OF THE STATE TOWARD ITSELF AND THE WORLD

In Part I we explored philosophically the nature of the state and its function as a state; in Part II we extended our investigation to a general consideration of the state as educator; in Part III we detailed our investigation by studying the state's educational relationships to the Church and to the family. In this present Part IV we wish to complete our work by a detailed analysis of the state's educational duties toward the third agency of education, itself, and toward the community of nations as a whole.

CHAPTER XII

THE STATE'S DUTIES TOWARD ITSELF

CIVIC EDUCATION OF THE POPULACE

EVERY government for its own well-being and that of its people must see to the adequate dissemination of civil information among all classes and age groups. That this obligation rests directly upon the state is easily seen upon consideration of the fact that matters civic stem immediately from the *civitas,* the state or government.[1]

Under the caption of civic information we would include a general knowledge of one's country, its form of government, and some grasp of its history. Included also would be civil rights and duties. Among the former can be mentioned the more important forms of legal protection and the rights to vote, trial, and freedom from search. Examples of civic duties would be the obligation to co-operate in a war effort and to know the laws of the land.

For illustrations of the discharge of this educational duty by the nations of the world we refer the reader to other sections of this study. Governments commonly carry out their programs of civic instruction through curriculum requirements in public and private schools and

---

[1] In his encyclical on education Pope Pius XI devoted a surprising amount of space to this function of the state: "In general also it belongs to civil society and the State to provide what may be called civic education, not only for its youth, but for all ages and classes. This consists in the practice of presenting publicly to groups of individuals information having an intellectual, imaginative and emotional appeal, calculated to draw their wills to what is upright and honest, and to urge its practice by a sort of moral compulsion, positively by disseminating such knowledge and negatively by suppressing what is opposed to it. This civic education, so wide and varied in itself as to include almost every activity of the State intended for the public good, ought also to be regulated by the norms of rectitude. . . ." Pp. 18–19.

through programs of adult education. In many countries much of this instruction is cared for in newspapers and magazines.

EDUCATION FOR GOVERNMENT SERVICES

The common welfare of any community requires that those to whom the government of that community is committed be well trained for the efficient performance of their various tasks. In a modern, highly complex state the vast diversity of offices and specialized services often render necessary separate schools for the education of government employees. We do not envision here the general, liberal arts education that is basic to any well-formed individual, but rather the specialized instruction, sometimes professional, that is needed for a particular class of jobs. Such would be, for example, schools for the training of policemen, diplomats, or forest rangers.

That the state has a right and duty to establish and operate such schools is, of course, beyond the pale of discussion. Just as any private employer has the full right to instruct his apprentice employee in the skills requisite for his job, so also may a government instruct its employees in the knowledge and skills needed for their charges. Pope Pius XI explicitly mentions this right in his encyclical on education.[2]

For the protection of a nation's integrity the government may likewise reserve to itself the establishment and operation of military schools for the training of officers and training camps for the formation of army, navy, and air force personnel. Not only does the common good of the country require these educational institutions, but the individual welfare of the soldier or sailor also requires them. Modern warfare is dangerous enough for the well-trained combatant; for the poorly trained it is almost suicide. Pope Pius XI refers to this governmental right also but at the same time cautions against an exaggerated nationalism in the execution of it. He condemns unwarranted violence and an exaltation of athleticism sometimes found in military training and points out that because of a false nationalism an excess is some-

---

[2] "This (educational monopoly) does not prevent the State from making due provision for the right administration of public affairs and for the protection of its peace, within or without the realm. These are things which directly concern the public good and call for special aptitudes and special preparation. The State may therefore reserve to itself the establishment and direction of schools intended to prepare for certain civic duties. . . ." P. 18. González spotlights the Holy Father's expression, "may reserve to itself," by pointing out that the state's right here is exclusive. *Op. cit.*, p. 811.

times present in giving a military turn to the physical training of boys and girls.[3]

For purposes of illustration we may view some of the governmental service schools maintained by the United States. Among the better known institutions are the United States Coast Guard Academy, New London, Connecticut; the United States Department of Agriculture Graduate School, Washington, D. C.; the United States Merchant Marine Academy, Kings Point, New York; the United States Military Academy, West Point, New York; the United States Naval Academy, Annapolis, Maryland; the United States Postgraduate School, Monterey, California;[4] the United States Air Force Academy, Denver, Colorado; and the Federal Bureau of Investigation Training Academy, Quantico, Virginia, and Washington, D. C.[5]

The magnitude of modern military educational enterprises may be glimpsed from a partial listing of institutions maintained by the Army of the United States:

> The Adjutant General's School, U. S. Army, Ft. Benjamin
> Harrison, Ind.
> The Armor School, Ft. Knox, Ky.
> The Army Medical Service School, Ft. Sam Houston, Tex.
> The Army War College, Carlisle Barracks, Pa.
> The Finance School, U. S. Army, Ft. Benjamin Harrison, Ind.
> The Infantry School, Ft. Benning, Ga.
> The Signal School, Ft. Monmouth, N. J.
> The U. S. Army Air Defense School, Ft. Bliss, Tex.
> The U. S. Army Artillery and Missile School, Ft. Sill, Okla.
> The U. S. Army Aviation School, Ft. Rucker, Ala.
> The U. S. Army Chemical Corps School, Ft. McClellan, Ala.
> The U. S. Army Cold Weather and Mountain School, Ft.
> Greely, Alaska
> The U. S. Army Command and General Staff College, Ft.
> Leavenworth, Kans.
> The U. S. Army Engineer School, Ft. Belvoir, Va.
> The U. S. Army Intelligence School, Ft. Holabird, Md.
> The U. S. Army Language School, Praesidio, Calif.
> The U. S. Army Ordnance School, Aberdeen Proving Ground, Md.
> The U. S. Army Primary Helicopter School, Camp Wolters, Tex.
> The U. S. Army Quartermaster School, Ft. Lee, Va.

---

[3] *Ibid.*

[4] *The World Almanac*, ed. Harry Hansen (New York: New York World-Telegram, 1955), p. 460.   [5] *Ibid.*, p. 308.

The U. S. Army Special Warfare School, Ft. Bragg, N. C.
The U. S. Army Transportation School, Ft. Eustis, Va.
The U. S. Army Women's Corps School, Ft. McClellan, Ala.
The Walter Reed Army Institute of Research, Washington, D. C.[6]

Other nations, of course, sponsor government service institutions, although they are not always as well developed as those in the United States. Indonesia, for example, has a University for Police Science, a Flying Academy, and an Academy for Foreign Affairs.[7] The Netherlands has institutions for training in foreign trade and diplomacy, the military sciences, and tax administration.[8]

ADULT EDUCATION

In view of what we have said in the first section of this chapter, it is clear that the state does have some sort of obligation in the field of adult education. But since there are so many areas of knowledge that can be either useful or necessary for an uneducated adult, it is impossible to determine before concrete circumstances are considered just where and when the state is obliged to furnish instruction. As a general guide, however, we may observe that whenever the common welfare of the community requires that the adult population or a notable section of it be given information of some kind, the government is bound to provide it. Such might be, for example, methodology in agriculture or preventive measures to be taken during a plague.

Programs in adult education are common among the nations of the world. The Nationalist Republic of China provides in its constitution that "all citizens beyond school age who have not received primary education shall receive supplementary education free, and shall also be supplied with textbooks by the government."[9] Cuba in 1950 embarked on an ambitious anti-illiteracy program embracing schools for adults literacy centers, volunteers giving literacy training, traveling teachers literacy societies, extracurricular activities, and night schools.[10] The Federal Republic of Germany encourages adult education and assure recognition of interest in adult education on the part of the churche

---

[6] The Army School Catalogue, DA Pam. 20–21 (Washington, D. C.: Department of the Army, 1957), pp. 583–599.

[7] Ministry of Information, *Basic Information on Indonesia,* p. 160.

[8] Idenburg, *Education in the Netherlands,* pp. 104–105.

[9] *Constitution of the Republic of China,* Dec. 25, 1947, article 160. Peaslee, I, p. 460

[10] Decree No. 1087 of Mar. 7, 1950, Chapters III–IV and Decree No. 2556 of Aug 21, 1950, U.N.Y. for 1951, pp. 55–57.

and other private agencies.[11] Norway supports a system of "folk high schools," both public and private, aimed at aiding adult education especially in the rural areas of the country.[12] Panama provides that "the State . . . will maintain a system of gratuitous complementary courses for adults, with the purpose of preventing and eliminating illiteracy and increasing the practical capacities of the working classes."[13]

REHABILITATION OF PRISONERS

An extremely specialized sort of education and perhaps the most difficult of all formational duties that lie upon the state is the re-education of criminals to a life useful to themselves and to society. There is, of course, not the least doubt that the state has not only a right but also a duty to rehabilitate its prison inmates. We may even say that the state has in this province a singular right and duty, for the incarcerated are of all citizens most removed from the possible influence and help of private enterprise. If they are to be reformed and reinstructed, it is the state that must to a large extent provide for that reforming and reinstructing.

Among criminologists the function of the prison has been conceived as threefold: protective for society, punitive for the criminal, and rehabilitative for the criminal. St. Thomas More was among the first to point out that prevention and education for the criminal were of greater importance than mere punishment.[14] During the past century much stress has been placed on the need for individualized study and care suited to the particular needs of each prisoner.[15] To carry out this new approach modern states must lean in their thinking toward greater emphasis on the educational and rehabilitating aspects of their corrective institutions.

Such seems to be the actual trend in today's prisons. Many nations have followed the lead of Belgium and Argentina and have established

---

[11] *Constitution of North-Rhine-Westphalia*, June 28, 1950, article 17, U.N.Y. for 1950, p. 102.

[12] Olaf Devik, "Norway," *Educational Yearbook, 1944*, ed. I. L. Kandel, pp. 258–259.

[13] *Constitution of the Republic of Panama*, Mar. 1, 1946, article 90. Peaslee, II, p. 712.

[14] Melvin J. Williams, *Catholic Social Thought* (New York: The Ronald Press, 1950), p. 373. Williams is not a Catholic.

[15] See "Prison," *Encyclopaedia Britannica*, XVIII (1951), 516; T. C. Clark, "Within Prison Walls," *Sign*, XXV (July, 1946), 38.

prison clinics staffed by social workers, psychologists, and psychiatrists.[16] To carry out more effectively the work of rehabilitation, prison staffs are in many places being improved. The United States Penitentiary in Atlanta, Georgia, for example, now has trained social workers as warden's assistants. The prison boasts also a supervisor of education with two assistants, a staff of teachers, a trained librarian, medical and dental officers, a psychiatrist, women nurses and several part time consultants.[17] Nonetheless, the over-all prison educational outlook in the United States seems to be far from ideal.[18]

In some countries the state board of education co-operates with the penal agency in carrying out the rehabilitation program of the prison. The Idaho State Board of Education has such an arrangement with the State Board of Correction in providing courses of study and/or vocational training to state penitentiary prisoners.[19] Yugoslavia seeks to rehabilitate its criminals through industrial or agricultural labor and through cultural, educational, and gymnastic courses.[20]

PROMOTION OF CULTURE

Under the caption of culture we wish to include the sponsorship of museums and art galleries, the promotion of research, and the maintenance of libraries. These three categories of cultural endeavor obviously contribute profoundly to the furtherance of the common welfare

[16] Thorsten Sellin, "Penal Institutions," *Encyclopaedia of the Social Sciences*, XII (1942), 63.

[17] *Ibid.*, p. 61.

[18] "The instruction of prisoners has long been academic and vocational. Academic education has but rarely transcended the level of the elementary school, although here and there in the United States high school subjects are taught, particularly in institutions for juvenile delinquents; university extension or correspondence courses are available in a few institutions. The average adult prison school in the United States is improperly housed and is taught by untrained inmate teachers using textbooks designed for children; the schools of juvenile institutions, however, ordinarily reach adequate standards. Vocational training is at a higher level than academic instruction; in some institutions it is intimately bound up with industrial and agricultural activities. Prison libraries are frequently overloaded with inspirational and religious literature, and adequate library service is still absent in most institutions. Practically no provisions for education exist in jails for short term prisoners and in workhouses." *Ibid.*, pp. 62–63.

[19] Idaho school law, Sec. 33–115, in Huston, *op. cit.*, under "Idaho," "1953 School Supplement," I, 7.

[20] *Execution of Penalties, Security Measures and Corrective Training Measures Act,* Oct. 20, 1951, introductory note. See Part II, Chapter II, articles 53–57, U.N.Y. for 1951, pp. 409–413.

of society. While they can be and often are maintained by private enterprise, the prohibitive cost involved in their sponsorship frequently makes state initiative imperative.[21]

The nations of the world do, as a matter of fact, frequently provide, and even in their constitutions, for the preservation and development of national culture. Cuba is a typical example in that its constitution provides for the care of cultural, artistic, and historical treasures and for national monuments and spots of natural beauty.[22] To direct this work Cuba ordained that "a national council on education and culture shall be created, which under the chairmanship of the minister of education and culture shall be charged with developing, technically orienting, or inspecting the educational, scientific, and artistic activities of the Nation."[23] Turkey provides for the care of its museums, historical art treasures, rare documents, and art collection through a Department of Antiquities and Museums, a division in the Ministry of Education.[24] The Department of Education in Sweden has four bureaus, one of them being in charge of "universities, academies, museums, archives. . . ."[25]

The promotion of research is carried on in Pakistan by a special Department of Scientific and Industrial Research.[26] In its constitution the state of Rio de Janeiro (Brazil) states that it "shall encourage scientific research; it shall establish and maintain institutions for this purpose and assist private initiative by means of Government subsidies and protection."[27] The government of India has embarked on a far-reaching program for the development of research. It is improving and enlarging The Indian Institute of Technology in Kharagpur and the Indian Institute of Science in Bangalore. The Research Training

---

[21] John Stuart Mill long ago observed that since society as a whole benefits from the learning of the professional and scholarly class, the state should come to their aid with financial support when such is needed. *Op. cit.*, pp. 976–977.

[22] "The Nation shall regulate by law the conservation of the cultural treasures of the Nation, its artistic and historic wealth, and shall especially protect national monuments and places notable for their natural beauty or their acknowledged artistic or historic value." *Constitution of the Republic of Cuba*, July 5, 1940, article 58. Peaslee, I, p. 537.

[23] *Ibid.*, article 59.

[24] Sassani, *Education in Turkey*, pp. 77–79.

[25] Lindegren, *Education in Sweden*, p. 3.

[26] Brian Holmes, "United Kingdom," *The Year Book of Education, 1954*, ed. Robert King Hall, N. Hans, and J. A. Lauwerys, p. 388.

[27] *Constitution of the State of Rio de Janeiro*, June 20, 1947, article 151, U.N.Y. for 1948, p. 22.

Scholarship Scheme, begun in 1949, is furnishing several hundred scholarships to qualified research workers. Grants of money have been given to universities to enable them to increase research personnel and facilities and to inaugurate postgraduate departments where they do not exist.[28]

Some countries provide in their law for the establishment of professional schools. Luxembourg declares in its constitution that it shall furnish its citizens with free professional courses.[29] Panama states that the government is to promote the establishment of technical, industrial, professional, agricultural, and commercial schools.[30] The constitution of Finland stipulates that the government must either maintain or subsidize institutions for the technical professions, agriculture, commerce, navigation, and the fine arts.[31]

In the province of libraries Japan provides subsidies for local public units that meet minimum standards but denies aid to privately controlled ones.[32] Several of the states of Australia (among them New South Wales, Victoria, and Queensland) offer subsidies to municipalities for the development of free lending libraries.[33] In the United States the state of Connecticut authorizes the state board of education to furnish library service to sections having inadequate facilities.[34]

COMPULSORY EDUCATION

The educational duties of the state toward itself as we have thus far considered them in this present chapter have not occasioned any difficult problems. Each of those duties is clear and hardly likely to give rise to controversy. We now, however, take up a question that does pose some difficulties and has in the past occasioned rather bitter controversy.

[28] K. G. Saiyidain and K. L. Shrimali, "India," *The Year Book of Education, 1954*, pp. 472–473.

[29] *Constitution of the Grand Duchy of Luxembourg*, Oct. 17, 1868, article 23 (as amended May 21, 1948), U.N.Y. for 1948, p. 142.

[30] *Constitution of the Republic of Panama*, Mar. 1, 1946, article 89. Peaslee, II, p. 712.

[31] *Form of Government of Finland*, July 17, 1919, article 81. Peaslee, I, p. 787.

[32] Act No. 118 of Apr. 30, 1950, U.N.Y. for 1950, p. 171.

[33] W. C. Radford, "Australia," *The Year Book of Education, 1952*, ed. J. A. Lauwerys and N. Hans, p. 294.

[34] The law states that the board of education may "establish and operate regional library service in sections having inadequate library services as centers for book-mobile and other book services to supplement existing facilities." Connecticut school law, Chapter 67, Sec. 1367, in Huston, *op. cit.*, under "Connecticut," I, 19–20.

But first we must clear the field of deadwood and obscurity. We may not shunt off the problem of compulsory education on the plea that the vast majority of parents do fulfill their obligation to educate their offspring and so there is no need to force them by law. On these grounds a writer in the last decade of the past century considered compulsory education as inopportune and unnecessary, although he did not argue that the state has no right in the matter.[35] Even granting for the sake of discussion that the great majority of parents do or would see to the adequate training and instruction of their children without compulsory laws, we are still left with the pertinent question as to whether the state may force education if and when parents neglect it.

The very expression, compulsory education, is open to diverse meanings and a discussion of it can therefore easily achieve no consistent purpose. In order to prepare the way for a clarification of our position, we wish to distinguish three possible meanings. First, the state determines a miminum amount of knowledge to be acquired by all normal children but does not determine where it is to be obtained. Second, the state establishes a minimum and states that it must be obtained in a school, public or private. Third, the state establishes a minimum amount of instruction and further determines that it shall be obtained in public schools alone.[36]

The usual discussion of compulsory education does not envision the last meaning we have given, and we likewise do not envision it here. The actual equivalent of this third meaning is nothing but state monopoly and that we have considered elsewhere in this study. We will retain, however, meanings (*a*) and (*b*), and we will clearly distinguish between them when we give our position at the end of this section. In the meantime the reader will have at times to examine closely the precise meaning held by the authors we shall cite for and against compulsory education. Often they are clear; sometimes they are not.

We will first examine the position of those writers who have opposed compulsory education in one or other of the two forms we have mentioned. The versatility of these men may be seen from the not insignificant number of different arguments they have advanced.

Messmer would not allow "the State *to compel all parents by a*

---

[35] Dennis T. O'Sullivan, "Is It Opportune?" *American Ecclesiastical Review*, VI (Apr., 1892), 308–309.

[36] S. G. Messmer, "Compulsory Education," *American Ecclesiastical Review*, VI (Apr., 1892), 281–282.

general law [italics his] to give to their children a certain minimum of secular instruction and to directly control such instruction." His reason seems to be that the home is private and the state has no right to take a deficiency for granted in the instruction given in the home since that instruction is also private. If, however, there is public reason to suspect a serious deficiency in private school or home instruction, the state may interfere as long as it has evidence.[37] Holaind agreed with this opinion.[38] Conway held that in modern circumstances parents are bound in conscience to secure both a religious and an elementary secular education, but he denied that the state may make laws to that effect. He allowed the state to interfere in the family to provide food, clothing, and education only in cases of utter neglect, which neglect is present only when the child is altogether abandoned.[39] Castelein required a "notorious indignity or incapacity" on the part of the parents before the state could enter the scene.[40]

The second group of arguments is characterized by a somewhat strange minimizing of the child's right to education. Cathrein reasoned that the state may not force parents to send their children to school because "it is more probable that children do not have a strict right to receive education from their parents, since an obligation of rigorous justice does not exist between parents and children as such — *qua tales.*"[41] His reason for denying a rigorous justice is based on the fact that children are in a way something of the parents (as St. Thomas points out), and hence the perfect otherness necessary for strict justice is absent.

Conway acknowledged a right in the child to receive education, but only to "essential" education, that needed for the attainment of its last end. Although parents are bound out of love for their children to give more than this bare minimum, the state may not force more, for more is not required in justice.[42] Dunne's view was similar to Conway's: ". . . when Catholic authors say the state may coerce parents who neglect the education of their children, they mean only moral educa-

---

[37] S. G. Messmer, "The Right of Instruction," *American Ecclesiastical Review*, VI (Feb., 1892), 112–114.

[38] *Op. cit.*, p. 12.

[39] *Op. cit.*, p. 30.

[40] "Seule, l'indignite ou l'incapacite notoire des parents appelle et justifie en cette mission (d'education) la subrogation de l'Etat." A. Castelein, *Droit Naturel* (Bruxelles: Albert Dewit, 1912), p. 644.

[41] *Op. cit.*, No. 668 and No. 194.

[42] *Op. cit.*, pp. 30–31.

tion, which is the only education children have a strict right to receive."[43]

Both Dunne[44] and Conway[45] held that the argument in favor of compulsory education stemming from the protection of the common good is invalid. The former pointed out that this argument supposes that without a compulsory law an insufficient number of people would use the schools to insure the safety of the state. He felt — and so did Conway — that the overwhelming majority of citizens would use free schools if such are provided. The latter also believed that the common good does not require that all persons in a state enjoy the benefits of literacy, but that the need for literacy will be adequately met by mere promotion of education by the state.

Charles F. Donnelly put the matter in slightly different terms. Testifying before the Massachusetts legislative committee on education in 1888 he made the point that parents ordinarily do not need to be coerced in the fulfillment of their substantial educational duties. "If one, two or three per cent of the population of Massachusetts neglect their natural obligations is it to be claimed or pretended that for the purpose of compelling that small percentage to do their duty you are going to pass a law in subversion of the natural rights of the citizen?"[46]

Another writer observed that it is not universally true that a person needs to know how to read and write in order to live a life of reasonable comfort. And since that is so, the state may not force those parents to give their children more whose children do not need more.[47] Jansen, a canonist, held the same opinion.[48] Dunne asks rhetorically how the state can know that education will benefit each and every citizen. "How do they know that it is going to benefit a boy to take him from a mountain home, where he might possibly live and die happily without ever seeing a book, and fill him full of knowledge and deviltry at a city school, with the possible result of living a rascal and dying a debauchee?"[49] Rickaby is more moderate. He acknowledges that in

---

[43] From his argument in the Quigley case, *op. cit.*, p. 424. We hardly need mention that Dunne's interpretation of Catholic authors is wide of the mark.

[44] *Op. cit.*, pp. 212–215.

[45] *Op. cit.*, p. 32.

[46] Massachusetts General Court, Committee on Education, a digest of the remarks of the Remonstrants at the hearings of the Legislative Committee on Education in March, 1888, p. 11.

[47] Rosetti cited in Holaind, *op. cit.*, p. 20.

[48] *De Facultate Docendi Institutiones Juridicae*, Thesis XXXIII, cited *ibid.*, p. 25.

[49] *Op. cit.*, p. 82.

many walks of life reading and writing are indispensable. In such walks of life if the parents neglect adequate training for their offspring, "the State may step in with compulsory schooling. Compulsory schooling for all indiscriminately, and that up to a high standard, is quite another matter."[50]

In looking back upon the triumph of compulsory education in western society Toynbee sees several unhappy consequences. One is an intellectual impoverishment, "a weak dilution of the elixir of intellectual life" that has flown from an attempt to bring instruction to the masses. A second is the "utilitarian spirit in which the fruits of Education are apt to be turned to account when they are placed within everybody's reach." Today, for many education becomes an instrument of "worldly ambition or of frivolous amusement." But for Toynbee the third consequence is the saddest. Universal education has cheated our educationalists by using their work to enslave the masses. To illustrate his point he cites the rise of the English yellow press as following universal compulsory education in twenty years, 1870 to 1890.[51] Since the introduction of universal education there has arisen the danger to the elementarily educated of being exploited either for the sake of private profit or political advantage. "Thus, in countries where the system of Universal Education has been introduced, the people are in danger of falling under an intellectual tyranny of one kind or the other, whether it be exercised by private capitalists or by public authorities; and, if they are to be saved from both of these two almost equally lamentable fates, the only third alternative is to raise the standard of mass-cultivation to a degree at which the minds of children who are put through the educational mill are rendered immune against at least the grosser forms of either private or public propaganda."[52] In this connection von Kuehnelt-Leddihn refers to Peter Viereck's observation that Hitler's Nazism could hardly have appealed to any but a highly literate nation.[53]

In the famous case, "State of Ohio vs. Patrick F. Quigley," Edmund F. Dunne in his pleading on behalf of Father Quigley offered a large

---

[50] Joseph Rickaby, *Moral Philosophy* (New York: Longmans, Green, and Co., 1912), pp. 358–359.

[51] Arnold J. Toynbee, *A Study of History*, 6th impression (London: Oxford University Press, 1955), IV, pp. 192–194.

[52] *Ibid.*, pp. 195–197.

[53] Erik von Kuehnelt-Leddihn, *Liberty or Equality* (Caldwell, Idaho: Caxton Printers, 1952), p. 163.

number of arguments against compulsory education, some of which we have already noted. Because those arguments are of unequal value, we will review here only the better of his remaining ones.

Compulsory education is a violation of the liberty of those who object to it, and a violation without sufficient reason. The state does not force other things for the reason that they might contribute to the common welfare. It does not, for example, compel people to own property.[54]

The family, second, is the natural educator and antecedent entirely to the state. "If a parent has the right to control the education of his child, then his neighbor will have no right to take control of the age at which that instruction shall begin, of what it shall consist, when and where it shall be given, nor for how long it shall continue."[55]

Furthermore, a state which through compulsory education laws requires attendance at schools which cannot be patronized in good conscience violates the rights of conscience. But some citizens cannot patronize state schools as they are constituted in the United States. And yet some parents are forced by compulsory education to use those schools either because there is no room in church schools or because the parents cannot afford the tuition costs of church schools. Since, therefore, compulsory education laws invade the rights of conscience they are invalid.[56]

Dunne argued further that the citizens of a state, before they can force education, must either agree as to what education is or, if they cannot agree, they must furnish schools to provide what each one conceives a real education to be. Only then may the majority compel the minority to patronize a school.[57]

In his next observation Dunne touches upon the problem of individual differences. No one standard of instruction will satisfy the needs and aptitudes of all pupils. If the standard is such that it will bring the best out of the bright, it will be oppressive, ruinous, and impossible for the great majority. If, on the other hand, the standard is leveled to the lowest in ability, there would be no means of compelling the parents

---

[54] Edmund F. Dunne in the Court of Common Pleas, "The State of Ohio vs. Patrick F. Quigley, No. 2918 of the Criminal Docket," Patrick F. Quigley, *Compulsory Education* (New York: Robert Drummond, 1894), pp. 48–49.

[55] *Ibid.,* pp. 50–54 and 74.

[56] In the Sixth Circuit Court of Ohio, *ibid.,* pp. 202–206. See this argument further developed, p. 413.

[57] *Ibid.,* p. 212.

of the majority to do their full parental duty.[58] Compulsory education, therefore, cannot meet the full needs of pupils.

Cathrein occupies a somewhat middle position, for he granted that in certain conditions the state may compel parents to see to it that their children learn reading, writing, and arithmetic. He allowed the state a right to define what least measure of knowledge is necessary for all and then to examine the children at a set age to see that they possessed it.[59]

We turn now to writers who have favored the right of the state to impose compulsory education. At the head of our list is Pope Pius XI who, in his encyclical on education said that "the State can exact, and take measures to secure that all its citizens have the necessary knowledge of their civic and political duties, and a certain degree of physical, intellectual and moral culture, which, considering the conditions of our times, is really necessary for the common good."[60] We must note, that while the Holy Father clearly teaches a state's right to determine a minimum of knowledge, he does not say whether or not it may demand that that minimum be obtained in a school.

González' commentary on this section of the Holy Father's encyclical is interesting in the number of distinctions he makes in applying the pontiff's doctrine. If the state has imposed a public monopoly in education, González holds that compulsory education is contrary to the natural law and that for two reasons: (1) the parents are denied the right to educate their children as they see fit; (2) the state arrogates to itself a direct right in education. If there is no public monopoly, he distinguishes three questions. (1) The state may impose an indirect obligation of minimum education by demanding that minimum as a condition for civic positions. (2) The state may *probably* impose a minimum education on all provided the parents be given a free choice as to the type of school patronized. Thus the state may indirectly compel attendance at a school when no other means of instruction is available to the parents. (3) Compulsory education is to be kept within modest limits; i.e., the state may not oblige all children of all conditions to a long or detailed education.[61]

The bishops of the United States in their pastoral letter of 1919

---

[58] Before the Supreme Court of Ohio, *ibid.*, p. 412. This argument is, of course, patently fallacious.

[59] *Op. cit.*, Nos. 666, 668.

[60] *Op. cit.*, p. 17.

[61] *Op. cit.*, pp. 817–818.

likewise supported compulsory education but did not determine where it is to be obtained: "The community has the right to insist that those who as members share in its benefits shall possess the necessary qualifications."[62] In their statement for 1955 the American hierarchy went into some detail on the question of compulsory instruction:

> If the state has a concurrent right to decree a minimal education for its citizens, as a vital necessity in a modern democratic society, that right does not extend to an arbitrary designation of the school or the educational agency.
>
> It is, rather, a general right, limited by the primary right of the parent to exercise his choice according to his best wisdom and his conscience. Indeed, it is worth remarking that while the state may usefully engage in the business of education, as demonstrated in our national experience, it has no authority either to monopolize the field or to arrogate to itself exclusive privileges or powers. The state, by definition, is not itself primarily an educative agency.[63]

The fiery archbishop of St. Paul, John Ireland, spoke out more than once in favor of compulsory education. On one occasion the prelate declared that "I unreservedly favor state laws making instruction compulsory."[64] On another he expressed the opinion that it is useless to argue with a man (Holaind) "who thinks that the knowledge of the three R's could be, without deep injustice and positive cruelty, neglected in the education of the child, and that the ignorant parent who is bringing up his child without such knowledge is not amenable to law."[65] Bishop John Lancaster Spalding likewise thought that the state's need for compulsory education to protect itself is so clear that "argument becomes ridiculous."[66]

Perhaps Bishop Spalding's remark helps to explain why supporters of compulsory education have not advanced as many diverse arguments in support of their opinion as their opponents have done. In any event, the former rest their case chiefly on the rights of the child and the protection of the common welfare.

---

[62] J. F. Leibell, ed., *Readings in Ethics* (Chicago: Loyola University Press, 1926), p. 853.

[63] *The Washington Post and Times Herald,* Nov. 20, 1955, p. B5.

[64] Cited by J. A. Barber before the Supreme Court of Ohio, Quigley, *Compulsory Education,* p. 547.

[65] *New York Herald Tribune,* Dec. 14, 1891, cited in Daniel F. Reilly, *The School Controversy* (Washington: Catholic University of America Press, 1943), p. 98.

[66] Reilly, *ibid.,* pp. 73–74. Among the early supporters of compulsory education were John Stuart Mill, *op. cit.,* p. 956, and Adam Smith, *op. cit.,* p. 328.

Today the necessity of an education to make one's way in a highly competitive world is viewed as a self-evident truth. There might be some controversy, however as to what exactly "making one's way" might be. On the lower rungs of the social and economic ladder a man might "make his way" with very little formal education, whereas on the higher rungs formal instruction is indispensable. Proponents of compulsory education would agree that all capable children should be given at least a chance at those higher rungs by an adequate education.

As an instance of the necessity of some minimum instruction for the common good of society one writer cited the thousands of immigrant parents who will not see to it that their children be instructed in the language of their adopted land.[67] Another approach was taken by Doughton. This writer offered three reasons compelling the state to guarantee to every child the fullest development possible: (1) The injustices of a grossly unequal distribution of wealth will be intensified unless the depressed classes be given full opportunity for cultural advancement. (2) Latent talent in all classes will be lost to society unless that talent be developed through adequate education. (3) The growing amount of leisure time will become a menace to society unless the state instruct the child in its proper use.[68]

To meet the objections of the opponents of compulsory education, Bouquillon acknowledged that circumstances could easily render forced instruction inopportune, dangerous, or actually harmful, but this admission, he pointed out, in no way destroys the validity of the principle.[69]

---

[67] "Whole districts in large cities or in the country are populated by men, women, and children, often as different from the average American, whose civil relations oblige him to exchange commodities with them, as any two societies on earth can be. Take an example. In some parts of the country, east and west, the Slavonic element predominates to such an extent that the natives could easily become the prey of disorders absolutely associated with illiteracy. Our laws are no longer promulgated by town criers or beadles in public assembly. People are expected to read them. All the affairs of trust, public and private, are transacted upon the supposition that a man has a common school education, and hardly any one would think of using precautions and safety measures which ignore the ability to read a public notice, or a letter warning him of the lapse of a privilege, and the like." H. J. Heuser, "Compulsory Education in the United States," *American Ecclesiastical Review*, III (Dec., 1890), 429–430.

[68] *Op. cit.*, pp. 440–441.

[69] "One may — and this is often done — without denying the principle of compulsory education, resist for reasons of opportuneness its application to one or the other country. It may be resisted as *useless* in a land where parents are generally zealous for

In order to derive some simplified conclusions from the preceding discussion and in order to make our own position clear, we will pinpoint our solution to the problem of compulsory education in a series of brief statements. 1. *The state has a right to determine a minimum amount of knowledge to be possessed by each normal child.* Our reasons: (*a*) A child has a right to a formation proportioned to the age and place in which it lives. Once a human being exists, it has a right to a reasonably complete existence, and today in most places such an existence cannot be had without some minimum education. (*b*) The welfare of most modern societies undoubtedly requires that the usual citizen be given an education. Not only is this necessary in order that the community be able to carry on its ordinary activities, but it is indispensable also if the community is to realize its full development by a use of the talents latent within it. (*c*) There will always be some parents who will neglect their educational duties if they are permitted to do so. Even if their number does not exceed two or three per cent of the general population, yet it is large enough to warrant the state's legislative attention. (*d*) The unfortunate effects of universal education mentioned by Toynbee can be remedied within the framework of compulsory instruction. We do not treat a headache by removing the head.

2. *The state does not have a* per se *right to determine where that minimum of instruction shall be obtained;* i.e., whether it shall be obtained in the home, in the private school, or in the public school. Our reasons: (*a*) No argument in favor of compulsory education proves that that education must be received in a school. The right of the child does not demand it, nor does the common welfare of so-

---

the schooling of their children, and neglect is rare. It may be resisted as *ineffective* in a land where reigns large liberty of customs and the people are restive under constraint. It may be resisted *as not quite equitable* in a land poorly provided with schools where consequently parents have not at hand the means of giving instruction to their children. It may be resisted as *unconstitutional* in a land where the State's innate right has been restricted by positive limitation in the premises expressed in the nation's charter. It may be resisted as *dangerous* in a land divided into political parties so fierce that schools might be used for partisan purposes. It may be resisted as *iniquitous* in a land governed by religious sectaries where schools might be made the engines of irreligious teachings. Doubtless those reasons and others of a like nature are of the gravest character, but they do not affect the principle itself, they affect only its application." Thomas Bouquillon, *Education: To Whom Does It Belong?* — A Rejoinder to the Civilta Cattolica, pp. 23–24. Italics in the original. The reader will note that Bouquillon's observations are of unequal value.

ciety.[70] (b) The parent is the primary educator and not the state. Hence it is the former who determines where education is to be received, not the latter.

3. Per accidens *the state may compel attendance at a school.* This would be true: (a) If parents cannot or do not provide the minimum instruction in the home. (b) If the schools furnished by the state satisfy the conscience of the parents.[71] (c) If home instruction is so widespread that the state cannot certify its adequacy. This condition will, however, probably never be realized.

LENGTH OF COMPULSORY EDUCATION

It is impossible to determine a priori just how much education parents are bound to give their children, and it is, consequently, also impossible to determine a priori just how compulsory education laws ought to read. This is so because the amount of education needed to preserve both the rights of the child and the welfare of society will vary widely from place to place and from time to time. We will note below the variations that do, as a matter of fact, occur in the legislation of the different nations and even in different sections of the same nation.

Closely allied, however, with this problem is the question of child labor laws. This is true because, when the state through child labor laws lengthens a youth's economic minority, it assumes the obligation to afford that youth full opportunity to spend his additional nonemployed years in an education profitable both to himself and to society.[72]

Child labor laws are generally conceived to have three purposes: (a) to provide for the safety of children by preserving them from occupations dangerous either morally or physically;[73] (b) to afford children the leisure necessary for a full and healthful development; and

---

[70] We may remark that the Church in her school legislation does not require attendance in any school, Catholic or otherwise. She does require a religious formation, but she does not determine where it is to be obtained. See canons 1372–1374.

[71] It will be noted that our position satisfies the objections of Dunne based on conscience.

[72] Doughton, *op. cit.,* p. 440.

[73] Sturges and Burn Manufacturing Co. v. Beauchamp, 231 U.S. 320, 58L ed 245, 34 S Ct 60, L.R.A. 1915A, 1196 (1913), Robert Adam Maurer, *Cases on Constitutional Law* (Rochester, N. Y.: Lawyers Cooperative Publishing Co., 1941), p. 673.

(c) to provide opportunity for an adequate education.[74] Lawmakers do well to bear these principles in mind not only when they fashion child labor laws but also when they form their legislation on compulsory education. The two can hardly be disassociated.[75]

REFUSAL OF ADMITTANCE TO THE PUBLIC SCHOOL

We may ask the question here whether the state is ever justified in refusing children entrance into its schools. As a general principle we think that an affirmative answer must be returned to this query. The state has this right whenever the individual good of the pupil or the common good of the group requires a refusal.

Among the reasons that would justify a refusal of admittance (temporary or permanent according to the nature of each individual case) to the public schools the following may be included: (1) Lack of mental capacity. We do not mean here mere dullness, but rather a feeble-mindedness that would preclude learning in any available institution. (2) Criminal activities and/or immorality. (3) Serious and repeated disciplinary infractions that disturb the work of the school. (4) Contagious disease. (5) Age extremes.

Conditions that do not seem to justify a school system in refusing admission include the following: (1) Mental dullness, as long as the pupil is able to profit to some appreciable extent from attendance at a school. (2) Poor achievement in classwork, at least as long as it is not due to gross neglect on the part of the pupil or is not seriously harmful to the purposes of the school. (3) Distance from the school, provided the provision of transportation would not constitute an undue liability on government finance. (4) Race. (5) Religion. (6) Poverty of the child's parents. If private charities are unequal to the task, the government is ordinarily obliged to furnish whatever food and clothing is necessary for the profitable attendance at school. Children of the very poor are in special need of education for it is only through instruction that they will be able to better their position and alleviate their drag on society.

---

[74] Federal Legislative Service, "School Laws Appendix," n.d., no place, Huston, op. cit., I, 1.

[75] Sweden has given considerable thought to these problems in its own context. See Ingemar During, The Swedish School-Reform, pp. 53–56.

COMPULSORY EDUCATION LAWS OF THE NATIONS
OF THE WORLD

While such was not always the case, laws compelling a minimum of education are found today almost universally among the community of nations. Saudi Arabia and Colombia are instances of the rare governments that provide free education but do not make it compulsory.[76] As we have already suggested, the laws of the nations show a great deal of variation. Some specify merely that a primary education is compulsory. Among these seem to be Argentina, Bolivia, Brazil, Costa Rica, Ecuador, Ireland, Korea, Portugal, Romania, Spain, Switzerland, and Uruguay.[77] Venezuela requires both primary and secondary.[78] Other nations speak in terms of years of actual instruction: Japan, nine years; Hungary and Iceland, eight years;[79] and Greece, six years.[80] Many other countries define their laws in terms of age spans: Great Britain and Northern Ireland, 5–15 years of age;[81] New Zealand, Chile, and Panama, 7–15 years;[82] Austria, France, Italy,[83] and Australia,[84] 6–14 years; Bulgaria, Cuba, Norway, Paraguay, Peru,[85] Sweden, and Denmark,[86] 7–14 years; and Thailand, 8–15 years.[87] Nova Scotia varies its regulations for urban and rural districts. In the former the compulsory period is from 6 to 16 years, while in the latter it is three years less, from 7 to 14 years.[88]

Considerable variety may be seen in the United States. Four states set the upper limit at 14 or 15 years of age; approximately two thirds

---

[76] Harry Hansen (ed.), *The World Almanac, 1956* (New York: New York World-Telegram, 1956), pp. 333, 341.

[77] *Ibid.,* pp. 334, 337, 342, 344, 359, 363, 372, 373, 374, 375, 381.

[78] *Ibid.,* p. 381.

[79] *Ibid.,* pp. 362, 354, 355.

[80] Evangelos G. Sakeris, "Greece, Education in," ed. Harry N. Rivlin, *Encyclopedia of Modern Education* (New York: Philosophical Library, 1943), p. 346.

[81] Hansen, *op. cit.,* p. 320.

[82] *Ibid.,* pp. 331, 339, 369.

[83] *Ibid.,* pp. 335, 348, 361.

[84] David Ross Jenkins, "Australia and New Zealand, Education in," Rivlin, *op. cit.,* p. 72.

[85] Hansen, *op. cit.,* pp. 338, 342, 369, 370.

[86] Hedda Korsch, "Sweden, Education in," and A. Th. Dorf, "Denmark, Education in," Rivlin, *op. cit.,* pp. 788, 224.

[87] Hansen, *op. cit.,* p. 376.

[88] Arch O. Heck, "Compulsory Education," ed. Walter S. Monroe, *Encyclopedia of Educational Research* (rev. ed., New York: The Macmillan Co., 1950), p. 295.

of the states require attendance to the age of 16; 8 states have determined the age of 17; and 6 states set the limit at 18.[89]

While almost every country in the world can point to constitutional or legislative enactments making education compulsory, many of them have been unable to implement those enactments. The Indonesian educational program, for example, *envisages* compulsory education for children 6 to 12,[90] and elementary education is only nominally compulsory in Iraq[91] and Albania.[92] The constitution of India provides for *future* free compulsory education.[93]

The law of the Netherlands is interesting especially in its treatment of acceptable exceptions. Significant is its respect for the objections parents may have to the type of education being offered in available schools.[94] The *Bombay Primary Education Act, 1947* lists among its exceptions illness, distance, a language barrier, adequate instruction received outside a school and the absence of a religiously unobjectionable school in the student's locale.[95]

---

[89] W. Virgil Nestrick, "Compulsory Attendance," Rivlin, *op. cit.*, pp. 178–179.

[90] Hansen, *op. cit.*, p. 357. Italics added.

[91] *Ibid.*, p. 358.

[92] *Ibid.*, p. 333.

[93] *Ibid.*, p. 356. Italics added.

[94] Exempt from the law are "children who have no fixed abode, i.e., the children of bargees and itinerants. . . . If a bargee remains more than two days in one and the same municipality, he is bound to send his children to school. . . . The following are also exempted: children who in the opinion of the doctors are not fit to attend school or who have no school within 4 kilometres of their homes (for children up to eleven years of age) or 6 kilometres (for those of eleven years and over). The law goes very far as regards its respect for the liberty of conscience of the parents; if they have serious objections to put forward concerning the education given in all the schools situated within a radius of 4 kilometres (2½ miles) from their residence (for children up to eleven years of age) and 6 kilometres (app. 4 miles) (for those of eleven years and over) they are relieved of the general obligation imposed by the Compulsory Education Law." Idenburg, *Education in the Netherlands*, pp. 17–18.

[95] Exceptions (b) and (f) in the law, the last two we have mentioned above, are especially interesting: "(b) where the child is receiving, otherwise than in an approved school, instruction which in the opinion of the school board is efficient or has received from the school board a certificate of having already completed his primary education up to the standard included in the scheme; (f) where there is no approved school in the locality to which the parent can send the child without exposing him to religious instruction to which the parent objects." Section 33, Replacement Series No. VIII, p. 83, sent to me by the Embassy of India, Washington, D. C., under date of Feb. 24, 1955.

LENGTH OF ATTENDANCE DURING SCHOOL YEAR

Closely connected with the number of years required for a minimum education is the number of days required in each school year. There is probably even more variation in this matter than in the previous. English law provides that in a case of infraction of the compulsory education law "the parent shall not be entitled to be acquitted under this subsection unless he proves that the child has made at least two hundred attendances during the period of twelve months. . . ."[96] In the United States forty-three states by 1945 were requiring children to attend school for the full term, while two others merely specified that authorities may require full term attendance. Nebraska required full attendance in some districts and partial in others and the two remaining states determined a definite period of attendance.[97] Actual practice has been so varied that in the decade of the thirties an average child in one state was receiving six more years of elementary schooling than an average child in another state.[98]

EDUCATION IN THE HOME

Many countries make explicit the right of parents to satisfy compulsory education laws by instruction in the home.[99] Egypt allows home instruction to supply for the school provided the proper authority be notified before the beginning of the school year and the local inspector find the instruction adequate.[100] Portugal states explicitly that compulsory elementary education may be imparted either in the home or in the private institution or in the state school.[101] The law of the Netherlands, while it makes an adequate elementary education compulsory, does not compel parents to send their children to any type of school.[102] Very few children actually avail themselves of this right.[103]

---

[96] *Education Act, 1944,* Part II, sec. 39.

[97] Heck, *op. cit.,* p. 295.

[98] Nestrick, *op. cit.,* p. 179.

[99] I did not notice in legal sources available that any nation denied this right in its legislation.

[100] *Elementary Education Act of 1951,* U.N.Y. for 1951, p. 80.

[101] *Political Constitution of the Portuguese Republic,* Mar. 19, 1933, article 43, U.N.Y. for 1951, p. 299.

[102] "No one is bound to send his children to school, provided he makes provision for their education by tuition at home." Idenburg, *op. cit.,* p. 16.

[103] *Ibid.*

English law binds parents to educate their children either in a school or otherwise.[104] Early school laws in the United States did not compel attendance at a school as long as parents saw to it that their offspring received the minimum instruction at home or in some other agency. Today each of the forty-eight states requires attendance in a school, either private or public. There are many exemptions provided in these laws, however, and tutoring at home is usually accepted as a justifiable cause for exemption.[105] American courts have likewise supported the practice of home instruction by parents or tutor.[106] An Illinois court, for example, asserted that those who wish to use private tutoring as a substitute for public education bear the burden of showing that they have provided adequate instruction in those subjects which have been prescribed by the state.[107]

AMOUNT OF FREE EDUCATION PROVIDED BY CONTEMPORARY GOVERNMENTS

It is difficult to say in many instances to what exact extent a government finances the complete education of its subjects. The obscurity is often due to the partial character of the aid given for the higher levels of instruction. On the one hand we may find a nation which charges a fee for public secondary education and on the other one which grants university scholarships to particular groups of students. Often the outside observer knows the amount neither of the fee nor of the scholarship. Our illustrations, therefore, ought not to be construed as necessarily typical of worldwide practice.

In the Union of South Africa's Cape Province public education is free up to the child's fifteenth year of age except in certain high schools and a few primary schools. The fees charged at the various secondary and high schools are scaled according to the locality in which a school is located and the financial condition of the citizens.[108] Danish parents

---

[104] "It shall be the duty of the parents of every child of compulsory school age to cause him to receive efficient full-time education suitable to his age, ability, and aptitude, either by regular attendance at school or otherwise." *Education Act, 1944*, Part II, sec. 36.

[105] Heck, *op. cit.*, pp. 290–291.

[106] *Ibid.*, p. 299.

[107] *People* v. *Levisen et al.*, 404 Ill. 574, 90 N.E. (2d) 213 (Ill. 1950), cited in Loughery, *op. cit.*, p. 128.

[108] Union of South Africa, *Education*, p. 24.

whose children attend public schools on the secondary level pay a small fee if their income exceeds a determined amount.[109] For a secondary education Swedish pupils likewise pay a fee which varies from school to school but is usually about forty to fifty crowns. Needy students are exempted from this charge.[110] Japan's recent education law explicitly rules out fees in primary and secondary schools conducted by the government and in institutions for the handicapped.[111] Tasmania, Australia in its *Education Act of 1952* provided that no fee shall be any longer charged for instruction in state schools of any kind.[112] England has no state universities, but the government aids privately owned and operated institutions both by direct grants and by scholarships.[113] Both Ceylon and Saudi Arabia offer free education on all three levels, primary, secondary, and higher.[114] Public institutions in the United States provide education on the primary and secondary levels free of charge, however they ask a partial fee on the higher level.

Nursery schools may be found in many countries today. Romania provides in its law for optional pre-school education for children from three to seven years of age.[115] Morris reports that Hungary in the years 1949–50 took care of 141,000 children from three to six years of age in state, municipal, and factory nurseries.[116] Among the duties that England assigns to its local education authorities is "the need for securing that provision is made for pupils who have not attained the age of five years by the provision of nursery schools or, where the authority consider [*sic*] the provision of such schools to be inexpedient, by the provision of nursery classes in other schools."[117] In England the nursery school is understood as meant for children from the ages of two to four inclusive.[118]

---

[109] Royal Danish Ministry for Foreign Affairs, *Denmark*, p. 80.

[110] During, *op. cit.*, p. 41. A Swedish crown in 1939 was equivalent in American money to .2680 cents.

[111] *School Education Law Number 26*, Mar. 31, 1947, article 6, mimeo. copy, n.d., no place, p. 1.

[112] U.N.Y. for 1952, p. 4.

[113] British Information Services, *Education in Great Britain*, pp. 29–31.

[114] Hansen, *op. cit.*, pp. 326, 333.

[115] *Education Reform Act*, Aug. 3, 1948, article 4, U.N.Y. for 1948, p. 180.

[116] Morris, *op. cit.*, p. 3.

[117] *Education Act, 1944*, Part II, sec. 8.

[118] *Ibid.*, sec. 9.

CHILD LABOR LAWS

The close relationship between compulsory education and child labor laws is nicely exemplified in the English and Indian laws on education, which laws themselves contain sections on the employment of children. "If it appears to a local education authority that any child who is a registered pupil at a county school, voluntary school, or special school, is being employed in such manner as to be prejudicial to his health or otherwise to render him unfit to obtain the full benefit of the education provided for him, the authority may, by notice in writing served upon the employer, prohibit him from employing the child, or impose such restrictions upon his employment of the child as appear to them to be expedient in the interests of the child."[119] Bombay State in India has a similar stipulation.[120] Poland forbids the employment of a person under sixteen years of age,[121] and the United States has generally adopted a fourteen to sixteen year minimum for employment during school hours.[122]

PROVISION FOR NEEDY STUDENTS

It is common in the modern world for a government to furnish food, clothing, and medical assistance to pupils who would otherwise be handicapped or even utterly unable to attend school. In some countries meals and medical assistance are given indiscriminately to all students. Finland furnishes to poor children shoes and clothing and to all children free medical and dental service. On school days they are served one free meal.[123] The government of Iraq in its regulation No. 62 of 1952 authorizes the Ministry of Education to provide needy students with food and clothing.[124] Ecuador furnishes "healthful and nourishing food" to students attending its rural teacher-training in-

---

[119] *Ibid.*, sec. 59.
[120] "Whoever knowingly takes into his employment, either on his behalf or on behalf of any person, any child in respect of whom the provisions of section 32 apply, so as to interfere with the education or instruction of such child shall, on conviction, be liable to a fine not exceeding twenty-five rupees." *Bombay Primary Education Act, 1947*, sec. 36.
[121] Decree of Aug. 2, 1951, U.N.Y. for 1951, p. 295.
[122] Harry N. Rosenfield, "Child Labor," Rivlin, *op. cit.*, p. 121.
[123] Kallio, *The School System of Finland*, pp. 11–12.
[124] U.N.Y. for 1952, p. 136.

stitutions.[125] Codignola reports that Italy in 1947 provided meals for 862,761 pupils in 10,825 schools.[126] Japan stipulates that "the city, town or village shall give necessary aids to the protectors of those school age children who are recognized to be difficult [*sic*] to attend school for financial reasons."[127] In the United States, Arizona provides necessary clothing and the means of transportation for children whose parents cannot provide them.[128]

[125] Regulation No. 206, Feb. 7, 1950, U.N.Y. for 1950, p. 72.
[126] Ernest Codignola, "Italy," *The Year Book of Education, 1952,* ed. J. A. Lauwerys and N. Hans, p. 397.
[127] Law No. 26, *op. cit.,* article 25, p. 4.
[128] Arizona school law, Sec. 54–1523, in Huston, *op. cit.,* I, 14.

CHAPTER XIII

THE STATE AND INTERNATIONAL
CO-OPERATION IN EDUCATION[129]

THE early ages in the history of organized society are characterized by localized government, localized government that knew little or nothing of organized relationships and co-operation with other units in the human family. As civilization grew and developed, however, contacts between geographical units became more frequent and more numerous. From tribal organizations city-states eventually evolved and then national states as we know them today.[130] This universalizing process has not ceased. It is going on today.

Modern scientific and technological developments have shrunk the world and made all of its inhabitants neighbors. Whereas the ancient Aztec was wholly unconcerned with (because ignorant of) his African and Asian and European contemporaries, the Latin American today cannot afford to ignore his fellow men in other lands. They profoundly influence his standard of living, his taxes, and his culture. He likewise influences theirs.

The age of isolationism is therefore gone forever. Both men and states must now consider themselves members of a worldwide community of nations and members possessed of international duties,

---

129 Wandycz has rightly observed that the study of international relations is one of the youngest of the members in the social science family. He views international relations as a separate and autonomous branch of political theory but one related to the main body. Piotr S. Wandycz, "The Theory of International Relations," *Review of Politics,* XVII (Apr., 1955), pp. 189, 191.

130 We are aware that this evolution was not lacking in periods of devolution. There was, for example, a retrogressive, deuniversalizing tendency in the Middle Ages in spite of a superficial appearance of unity in the Holy Roman Empire. We wish to indicate here merely an over-all process.

rights, and privileges. Gone, too, as a consequence is the concept of absolute sovereignty. Legalists have for some time now recognized the fact that no nation may consider itself free of obligations toward its sister nations, that it enjoys supreme jurisdiction and authority in all spheres. Pope Pius XII himself has insisted that in the community of nations "every state becomes a part of the system of international law, and hence of natural law. . . . Thus the individual nation no longer is — nor was it ever — 'sovereign,' in the sense of being entirely without restriction."[131] He has spoken also of the "erroneous concept of an absolutely autonomous sovereignty divested of all social obligations."[132]

This obligation of states to view themselves as members of an international community arises, of course, from the very nature of man, from the natural law. Legal positivists, as a matter of fact, have been hard pressed to explain without recourse to natural law how there can be obligations between the nations of the world. If, as they hold, all law is positive law and stems from the authority of the state, there can be no international law because there is no international state. On this basis one is unable to justify the Nuremberg trials for there was no international law under which to judge the accused.[133]

Boyer wisely builds his demonstration of the natural law character of international rights and duties on two sound premises: (1) There is a natural law obligation wherever there are necessary relationships between subjects capable of rights. (2) The nations of the world both enjoy necessary relationships and are the subjects of rights. It therefore inescapably follows that the rights and duties existing between national states stem from the very nature of the international community, which is to say from the international natural law.[134]

The international relationships we wish to discuss here lie in the field of educational co-operation. The reasons that indicate the necessity

---

[131] Robert C. Pollock, ed., *The Mind of Pius XII* (New York: Crown Publishers, 1955), p. 79.

[132] "Christmas Message, 1948," *Catholic Mind*, XLVII (Mar., 1949), 183.

[133] Messner, *op. cit.*, pp. 446–447.

[134] "Ibi habetur ius naturale ubi necessariae sunt relationes inter subiecta iurium. Atqui necessariae sunt relationes inter nationes, quae sunt subiecta iurium. Ergo datur ius naturale." The minor is, of course, evident. He explains his major as follows: "Ubi enim relationes necessario habentur, hoc ipsum systema relationum ad ampliorem societatem pertinet novamque communitatem creat vel supponit: relationes enim inter subiecta iurium non haberentur si non esset aliquis finis communis ad quem habendum haec subiecta sese iuvare vel a quo habendo sese invicem impedire possint." *Op. cit.*, p. 568.

for co-operation among the nations in matters educational are many. We will divide these reasons into those which are more general in character and those which are specifically educational.

First the general. The common human nature that all men share regardless of their creed or color is an unmistakable bond demanding that they be interested in their fellows and that they prove their interest by action when such be indicated. The technological closeness of states today makes this nature-bond such that it demands an issue into practice. Pope Pius XII has underlined the importance of this unity, this bound-togetherness of the human family.

> A disposition, in fact, of the divinely sanctioned natural order divides the human race into social groups, nations or states, which are mutually independent in organization and in the direction of their internal life. But for all that, the human race is bound together by reciprocal ties, moral and juridical, into a great commonwealth directed to the good of all nations and ruled by special laws which protect its unity and promote its prosperity. Now no one can fail to see how the claim to absolute autonomy for the state stands in open opposition to this natural law that is inherent in man — nay, denies it utterly — and, therefore leaves the stability of international relations at the mercy of the will of rulers, while it destroys the possibility of true union and fruitful collaboration directed to the general good.[135]

The natural bond of unity tying states together, therefore, founds an obligation for the state to co-operate with and aid other states in educational and cultural endeavors.

On the supernatural level the nations are united in an even more compelling bond, the bond of potential or actual membership in the Mystical Body of Christ, the Catholic Church.[136] In this Body there is first of all a unity deriving from a collaboration of members toward one supernatural end, the beatific vision. There is an externally manifested unity flowing from a profession of the same faith, a participation in the same sacraments and sacrifice, and an obedience to the same

---

[135] *Summi Pontificatus,* Oct. 20, 1939 (Washington: N.C.W.C., 1939), Nos. 65, 66. We have corrected a misprint in the N.C.W.C. edition which reads "way" instead of "law" in No. 66. See *Acta Apostolicae Sedis,* XXXI, p. 554.

[136] Brickman has observed that Christianity has been "an international force toward educational unity from its beginnings until the Reformation." If he had been more exact and said Catholicism instead of Christianity, he could have brought his latter limit to the present date. See William W. Brickman, "International Education," *Encyclopedia of Educational Research, op. cit.,* p. 618.

Roman Pontiff. In addition to these juridical bonds there are the still more sublime ones issuing from the three theological virtues and the indwelling of the Soul of the Body, the Holy Spirit.[137]

Catholics, therefore, have special reasons for generous co-operation in solving the educational and cultural problems that beset the nations of the world. There is almost no country lacking in a substantial number of actual members of the Mystical Body, and none lacking in potential ones.

Our third general reason for holding that the state is obliged to participate in education on an international level is the consequent improvement in international relations and understanding. In its charter the United Nations Educational, Scientific, and Cultural Organization states that "ignorance of each other's ways and lives has been a common cause, throughout the history of mankind, of that suspicion and mistrust between the peoples of the world through which their differences have all too often broken into war."[138] It seems obvious, however, that mere understanding will hardly suffice, and that without good will and a spirit of tolerant understanding it "may be sterile in achieving the goal at which it is finally aimed."[139]

Among the fruits of improved international understanding perhaps the very first and the most crucial is a reduction of the probability of war. It was this that Pope Pius XII had in mind when he declared that "the educating of public opinion to look at things as they are and to consider truth dispassionately, with calm and dignity, is one of the essential conditions for the smoothing down of opposition, for bringing peoples together and for peace."[140]

The final general reason indicating the need for international co-operation in education lies in the insufficiency of the modern state. That our contemporary nations individually taken cannot assure the peace is more than patent in the light of sad experience. To a lesser extent we may also say that a state singly taken is culturally, scientifically, and educationally inadequate. So much is this true that Maritain doubts that modern states can be called perfect societies.[141]

---

[137] Pope Pius XII, *Mystici Corporis*, June 29, 1943 (Washington: N.C.W.C., 1943), Nos. 67–73, 78–80.

[138] Preamble of the Charter.

[139] A. LeRoy Bennett, "Education for International Understanding — Challenge to Unesco," *School and Society*, 75 (May 17, 1952), 308–309.

[140] Address to the Foreign Press Association, Pollock, *op. cit.*, p. 89.

[141] We are using the term in the philosophical sense. A perfect society is one that

He remarks that

> . . . when the particular bodies politic, our so-called national States, grown incapable of achieving self-sufficiency and assuring peace, definitely recede from the concept of perfect society, then the picture necessarily changes: since it is the international society which must become hence forth the perfect society, it is not only on a *moral,* but on a *juridical* ground that the obligations of the particular bodies politic, once they have become parts of a politically organized whole, will have to fulfill their obligations toward this whole . . .[142]

The specific educational grounds for urging international co-operation in matters intellectual are both many in number (we will suggest just a few) and briefly told. (1) Educational contacts with other states can hardly fail to broaden a government's approach to the problems of its educational system. National narrowmindedness can be both unsuspecting and naive. Many Americans, for example, seem utterly unaware that there is any other workable plan for the distribution of educational tax money than the American plan. Our above examination of this problem as it is solved in the nations of the world suggests how contact can dissipate provincialism. (2) Through a mutual interchange of national cultures the world of the arts grows and develops. (3) Co-operation can aid in a healthy reduction of nationalist bias in text books. (4) International contacts in the learned sciences (theology, philosophy, medicine, physics, law, etc.) have already gone far in speeding the advance of these areas of endeavor. Further and even more thorough co-operation will accelerate this advance. (5) As Maritain has remarked, "matter goes faster than the spirit."[143] Technical progress in the physical sciences has already made the world economically one at least to a point; it remains for education to make it culturally one.

Our last observation and the ones also that precede it by no means bespeak an educational uniformity that would embarrass or meddle in the refreshing educational and cultural differences that set one nation off from another. A diplomat and historian has stated that a genuine internationalism "presupposes a prime loyalty of the individual to his national state, a cherishing by him of his national lan-

---

has as an end some good complete in its order and means sufficient to achieve that end.
[142] Jacques Maritain, *Man and the State* (Chicago: University of Chicago Press, 1951), p. 198.
[143] *Ibid.,* p. 191.

guage and his national traditions, a lively patriotism within him; the internationalist aims to build his world-state with national blocks."[144] In this connection Pope Pius XII has counseled the nations of the world to exercise a respectful reserve and regard for the wholesome traditions and cultures of peoples if real harmony is to be achieved among them.[145]

The obligation of the nations of the world to work together for the promotion of the common good of all mankind is, as we have already remarked, an obligation stemming from the very nature of man, from natural law. Yet this is not to say that natural law says everything that must be said about the matter. There remains for the international community the need to work out a code of positive law that will pinpoint and detail the natural law. In many cases, however, there will be no necessity to detail natural law by positive legislation since that work will have been done by the custom of nations acting among themselves.[146] These customs under certain conditions can, of course, attain the status of real law.

One of the very first to write on the theory of international law, Francis Suarez (1548–1617), nicely summarizes the origin and foundation of it.

> Although the human race is divided into various peoples and nations, it is always possessed of some unity, not only specific but also quasi-political and moral. The natural precept of mutual love and mercy, which extends to all men, even to foreigners of every nation, bespeaks that unity. For this reason even though each complete state, nation, or kingdom is in itself a perfect community made up of its own members, nonetheless because it belongs to the human race each is in some way also a member of the whole community of nations. Never are these states taken singly so self-sufficient that they do not need mutual help, association, and interchange. Experience shows that sometimes they need that help merely to get along better or for greater utility, but at other times they need it out of real necessity or indigence. Hence they need some law to direct and order their relationships and interchanges. And although for the most part this law will be introduced by natural

---

[144] Carlton J. H. Hayes, *Essays on Nationalism* (New York: Macmillan Co., 1941), p. 271.

[145] "Catholics and International Life," an address given under the auspices of Italian Catholic Action, July 23, 1952, *Catholic Action*, 34 (Sept., 1952), 11.

[146] Suarez, *Tractatus De Legibus ac Deo Legislatore* (Neapoli: Typis Fibrenianis, 1872), Liber II, Caput XX, 1.

reason, yet such is not always adequate. Some laws, therefore, may be introduced by custom.[147]

We may speak of the obligation of nations to co-operate in the promotion of the common universal good as an obligation of natural international justice.[148] Messner sees two principles lying as the foundation of a society of nations. The first is that no nation may be refused admittance into the international community as long as it is willing to co-operate peacefully with its fellow nations. The second excludes isolationism and therefore requires all states to participate in the securing of the common welfare since the participation of all is needed.[149]

The ways in which the governments of the world may co-operate in furthering educational, cultural, and scientific endeavor on a supranational level are many and varied. We will list some of them by way of illustration: (1) Granting of scholarships to citizens for the purpose of study in foreign lands. (2) Facilitating through appropriate legislation the exchange of teachers and students. (3) Participating in international fairs, expositions, and exhibits. (4) Originating research studies in educational, cultural, and scientific fields and sharing with other nations the useful information deriving from these studies. (5) Co-operation in the international promotion of educational movies, television, and radio. (6) Sponsorship of a public relations program aimed at foreign lands. We have in mind here some sort of department of information that would make available to other nations accurate and interesting data and insights dealing with its country. (7) Co-operation with the various international learned organizations and federa-

---

[147] "Humanum genus quantumvis in varios populos et regna divisum, semper habet aliquam unitatem non solum specificam, sed etiam quasi politicam et moralem, quam indicat naturale praeceptum mutui amoris et misericordiae, quod ad omnes extenditur, etiam extraneos, et cuiuscumque nationis. Quapropter licet unaquaeque civitas perfecta, respublica, aut regnum, sit in se communitas perfecta, et suis membris constans, nihilominus quaelibet illarum est etiam membrum aliquo modo huius universi, prout ad genus humanum spectat; nunquam enim illae communitates adeo sunt sibi sufficientes singillatim, quin indigeant aliquo mutuo iuvamine, et societate, ac communicatione, interdum ad melius esse maioremque utilitatem, interdum vero etiam ob moralem necessitatem et indigentiam, ut ex ipso usu constat. Hac ergo ratione indigent aliquo iure, quo dirigantur, et recte ordinentur in hoc genere communicationis et societatis. Et quamvis magna ex parte hoc fiat per rationem naturalem, non tamen sufficienter et immediate quoad omnia; ideoque aliqua specialia iura potuerunt usu earumdem gentium introduci." *Ibid.*, Liber II, Caput XIX, 5.

[148] Messner, *op. cit.*, p. 431.

[149] *Ibid.*, p. 432.

tions in their activities and congresses. (8) Sponsorship within its own boundaries of public educational programs aimed at a better understanding and appreciation of foreign peoples, their lives, views, and problems. (9) Granting of financial aid to other countries for educational purposes when such is feasible. (10) Other more detailed ways in which nations can aid one another are suggested by a recent educational writer: co-operation in the translation of famous books; assisting a wide distribution of classical paintings by making catalogues of reproductions; facilitating the purchase of books and educational films from one another.[150]

The activities of contemporary states in the field of educational co-operation more than adequately illustrate the principles we have considered.

The Corporacion de Bibliotecarios, Archiveros y Conservadores de Museos del Caribe, created in 1940 by the Second Inter-American Caribbean Meeting held in Ciudad Trujillo, Dominican Republic, serves as a co-ordinating agency for the librarians, archivists, and curators of museums in that sector of the western hemisphere.[151] An interesting account of the purposes and functions of this organization is given in Article I of its statutes:

(a) To adopt, after studying the question, a system providing for classification and cataloguing of the libraries, archives, and museums of the Caribbean region;

(b) To obtain copies of the catalogues already in existence in the libraries, archives, and museums of the Caribbean countries with a view to the compilation of accumulative catalogues based on them, copies of which may be distributed by the Corporation in either complete or partial form. . . .

(c) To obtain copies (photographic, micrographic, or produced by some other process) of documents existing in the Caribbean countries, or located elsewhere but concerned with Caribbean culture; and to consider the procedure for distributing such materials, in complete or partial form, . . . to the various libraries, archives, and museums of the Caribbean region;

(d) To establish among the different museums of the Caribbean

---

150 Herbert J. Abraham, "A Letter to Jennifer," *National Education Association Journal,* 43 (Jan., 1954), 14.

151 Ruth D. Masters, ed., *Handbook of International Organizations in the Americas* (Washington: Carnegie Endowment for International Peace, 1945), p. 63.

countries the practice of exchanging original works of art, copies of pictures, and all kinds of replicas;

(e) To induce the various Caribbean Governments to establish scholarships that will encourage the study of art;

(f) To hold meetings, conventions, or congresses of librarians, archivists, and curators of museums of the Caribbean region, at such times as shall be considered appropriate;

(g) To arrange for the proper housing of the contents of Caribbean libraries, archives, and museums;

(h) To take steps in order to ensure the proper attention on the part of states, provinces, or municipalities, to the needs of the various libraries, archives, and museums;

(i) To encourage the study of library science and of subjects relating to the scientific care and administration of archives and museums;

(j) To encourage the publication of all kinds of bibliographical works;

(k) To solicit the cooperation of all organisms, official or unofficial, engaged in activities similar to those of the Corporation.[152]

A program of international public relations is carried on in the United States by the United States Information Service and the Office of International Information and Cultural Affairs.

Among the many foreign educational and cultural activities sponsored by the United States Information Agency are the following: bookmobile services, book translation programs, the Voice of America broadcasts, television programs, films on American culture and current affairs, publication of *America Illustrated,* support of tours by American celebrities, participation in trade fairs, maintenance of reading rooms, and the issuance of press releases.[153]

One of the most natural and beneficial modes of international cultural exchange is that between nations sharing a common set of interests and a common background. The Portuguese Cultural Institute of Rio de Janeiro is a concretization of an effort of two nations with

---

[152] *Ibid.,* p. 64. One can easily see the considerable educational and cultural benefits that can flow from international co-operation of this type.

[153] *U. S. Information Agency* (Washington: Government Printing Office, 1956), *passim.* This agency issues periodic reports on its activities. See, for example, *U. S. Information Agency,* 7th Review of Operation (Washington: Government Printing Office, 1957). See also Franklin L. Burdette, "U. S. Information Agency and Advanced Learning Abroad," *Higher Education,* XIII (Nov., 1956), 45–58, and for another governmental agency, Oliver J. Caldwell, "International Education Activities of the Office of Education," *Higher Education,* XII (Sept., 1955), 4–6.

a common heritage to further their Luso-Brazilian culture. Interestingly enough, these two countries on December 6, 1948 concluded an Agreement for Intellectual Cooperation.[154]

In the field of scientific collaboration the Higher Council for Scientific Research, created by the Spanish government in 1939, facilitates relations between foreign and Spanish scientists and provides both with mutual reports. The contacts between the countries "consists of visits by Spanish scientists and scholars to universities and cultural centres in different countries, and invitations to eminent foreigners to give courses and lectures in Spain. . . ."[155]

The benefits to be derived from direct co-operation between two countries is well exemplified by the United States Education Mission to Japan in 1947. This 27-member mission toured Japan for a month and then submitted a plan for the reorganization and modification of Japanese education. Though we need not view all of its recommendations as ideal, the plan was well received by the Japanese and has had a profound influence on postwar educational development in their country.[156]

The international exchange of both students and teachers is today conducted on a large scale. One survey reports 54,041 persons engaged in exchange programs involving the United States during the year 1955–1956. Of these exchanges, "43,309 were foreign citizens in the United States — 36,494 students at institutions of higher education, 6033 doctors training at hospitals, 782 teachers and researchers who were at colleges and universities as visiting faculty members." Americans abroad numbered 10,732 — "9457 students at foreign institutions of higher education and 1275 faculty members from United States institutions abroad on teaching or research assignments."[157] Before it was overrun by Communism, China had established a Division of Cultural Relations in its Ministry of Education. Among its purposes were the promotion of an exchange of professors and students and the direction of Chinese overseas higher education.[158]

---

[154] *Portugal,* "The Portuguese Cultural Institute in Brazil," Numbers 210–211 (January-February, 1956), 49.

[155] Diplomatic Information Office, *Fifteen Years . . . ,* pp. 34–35.

[156] Ministry of Foreign Affairs, *Japan's Problems,* p. 28.

[157] Institute of International Education, *Open Doors* (New York: Institute of International Education, 1956), p. 4. The arguments in favor of a vigorous foreign student exchange program are gathered in *Expanding University Enrollments and the Foreign Student* (New York: Institute of International Education, 1957).

[158] Chih Meng, "China," *Educational Yearbook, 1944,* ed. I. L. Kandel, p. 63.

As an illustration of an international, governmentally sponsored association for the advancement of a particular field of learning we may cite the Pan American Institute of Geography and History with head-quarters in Mexico City. This organization has among its purposes the aiding of publication of geographical and historical studies, the facilitation of contacts between organizations in member states, and the initiation and co-ordination of investigations and scientific discussions.[159]

To date the most comprehensive attempt to solve educational prob-lems on an international scale is to be found in the work of the United Nations and the United Nations Educational, Scientific, and Cultural Organization attached to it. The former carries out its educa-tional endeavors through the Economic and Social Council, which Council is responsible under the General Assembly for carrying out the functions of the United Nations in social, economic, health, and educational matters. Among the purposes of the United Nations as outlined in its charter is the achievement of "international cooperation in solving international problems of an economic, social, cultural, or humanitarian character. . . ."[160] Later on in this same charter we read that the "Economic and Social Council may make or initiate studies and reports with respect to international economic, social, cultural, educational, health, and related matters and may make recommenda-tions with respect to any such matters to the General Assembly, to the Members of the United Nations and to the specialized agencies concerned."[161]

The United Nations Educational, Scientific and Cultural Organiza-tion is an association distinct from, yet closely allied with the United Nations.[162] Its aim is specifically educational: "To contribute to peace and security by promoting collaboration among the nations through education, science and culture in order to further universal respect for justice, for the rule of law and for the human rights and fundamental freedoms which are affirmed for the people of the world, without dis-tinction of race, sex, language or religion, by the Charter of the United

---

[159] Masters, *op. cit.*, pp. 307–308.

[160] *Charter of the United Nations,* Chapter I, Article I.

[161] *Ibid.,* Chapter X, Article 62.

[162] A brief account of the nature and history of Unesco together with a survey of the attacks that have been made against it may be found in " 'Unesco' Under Fire — But What Is It?" *U. S. News and World Report,* 39 (Nov. 4, 1955), pp. 67–68.

Nations."[163] Unesco, however, does not view itself as enjoying any right to interfere in the internal educational affairs of member states. In Article I of its constitution it specifically states that "with a view of preserving the independence, integrity, and fruitful diversity of the cultures and educational systems of the states members of this organization, the organization is prohibited from intervening in matters which are essentially within their domestic jurisdiction."

The accomplishments of the United Nations Educational, Scientific and Cultural Organization in raising the educational level of the world are impressive in their scope if not in actual results obtained. Among those accomplishments we may mention the following: (1) Organization of summer school sessions for teachers of several nations; e.g., Mexico, United States, England, Belgium.[164] (2) Aid given to scientific organizations for the publication of international learned periodicals.[165] (3) Technical assistance sent to backward countries in the persons of trained experts in the various sciences.[166] (4) Dispatch of educational personnel to needy countries to aid in the training of native teachers and the formation of effective public school systems.[167] (5) Aid extended to several nations for the organization and establishment of model libraries.[168] (6) In order to combat illiteracy, the establishment of Fundamental Education Centers in Mexico for Latin America and in Egypt for Arab countries.[169] (7) Extension of help to teachers seeking accurate information about countries other than their own.[170] (8) Establishment of science co-operation offices for the benefit of industries and universities.[171] (9) Help extended to member governments for the development of fundamental education: reading, writing, and the basic rules of health.[172] (10) Sponsorship of inter-

---

[163] *Constitution*, Article I. A detailing of this purpose may be found in Leland M. Goodrich and Edvard Hambro, *Charter of the United Nations* (2nd rev. ed., Boston: World Peace Foundation, 1949), pp. 334–336.

[164] Abraham, *op. cit.*, p. 14.

[165] *Ibid.*

[166] *Ibid.*, p. 15.

[167] *Ibid.*

[168] *Ibid.* See also Bennett, *op. cit.*, p. 310.

[169] Robert H. Reid, "Box Score on the U. N., 1945–1954," *National Education Association Journal*, 43 (Sept., 1954), 347.

[170] Educational Policies Commission, National Education Association, *National Education Association Journal*, 42 (Feb., 1953), 78.

[171] *National Education Association Journal*, "What They Ask About Unesco," 41 (Oct., 1952), 441.

[172] *Ibid.*

national seminars for educators. Unesco has also helped member nations "improve teaching materials and textbooks, promoted international cooperation among universities, and acted as an international clearing house for information on education."[173] (11) Initiation of a publications program. One writer speaks of "well over a thousand books, reports, periodicals, and pamphlets" having been put into print by Unesco in its first six years of existence.[174] (12) Gathering and disseminating in an annual report information on the opportunities for the exchange of persons. This annual volume lists more than 30,000 such opportunities.[175]

As we have already suggested, the actual results achieved by Unesco may not be overpoweringly impressive, but they are decidedly steps in the right direction. They indicate that the nations of the world are acutely aware of the significance of educational co-operation on an international basis. That awareness is healthy.

---

[173] *Ibid.* See also Bennett, *op. cit.,* p. 311, for an account of the limited success that has accompanied some of these ventures. For a description of one of these international seminars see Theodore Andersson, "The Unesco Seminar on the Teaching of Modern Languages," *School and Society,* 77 (June 27, 1953), 408–410.

[174] William W. Brickman, "Unesco Developments and Achievements," *School and Society,* 76 (Nov. 29, 1952), 343.

[175] Bennett, *op. cit.,* p. 310.

CHAPTER XIV

SUMMARY AND CONCLUSIONS

THE state, an organized group within the community, has as its purpose the carrying out of the end of society, which end is the common good. Through its organization and its coercive power the state assures internal and external peace, thus laying the absolutely basic condition for the attainment of human ends. Such is its protective function. The state exercises its promotive function by supplying the help and direction the individual needs for the achievement of his purpose.

To guide a government in its prudential choice of the best means to achieve the common good of society, natural law philosophy offers the principle of subsidiarity. In its positive aspect subsidiarity, we have noted, means that the state is to help individuals and lesser societies to do what they cannot do efficiently for themselves. Because private persons are unequal to the task of providing the means of modern transportation (highways, air regulations, etc.), an obligation lies on the state to build adequate roadways and to co-ordinate air traffic. In its negative aspect subsidiarity requires that the state aid private persons only when they are either unable or unwilling efficiently to execute a needed project. For this reason the state may not rightly interfere in an educational enterprise of private citizens as long as that enterprise is being adequately cared for.

The principle of subsidiarity applies not only to the sovereign state but to all lesser governmental units and agencies as well. A national government should not do what a regional government finds possible, nor should the latter undertake what falls within the competency of a local government. The principle of subsidiarity is thus a bulwark both against the individualistic *laissez-faire* state and against the all-embracing paternal state.

We have pointed out that in broad lines there are two extreme philosophies regarding the state's function in education. The individualist holds that the state has no role (or at most an extremely limited one) to play; the statist declares that it alone has any competency. We have rejected both views as unrealistic.

The state does have a role in education but one quite different from that of the Church and the family. The state is not of its nature a direct educator as are Church and family. Its direct function is the promotion of the common good and cannot, therefore, be education. From the reverse point of view we can see the same truth. The Author of nature and supernature has already committed the direct function in education to two other agencies, Church and family. There remains of necessity only an indirect function for the state.

If there is a basis for the state's participation in education, that basis must be built on a principle distinct from the principles undergirding the Church's and the family's role. The state, unlike the Catholic Church, has not received a direct divine commission to teach, and, unlike the parent, it does not communicate life. It is reasonable, therefore, to seek the foundation of the state's educational function in the end or the purpose of the state: the protection and the promotion of the common good.

The state's first and most basic function in education is so to dispose and regulate the factors operating in society that the primary educators may do the work God and nature have assigned to them. It must protect the educational rights of the Church and the family. The state's second basic function is to promote by positive means the citizen's educational welfare. This it does in a number of ways: (1) by assisting the initiative of Church and family; (2) by the establishment of public schools when such are needed; (3) by exacting a minimum of education in its citizens; (4) by maintaining institutions necessary for the training of governmental personnel; and (5) by sponsoring a program of civic education aimed at the populace at large.

After demonstrating the proposition that the state has a validly based role in education, we proceeded to show that this role is essentially subsidiary. Applied to the present question subsidiarity means that the state is to enter the field of education only when that entrance is necessary or at least beneficial to the common welfare. A government is to supplement the work of the primary educators, Church and family, whenever and wherever the latter are unable or unwilling adequately to carry out the full mission entrusted to them.

The subsidiary function of the state as educator is, consequently, firmly set against the notion that the state is the primary educator of children. It is no more such an educator than it is the primary farmer or physician. If private endeavor fails to farm or to heal efficiently, the state may step in and supply what is lacking, but it may go no further. So also, if private initiative is unequal to the entire educational task, the state may and must supply what is lacking, but nothing more.

In the body of our text we have noted a number of reasons underlying the principle of subsidiarity, both as viewed in itself and in its application to matters educational. One only we would like to re-emphasize here. An unnecessary entrance of the state into education can easily result in an intrusion into the rights of conscience. A parent has a conscientious right to give his child the type of education he deems best, and as long as that parent may choose the school to which he may send the child, that right is likely to be honored. But if the state *establishes* public schools where mere *assistance* is needed to establish and maintain private schools, the parent may be forced by economic pressure to patronize a school of which he does not approve. That this is no empty observation is readily seen in pluralistic societies where the government assists private educational endeavor as it ought. In these countries private institutions are many and well attended, indicating thereby their popularity with parents.

From our study we may conclude that while the state is an educator neither by definition nor by nature, yet it does have a vital and noble role to play in matters scientific, cultural, and instructional. As is true in the whole function of government, the state's role in education is a supplementary, subsidiary one. Its nobility lies in its co-operation with the primary agencies of education, not in its supplanting of them.

The contemporary picture of the state's function in education as it is painted on the concrete canvas of international society is far from harmonious and homogeneous. Some nations, as we have seen, deny the most basic principles of human freedom and dignity in their provisions for the agencies of education. Yet on the other hand it is encouraging to note the large number of nations that recognize in their laws the educational philosophy of state that we have presented in this study. That recognition, to be sure, varies in completeness, but it is nonetheless there. It is a root from which further growth can issue.

Because the state's functions in education are of key importance, they solicit the attention and active interest of the whole citizenry of each country. A government's duties are only one facet of the problem; the correlative role of the citizen is the other. A close and understanding concurrence among all concerned can issue in nothing but a positive promotion of the general welfare, natural and supernatural.

BIBLIOGRAPHY

Archer, R. L. (ed.), *Rousseau on Education* (New York: Longmans, Green and Co., 1916).

Bear, Robert M., *The Social Functions of Education* (New York: Macmillan, 1937).

Bestor, Arthur, *The Restoration of Learning* (New York: Alfred A. Knopf, 1955).

Bouquillon, Thomas, *Education: To Whom Does It Belong?* — A Rejoinder to the Civilta Cattolica (Baltimore: John Murphy and Co., 1892).

——— *Education: To Whom Does It Belong?* (Baltimore: John Murphy and Co., 1891).

——— *Education: To Whom Does It Belong?* — *A Rejoinder to Critics* (Baltimore: John Murphy and Co., 1892).

British Information Services, *Education in Great Britain* (New York: British Information Services, 1958).

Broudy, Harry S., *Building a Philosophy of Education* (New York: Prentice-Hall, 1954).

Cambridge Summer School of Catholic Studies, *Church and State* (London: Burns, Oates and Washbourne, 1936).

Cappello, Felix M., *Summa Iuris Publici Ecclesiastici* (Rome: Gregorian University, 1943).

Castelein, A., *Droit Naturel* (Bruxelles: Albert Dewit, 1912).

Cathrein, Victor, *Philosophia Moralis* (8th ed.) (Friburgi Brisgoviae: B. Herder, 1911).

Catlin, George, *The Story of the Political Philosophers* (New York: McGraw-Hill, 1939).

Cavagnis, Felix, *Institutiones Iuris Publici Ecclesiastici* (Rome: Typis Societatis Catholicae Instructivae, 1889).

Ciarlantini, Lino A., *The Liberty of the School and Family Education* (New York: Educational Publishers, 1954).

Cloyd, David E., *Benjamin Franklin and Education* (Boston: D. C. Heath, 1902).

Cocchi, Guidus, *Commentarium in Codicem Iuris Canonici,* 3rd ed. (Torino: Marietti, 1933).

Communist International, *Blueprint for World Conquest* (Washington: Human Events, 1946).

Confrey, Burton, *Secularism in American Education* (Washington: Catholic University of America Press, 1931).

Conway, James, *The Respective Rights and Duties of Family, State and Church in Regard to Education* (New York: Fr. Pustet, 1890).

Coronata, Matthews, 4th ed. rev., Vol. II: *Institutiones Iuris Canonici* (Taurini: Marietti, 1951).

Counts, George S., *The American Road to Culture* (New York: John Day Co., 1932).

Cox, John F., *A Thomistic Analysis of the Social Order* (Washington: Catholic University of America Press, 1943).

Cronin, John F., *Social Principles and Economic Life* (Milwaukee: Bruce, 1959).

Cronin, Michael, *The Science of Ethics,* Vol. II (Dublin: M. H. Gill and Son, 1929).

Cubberley, Ellwood P., *State School Administration* (Boston: Houghton Mifflin Co., 1927).

Doughton, Isaac, *Modern Public Education, Its Philosophy and Background* (New York: Appleton-Century-Crofts, 1935).

Doyle, John J., *Education in Recent Constitutions and Concordats* (Washington: Catholic University Press, 1933).

Driscoll, John A., *Rights and Duties — Their Foundation* (New York: The Paulist Press, 1948).

Dunning, William Archibald, *A History of Political Theories,* 3 vols. (New York: Macmillan, 1920).

During, Ingemar (ed.), *The Swedish School-Reform, 1950* (Uppsala, Sweden: Appelbergs Boktrycheriaktiebolog, 1951).

English Government, *Education Act, 1944* (London: Her Majesty's Stationery Office, n.d.).

Evans, Joseph W., and Ward, Leo R. (editors), *The Social and Political Philosophy of Jacques Maritain* (New York: Charles Scribner's Sons, 1955).

Findlay, J. J., *The Foundations of Education,* 2 vols. (New York: Henry Holt, 1925).

France, no author (France: Herbert, 1952).

Gabel, Richard J., *Public Funds for Church and Private Schools* (Washington: Catholic University Press, 1937).

Gettell, Raymond G., *History of Political Thought* (New York: Century, 1924).

Goodrich, Leland M., and Hambro, Edvard, *Charter of the United Nations,* 2nd ed. rev. (Boston: World Peace Foundation, 1949).

Government of Denmark, *Denmark, 1952* (Copenhagen: Royal Danish Ministry for Foreign Affairs and the Danish Statistical Department, 1952).

Government Information Office, *The Union of South Africa* (New York:

Union of South Africa Government Information Office, n.d.).

Gredt, Joseph, *Elementa Philosophiae*, 10th ed. rev., 2 vols. (Friburgi: Herder, 1953).

Grieder, Calvin, and Romine, Stephen, *American Public Education* (New York: Ronald Press, 1955).

Grindel, Carl W. (ed.), *Concept of Freedom* (Chicago: Henry Regnery Co., 1955).

Haas, Francis J., *Man and Society*, 2nd ed. (New York: Appleton-Century-Crofts, 1952).

Hall, Robert King, Hans, N., and Lauwerys, J. A. (editors), *The Year Book of Education, 1953* (Yonkers-on-Hudson: World Book Co., 1953).

—— *The Year Book of Education, 1954* (Yonkers-on-Hudson: World Book Co., 1954).

Hallowell, John H., *Main Currents in Modern Political Thought* (New York: Henry Holt and Co., 1950).

Hansen, Allen Oscar, *Liberalism and American Education* (New York: Macmillan, 1926).

Hayes, Carlton J. H., *Essays on Nationalism* (New York: Macmillan, 1941).

Hellin, Joseph, and González, Irenaeus, *Philosophiae Scholasticae Summa* (Matriti: Biblioteca De Autores Cristianos, 1952).

Hill, Owen A., *Ethics, General and Special* (New York: Macmillan, 1920).

Holaind, R. I., *The Parent First* (New York: Benziger Bros., 1891).

Huston, Wendell, *School Laws of the Forty-Eight States*, 2 vols. (Seattle: Wendell Huston Co.).

Idenburg, Philip J., *Education in the Netherlands* (The Hague: Netherlands Government Information Service, 1954).

Indonesian Ministry of Information, *Basic Information on Indonesia* (Djakarta: Ministry of Information, Republic of Indonesia, 1953).

Institute of International Education, *Open Doors* (New York: Institute of International Education, 1956).

Johnson, Alvin W., and Yost, Frank H., *Separation of Church and State in the United States* (Minneapolis: University of Minnesota Press, 1948).

Juhasz, William, *Blueprint for a Red Generation* (New York: Mid-European Studies Center, 1952).

Kallio, Niilo, *The School System of Finland*, 3rd ed. (Helsinki: Suomalaisen Kirjallisuuden Seuran Kirjapainon Oy, 1952).

Kandel, I. L. (ed.), *Educational Yearbook, 1932* (New York Teachers College, Columbia University, 1933).

—— *Educational Yearbook, 1944* (New York: Teachers College, Columbia University, 1944).

Kelsen, Hans, *The Communist Theory of Law* (New York: Frederick A. Praeger, Inc., 1955).

Ketteler, Wilhelm E., von, *Public Schools or Denominational Schools* (New York: Benziger, 1892).

Kreilkamp, Karl, *The Metaphysical Foundations of Thomistic Jurisprudence* (Washington: The Catholic University of America Press, 1939).

Lauwerys, J. A., and Hans, N. (editors), *The Year Book of Education, 1951* (London: University of London, 1951).

―――― *The Year Book of Education, 1952* (London: University of London, 1952).

Leibell, J. F. (ed.), *Readings in Ethics* (Chicago: Loyola University Press, 1926).

Leo XIII, Pope, *Rerum Novarum* (Washington: N.C.W.C. n.d.).

Lindegren, Alina M., *Education in Sweden,* U. S. Office of Education, Federal Security Agency, Bulletin 1952, No. 17 (Washington: U. S. Government Printing Office, 1952).

Loughery, Sr. M. Bernard Francis, *Parental Rights in American Educational Law: Their Bases and Implementation* (Washington: Catholic University Press, 1952).

MacIver, R. M. (ed.), *Great Expressions of Human Rights* (New York: Harper, 1950).

Maritain, Jacques, *Man and the State* (Chicago: University of Chicago Press, 1951).

―――― *The Person and the Common Good* (New York: Charles Scribner's Sons, 1947).

―――― *The Rights of Man and Natural Law* (New York: Charles Scribner's Sons, 1947).

―――― *The Things That Are Not Caesar's* (New York: Charles Scribner's, 1930).

Massachusetts General Court, Committee on Education. A digest of the remarks of the Remonstrants at the hearings of the Legislative Committee on Education in March, 1888, n. pub., n. date.

Masters, Ruth D. (ed.), *Handbook of International Organizations in the Americas* (Washington: Carnegie Endowment for International Peace, 1945).

Mead, Edwin D., *The Roman Catholic Church and the Public Schools* (Boston: George H. Ellis, 1890).

Meiklejohn, Alexander, *Education Between Two Worlds* (New York: Harper and Bros., 1942).

Messner, J., *Social Ethics* (St. Louis: B. Herder Book Co., 1952).

Meyer, Hans, *The Philosophy of St. Thomas* (St. Louis: B. Herder, 1944).

Mill, John Stuart, *Principles of Political Economy* (London: Longmans, Green and Co., 1936).

Ministry of Foreign Affairs, *Japan's Problems* (Tokyo: Public Information and Cultural Affairs Bureau, 1954).

Monroe, Walter S., *Encyclopedia of Educational Research,* rev. ed. (New York: The Macmillan Co., 1950).

Moody, Joseph N. (ed.), *Church and Society* (New York: Arts, Inc., 1953).

Morris, Max, *Hungary Builds a New Education,* 2nd ed. rev. (London: Hungarian News and Information Service, 1952).

Nicolau, Michael, and Salaverri, Joachim, *Sacrae Theologiae Summa* (Matriti: Biblioteca de Autores Cristianos, 1952), Vol. I.

Oregon School Cases (Baltimore: Belvedere Press, 1925).

Ottaviani, Alfredo, *Institutiones Iuris Publici Ecclesiastici* (Vaticanis: Typis Polyglottis, 1936), 2 vols.

Parsons, Wilfrid, *The First Freedom* (New York: Declan X. McMullen Co., 1948).

Peaslee, Amos J., *Constitutions of Nations* (Concord, N. H.: Rumford Press, 1950), 3 vols.

Pius XI, Pope, *Quadragesimo Anno* (Washington: N.C.W.C., n.d.).

Pius XII, Pope, *Summi Pontificatus* (Washington: National Catholic Welfare Conference, 1939).

Plato, *The Works of Plato,* Irwin Edman, ed. (New York: Tudor Pub. Co., 1934).

Pollock, Robert C. (ed.), *The Mind of Pius XII* (New York: Crown Publishers, 1955).

Quigley, Patrick F., *Compulsory Education* (New York: Robert Drummond, 1894).

Regatillo, E. F., and Zalba, M., *Theologiae Moralis Summa* (Matriti: Biblioteca De Autores Cristianos, 1952), Vol. I.

Reilly, Daniel F., *The School Controversy* (Washington: Catholic University Press, 1943).

Renard, Henri, *The Philosophy of Morality* (Milwaukee: Bruce Pub. Co., 1953).

Republic of Indonesia, *Basic Information on Indonesia,* Ministry of Information, n.p.; n.d.

Rickaby, Joseph, *Moral Philosophy* (New York: Longmans, Green and Co., 1912).

Rivlin, Harry N. (ed.), *Encyclopedia of Modern Education* (New York: Philosophical Library, 1943).

Rommen, Heinrich A., *The Natural Law* (St. Louis: B. Herder, 1948).
——— *The State in Catholic Thought* (St. Louis: B. Herder Book Co., 1950).

Rugg, Harold, *Culture and Education in America* (New York: Harcourt, Brace and Co., 1931).

Sassani, Abul, H. K., *Education in Turkey,* U. S. Office of Education,

Federal Security Agency, Bulletin 1952, No. 10 (Washington: U. S. Government Printing Office, 1952).

Simon, Yves R., *Philosophy of Democratic Government* (Chicago: University of Chicago Press, 1951).

Smith, Adam, *An Inquiry Into the Nature and Causes of the Wealth of Nations* (Edinburgh: Thomas Nelson, 1840).

Spanish Diplomatic Information Office, *The Concordat Between Spain and the Holy See* (Madrid: 1953).

—— *Fifteen Years of Spanish Culture* (Madrid: Diplomatic Information Office, 1952).

Spencer, Herbert, *Social Statics* (New York: D. Appleton and Co., 1892).

Sturzo, Luigi, *Church and State* (New York: Longmans, Green and Co., 1939).

Suarez, Franciscus, *Tractatus De Legibus ac Deo Legislatore* (Neapoli: Ex Typis Fibrenianis, 1872).

Thayer, V. T., *The Attack Upon the American Secular School* (Boston: Beacon Press, 1951).

—— *Religion in Public Education* (New York: Viking Press, 1947).

Unesco, *Human Rights* (New York: Columbia University Press, 1949).

Union of South Africa, *Education,* a preprint from the *Official Yearbook of the Union of South Africa* (Pretoria: Government Printer, 1947).

United Nations, *Yearbook on Human Rights for 1948* (Lake Success, N. Y.: United Nations, 1950).

—— *Yearbook on Human Rights for 1950* (New York: United Nations, 1952).

—— *Yearbook on Human Rights for 1951* (New York: United Nations, 1953).

—— *Yearbook on Human Rights for 1952* (New York: United Nations, 1954).

Uzcategui, Emilio, *Compulsory Education in Ecuador* (Paris: UNESCO, 1951).

Vacant, A., Mangenot, E., Amann, E., *et al., Dictionnaire de Theologie Catholique* (Paris: Librairie Letouzey et Ane, 1903–1950), 15 vols.

Von Kuehnelt-Leddihn, Erik, *Liberty or Equality* (Caldwell, Idaho: Caxton Printers, 1952).

Ward, Lester F., *Pure Sociology* (New York: Macmillan, 1903).

INDEX

Academic freedom, and Communism, 46 f, 173; in educational organization, 113 f; and political factions, 76; and the state, 172 ff

Adult education, and the state, 184 f

Afghanistan, on inspection of private schools, 133

Albania, and compulsory education, 201; educational philosophy of, 81 f; on establishment of private schools, 99

Argentina, and compulsory education, 200; educational philosophy of, 86; and the rehabilitation of prisoners, 185 f

Aristotle, on man's social nature, 11

Australia, and compulsory education, 200; and education of exceptional children, 171; and free education, 204; public school religious instruction in, 157 f; and support of libraries, 188

Austria, and compulsory education, 200

Auxiliary services, 124 f; and the state, 205 f

Belgium, and aid to private education, 120; and the rehabilitation of prisoners, 185 f

Benedict XV, on the state and the private school curriculum, 134 *n*

Bible reading, in public schools, 148, 151, 154 ff, 159

Bolivia, and compulsory education, 200; and the curriculum of private schools, 135; and education of exceptional children, 171; educational philosophy of, 85; and granting of degrees, 140

Brazil, and aid to private education, 121; and compulsory education, 200; and compulsory establishment of private schools, 139; and education of exceptional children, 171; and international co-operation in education, 215 f; and promotion of research, 187; public school religious instruction in, 159; on residence of political authority, 18

Bulgaria, and compulsory education, 200; educational philosophy of, 82

Burma, public school religious instruction in, 153

Canada, and aid to private education, 122; and decentralization in public education, 168; educational philosophy of, 88; public school religious instruction in, 158; religion in state schools, 102 f

Caribbean nations, and co-operation in education, 214

Catholic Church, and teaching of morality, 175 f

Catholic position on state as educator, 61 ff

Catholic schools, bases for right to exist, 57

Catholic teaching on the Church as educator, 55 ff

Censorship, and the state, 172 ff

Centralization in public education, 161 ff; advantages of, 162; disadvantages of, 163 f

Certification, of private school teachers, 141 ff

Ceylon, and aid to private education, 122; and certification of teachers, 142; and free education, 204; public school religious instruction in, 158

Child labor laws, 198 f, 205

Chile, and aid to private education, 118; and compulsory education, 200; educational philosophy of, 85

China, adult education in, 184; and aid to private education, 120; and international co-operation in education, 216

Church, and Communism, 46 f; and conservative statism, 47 f; in education, protected by state, 63, 97 ff; and educational freedom, 98 ff; and family rights, recognized by modern states, 85 ff; and ordinary secularistic statism, 50 ff; and public schools, 144 ff; rights in education in relation to family's rights, 60 f; and society, 11

Church, as educator, Catholic position, 55 ff; function in education and state aid, 69 ff

231